AFRICA'S PAST, OUR FUTURE

AFRICA'S PAST,
OUR FUTURE

Kathleen R. Smythe

Indiana University Press

Bloomington and Indianapolis

This book is a publication of

Indiana University Press
Office of Scholarly Publishing
Herman B Wells Library 350
1320 East 10th Street
Bloomington, Indiana 47405 USA

iupress.indiana.edu

Library of Congress Cataloging-in-Publication Data

Smythe, Kathleen R., [date] author.
    Africa's past, our future / Kathleen R. Smythe.
        pages cm
    Includes bibliographical references and index.
    ISBN 978-0-253-01647-8 (cl : alk. paper) — ISBN 978-0-253-01655-3
(pb : alk. paper) — ISBN 978-0-253-01661-4 (eb)   1. Africa—
History.   2. Africa—Civilization.   3. Africa—Social life and
customs.   I. Title.
    DT20.S57 2015
    960
                                                      2015012043

1 2 3 4 5 20 19 18 17 16 15

To my friends in Tanzania and Kenya,
who shared with me their cultures, worldviews, and
social networks

Contents

Acknowledgments

THIS BOOK IS the result of years of intellectual and spiritual exploration at Xavier University, where I have made my academic home since 1997. Students in my African history survey pushed me to answer the question "Why should a student in Cincinnati, Ohio, study African history?" Their embrace of African history and the perspective that it brings not only to the continent's history but also to our own history helped to launch the project and continued to make it feel important and worthwhile. I am particularly thankful to several classes of students that helped to shape the manuscript with their sincere interest and candor.

Xavier's Jesuit mission provided the spiritual and personal space to explore my deep-seated interest in sustainability and to bring personal and vocational responses into dialogue with those engaged in similar and related quests. A sabbatical in the fall of 2012 provided the space and time to finalize the manuscript for external review. The university also funded attendance at several conferences, where I presented chapters from the book and gained opportunities to have some of the material published in advance of the full manuscript.

The intellectual flexibility, curiosity, desire, and talent for merging teaching, research, and service, together with the support of my departmental colleagues, chairs, other colleagues, and staff at Xavier, contributed, wittingly or not, to this project as well. A senior colleague, John Fairfield, is both an excellent teacher and a fine example of a curious scholar. He set a high bar in the classroom and in terms of broad, engaged scholarship. It is his embodiment of these traits that laid the foundation that helped me to consider undertaking this kind of book. More than ten years ago, I shared some survey class material with colleagues Julia O'Hara and Brandon LaRocque and upper-class material with Christine Anderson and in so doing began to see the wider relevance for much of the material in the survey course. O'Hara, a Latin Americanist and gentle colleague, has been a constant source of conversation and insight about the ways our fields intersect and diverge. About ten years ago, ethicist James Buchanan asked me to guest teach in his globalization class. Doing so required learning more about how American and European scholars talked about globalization and launched an investigation into economics that still absorbs me to this day. I am grateful for his initial invitation and support. I have learned from him, economist Jamal Abu-Rashed, theologian Gillian Ahlgren, and political scientist Anas Malik in several different iterations of the course. Theologian Marie Giblin and I taught a faculty workshop on Africa and globalization and then worked on a research project in

Tanzania on development aid that opened up a related line of inquiry around development aid and service learning. I led two academic service learning semesters in Ghana and benefited from the experience, questions, and support of director Irene Hodgson; my co-trip leader, biologist Jen Robbins; and the faculty on the Advisory Committee, particularly economist Amit Sen, Anas Malik, theologian Walker Gollar, and historians Christine Anderson and Julia O'Hara. The students on both trips allowed me to relive my first immersion experience in Africa and to be a guide for them on their transformative experience. How U.S. citizens, government, non-governmental organizations, and corporations impact and relate to Africa remains a deep and vexing question.

I had the privilege of working closely and becoming friends with theologian Elizabeth Groppe on a curricular program for three years and learned much from her about engaged scholarship and engaged living. I am grateful for the high bar she has set both personally and professionally. I also worked closely with Dave Lococo, Director of Physical Plant, as we co-chaired Xavier's Sustainability Committee for four years. The work we did together building a sustainability program deeply influenced the way I think about a university campus, what can and should be learned there, and from whom. Dave embodies transdisciplinary learning; he is an engineer with a theologian's questions.

As the project developed, historian Brandon Lundy's interest in an overview article derived from the text helped to boost my confidence, and reviewers' comments helped to sharpen my arguments. Historian Nicholas Creary attended a paper presentation of the content from chapter 3 and asked to use it and the other extant chapter in his classes and has been doing so for a number of years. His response and that of his students provided me with a concrete sense that I was writing for a wider audience and that I had colleagues who would be able to use the material. Geographer Heidi Frontani and I reconnected and discussed our research projects and found much overlap in our teaching and writing. Her contributions to two chapters in the book are integral to its final shape, and I appreciate both her work here and her friendship. Another historian colleague and friend, Jan Shetler, has been a keen supporter of the project as well. One of the roots of the book was an article I wrote on teaching Africa in world history. Jan made useful suggestions on a draft of that article, helping to shape several of the chapters herein. She read an earlier version of the manuscript, guiding it into a much better text than it would have been otherwise. She assigned the unpublished manuscript in her African history class and her students made very thoughtful and sometimes provocative comments on an almost final version of the manuscript. I appreciate their and her engagement with the text and its ideas and philosophy.

I am grateful to the many friends, acquaintances, and writers who read parts of the manuscript, heard parts of it in sermons, or used parts of it in their own teaching efforts and encouraged me to get it out into the world. I thank my parents and congregants at two Unitarian churches: St. John's in Cincinnati, Ohio, and Door County Fellowship in Wisconsin. In addition, I am grateful to the students who were not enrolled in the survey course but asked about my research and read chapters in their spare time and then shared their reactions with me. Such interest was deeply appreciated.

Dee Mortensen, editor at Indiana University Press, expressed interest in the project when it was in its early stages and, beginning several years ago, provided logistical and moral support as the manuscript went through multiple rounds of review. I am very grateful for her unflagging faith in the project.

Finally, this book emerged at this time in my life because I had two growing children who had already accompanied me to Africa twice and who wished to stay home rather than interrupt their school years and friendships again. For accompanying me to Africa and making those experiences part of our family's fabric, I am grateful to my children and my husband.

AFRICA'S PAST, OUR FUTURE

Introduction

In the past it has not mattered greatly what people believed about themselves and their societies, since nothing that followed from these beliefs could have endangered the species. Man is now rapidly approaching the point—and it will come in the lifetimes of his children—when, unless he takes survival consciously into his own hands, he may not survive as a species. This requires a revolution in thinking as serious as the Copernican revolution.

Robin Fox, *Encounter with Anthropology*

In fact, in ecological terms, the current situation is an extreme deviation from any of the durable, more "normal," states of the world over the span of human history, indeed over the span of earth history. If we lived 700 or 7,000 years, we would understand this on the basis of experience or memory alone. But for creatures who live a mere 70 years or so, the study of the past, distant and recent, is required to know what the range of possibilities includes, and to know what might endure.

John McNeill, *Something New under the Sun*

Our largest stories are those of cosmology. Whatever tales we tell about the origin and flow of the universe, and about our place in the scheme of things, will shape our sense of how we should behave.

Scott Russell Sanders, *A Conservationist Manifesto*

In the moment of crisis, the wise build bridges and the foolish build dams.

Nigerian proverb

THIS BOOK IS based on the belief that our future welfare depends on a deep and informed understanding of the human past. The African proverb above suggests that the way forward is through broad understanding rather than narrow thinking. To paraphrase writer Scott Russell Sanders's words, this book tells a new story about our civilization's place in the scheme of things, using African history. Africans, our earliest human ancestors, offer us the longest perspective on history of any people on the planet, and they challenge some fundamental modern (and sometimes Western) assumptions about how human beings have lived together for millennia.

In the first epigraph, anthropologist Robin Fox argues that the stories humans tell about the past are more critical than ever. In the new era, the Anthropocene, humans are impacting the Earth's ecosystems at levels never before seen in history. Due to population size, technology, and consumption, humans are very powerful and very destructive. In the second epigraph, world historian John R. McNeill notes that as beings with relatively short life spans, humans are handicapped by an inability to realize how different the last few hundred years have been from the rest of human history. While the last 200 years had a significant impact on the environment, McNeill's work focuses on the twentieth century as an unprecedented era in terms of environmental destruction.

The Great Acceleration, a product of the International Geosphere-Biosphere Programme, emphasizes the changes that have taken place globally over the last 60-plus years. Their research illustrates links between the loss of biodiversity and the gross domestic product (one measure of a national economy based on goods and services produced, whether or not they are beneficial to people or the planet) and between the destruction of rainforest and the amount of carbon dioxide released into the atmosphere. As a result of these rapid and profound changes, global citizens face unprecedented challenges, such as a mass sixth species extinction, runaway global climate destabilization (due to accumulation of greenhouse gases in the atmosphere), and large-scale, irreversible loss of topsoil and nutrients (such as phosphorus) that are essential to agricultural production. Moreover, these changes have led to increased economic inequality across the globe, both within and among countries. Resource extraction and consumption have increased, and many in the globalized capital class and localized marginalized majority (to use terms introduced by development scholar Wolfgang Sachs) feel increasingly powerless to be agents of change in their own communities, let alone across the globe. Thus, the last 50 years have been marked by several trends that have proven detrimental to healthy people, communities, and the planet's biosphere. To put it more strongly, humans have created a situation in which we might be the architects of our own destruction. To prevent this from happening, both scholars and citizens need comprehensive, imaginative ideas that bridge culture and time.

Most people, whether age 20 or 60, have seen tremendous cultural and technological changes in their lifetimes, and the pace of change is only accelerating. Such change, a result of our ability to create and innovate, is an integral facet of our humanity. But the rate of change means that few understand the relatively slow pace at which societies and earlier human species moved. Most of what appears as our culture and way of being seems not more than a few hundred years old. But many social structures and skills, while not immutable, were laid down by our ancestors millennia ago. Understanding those structures and skills is just as important to our everyday lives as computers and cell phones.

Imparting to others the uniqueness of the current historical moment is one of the challenges historians face. These challenges, and others not mentioned here, are only clear within a much longer view of history than what is normally considered. They suggest a need to learn about other cultures and ideas that have not been as closely associated with the Great Acceleration as those in the West. Humans have the capacity to either remake their world or continue along the same path. If the former is desired, African history is in a unique position to make significant contributions to a new view of humans' place in the world. This book examines long-standing traditions and ideas in African history as sources of wisdom and creativity for those caught in practices, ideas, and institutions that are not sustainable in social, economic, or ecological terms.

This is not a call for a return to some preindustrial past. Instead, older societies and those of different cultural backgrounds are crucial to understanding what kinds of behavior, institutions, and values are truly sustainable. An alternative view or language requires returning to the past, for students and scholars have no other place to turn. Insofar as the past departs from our modern paradigm, it offers us alternative ones. It can also provide creative and imaginative ideas and possibilities, freeing us from the structures and limitations that bind us both in terms of our own cultural traditions and experiences. For example, anthropologist Joe Henrich's recent work combining ethnographic and cognitive research methods demonstrates that although the majority of psychology research is based on Western subjects (96 percent of subjects from 2003 to 2007 in the top six psychology journals), many from the United States, the way Americans think about themselves and others is unique even within the unusual subpopulation of Westerners. This is another good reason to pay attention to the way Africans and others think about themselves and their societies, as they are closer to the human norm than those who often feature in American history classes.

This book uses history in the service of current compelling needs. The challenge is to present the information herein as part of a changing mosaic and not as primordial practices. Rather than return to an ancient, simple past, this book is a call to recognize and operate within a historical understanding that offers more diversity than the Western historical trajectory. If scholars look to the thoughts and practices of ancient Greece for a better understanding of our contemporary ideas about democracy, then they can benefit just as much by examining how populations adapted to climate change or arranged kinship, with a focus on women and their roles in society, for guidance on how to face climate change or rethink social arrangements now.

This book is a result of teaching an introductory African history survey. For almost the past two decades, I have sought to make what might seem a remote and unrelated study of early African history relevant to understanding students' everyday experiences in the United States and elsewhere in the early twenty-first century. African history is essential to developing a new view of our place in the world for four reasons.

Four Major Contributions of African History

First, the *longue durée* (literally, "long duration") of African history offers the distance and perspective that twenty-first-century citizens need to understand the uniqueness of this particular moment in history. Long-term views make visible the tremendously difficult environments and challenges that humans have overcome on the journey to the modern world. For example, almost all the foods eaten today were domesticated about 10,000 years ago. Almost everything in the modern diet is a result of the hard, experimental work of developing new kinds of domesticated plants and animals from wild ones. While our modern food system has produced many different kinds of processed foods, such as cheese crackers, energy drinks, and lunch meat, these are the result of using ingredients that initially came from plants and animals that have long been staples of the human diet.

In the mid-twentieth century, historian Fernand Braudel, considered one of the founders of the *longue durée* approach, called for better integration of the social sciences and history so scholars might discover long-term, large-scale world historical change that would illuminate the past and society's future possibilities. He wanted to include the study of geography, natural resources, and material processes as part of historical study. His vision was broad and influential. Among his beliefs was that "if one wants to understand the world, one has to determine the hierarchy of forces, currents, and individual moments, and then put them together to form an overall constellation." This book is, among other things, one of many answers to such a vision. There are a number of ways in which this book parallels Braudel's thinking. The parts of the book, the *longue durée,* the middle time frame, and more recent history ("traditional history," in Braudel's words) concerned with brief time spans, specific events, and individuals take a page from Braudel's work. This book's commitment to bridging academic disciplines, while focusing on historical change as the ultimate foundation upon which ideas and institutions are developed, reworked, and discarded, is also drawn from Braudel. Finally, for Braudel, history is the sum of all histories, including those that are often neglected in time (the distant past) and space (Africa).

The second reason African history is so important and useful in developing a new sense of our place in the world is that historians of the continent have used new methods of obtaining and reading the historical record. African historians have forged a new path that has allowed it the freedom to construct narratives that are different from those for Western histories. African histories are grounded in specific methodologies, such as historical linguistics and anthropology. Such methodologies lead to different ways of thinking about and understanding history. Historical linguistics, for example, identify points of culture contact and diffusion through shared words and ideas. They also help identify long-standing ideas and traditions, such as the value of clans and lineages or the role of gatherer-hunter peoples (often considered part of prehistory rather than history because they kept no written records) in helping farmers survive in a new locale. Oral traditions—stories told about events that took place in the distant past—also make important contributions. They are a window into one of the defining aspects of African history: maintaining history orally. Students and teachers in the United States are inheritors of a centuries-long approach to learning that gives primary importance to the written word. Thus, it is hard to imagine the mental capacity that African oral historians, if not all Africans, possessed when the only place to store information was their minds. *Griots* (oral historians) in West Africa, for example, told historical accounts that could last for days. The audience would actively participate through call and response and singing. African history, particularly early African history, then, becomes a study of cultures (including religion and social organization), ideas, economic adaptation, and technologies rather than a study of classes, royalty, church history, and conflict.

Moreover, as Neil Kodesh points out in his study of Buganda, because of the different nature of sources available for European history and African history, the narratives will never be commensurate. Historians might not be able to explicitly compare the eighteenth-century history of a European society with the eighteenth-century history of an African society. But they can produce histories that explain the ideas and practices that have informed transformations in African societies, and readers can benefit from the narratives produced by both histories.

The third reason African history is important is that traditions and ideas that cultures have held for thousands of years, like some I explore in this book, are literally sustainable—that is, they are adapted to a particular environment and people and their needs over the long term. These are often ideas and ways of doing and thinking that have endured over long periods of time because "they were continuously and collectively reinterpreted and expressed in any given moment," as historian Rhonda Gonzales writes in her book on East African societies over the *longue durée*. Thus, African history offers us alternative models for thinking about cultural contact and societal and political organization, among other things. Through exploration of heterarchy (horizontal organization) as opposed to hierarchy (vertical organization), societies where multiple sources of power coexisted and provided a sense of belonging and contribution to societal welfare become visible. African historian John Lonsdale has noted that the art of living relatively peaceably in societies without state structures is one of Africa's distinctive contributions to human history. Heterarchical societies illuminate various forms of political power, and matrilineal societies promote different kinds of family values, such as the importance of siblings and the value of redistribution of resources rather than accumulation within a nuclear family. In such societies, one's natal lineage remained of primary importance throughout life. In terms of political organization, imagine what readers might learn from states founded on the wisdom pastoralists have accumulated over hundreds of years or from informal vendors in urban Africa.

Africans do not have a better history than any other part of the world; they simply have an underappreciated history. African history tends to come with a lot of misinformation and prejudiced ideas for reasons that will become clear in this book, but mostly it is due to Africans' involvement in the Atlantic slave trade and then colonization. Ironically, the different sources covered in this book have also contributed to the field's marginalization. Most scholars trained in more mainstream historical methods find it difficult to incorporate historical evidence from a variety of fields, such as archaeology and historical linguistics. Yet, this interdisciplinary perspective is an integral part of African history and the ideas presented here.

In addition to making African history relevant to contemporary discussions regarding political and economic models and choices, this book also seeks to contribute to a new approach to education, one that takes our current economic, social, and political context as the starting point for building a curriculum relevant to current problems. This is the fourth reason African history can help us navigate the future. There are many critics of our educational system who have a variety of complaints. The critiques relevant here are those that contend that our education system must carry some of the blame for our current situation. Instead of education aimed solely at jobs and success, many call for an education that takes the environment and human survival more seriously. Population biologist Paul Ehrlich and environmental studies professor David Orr see a need for education with different subjects and different emphases than we currently have. Three of Orr's educational principles are particularly relevant to this book: all education would be environmental education; mastery of one's person, not mastery of a subject, would be the goal; and knowledge carries with it the responsibility to use it well in the world. Thus, students would not be able say they know something until they understand the effects this knowledge has on real people and their communities.

This book is based on the concept that African history can contribute to such principles of education. Early Africans appreciated the value of their natural world. They adapted to harsh and differing environments and came to understand their promises and limits. Thus, African history over the long run is environmental history. This book is, at its most fundamental level, about the environment and human sustainability within particular environmental constraints. History demonstrates, as Jared Diamond has recently illustrated, that civilizations that do not adapt to the peculiarities of their environments will eventually collapse.

There is much here that will challenge readers' way of being in the world; learning about Africa will lead to broader understanding of an individual's place in the world. Instead of seeing "our culture as the pinnacle of human achievement," to use David Orr's words, readers can realize the grandeur and achievements of past societies. A sense of humility and gratefulness for all the achievements of the past is in order to approach the future with humility and grace rather than the hubris that has marked the last centuries. Knowing who we are and where we came from in the broadest possible terms will provide the necessary resources for building the future.

To Orr's third point, the practices of foreigners past and present have had massive implications for Africans and their communities, implications that few North Americans are aware of. As the last section of the book demonstrates, ideas, such as development, have been powerful forces in dozens of nation-states and for millions of their citizens over the last six decades. A seemingly benign, if not beneficial, term, the concept of *development* has been a mechanism for ensuring economic and political dependence on former colonial powers and now emerging nations, like China, as the race for global resources continues. Development has not been the answer to Africa's problems, but it has been a detriment to Africans' governments' attempts to build self-sufficiency and civil society.

Twenty-five years ago, Ehrlich and psychologist Robert Ornstein called for a "Curriculum about Humanity." Such a curriculum would include thinking about our collective life as a species over millennia. This would involve studying the functioning of our brains and nervous systems to understand the shortcuts in perception and processing that occur that make it difficult for us to understand and act on long-term problems. In chapter 1, human evolution gives us a foundation for understanding our biological inheritance, including the gifts and limitations of our brains. Ehrlich and Ornstein also believed it was important to study where our food comes from. The development of agriculture is the subject of chapter 2. They called for cultural diversity across the curriculum, among other things. This book is a response to the call for cultural diversity in our classrooms in the broadest sense, ensuring that an often neglected continent receives attention in its own right and is considered as a resource for the welfare of a common human future.

Thus, one of the goals of this book is to contribute to a radical direction in higher education. It will lead students to question many of the assumptions that undergird their understanding of our society, their families, and the way they plan to make their way in the world. Such questioning is a necessary part of creating a new world order. This book is openly political and biased. It is for teachers who are in the classroom because they want to change the world and for students who are open to being changed.

Organization of the Book

This book is in three parts. Part 1 is titled "The *Longue Durée.*" African history returns us to our earliest human roots. From there the various monumental challenges that developing hominins (the current term for humans and all their ancestors) and then humans overcame to create the societies and technologies, such as agriculture and livestock keeping, that many take for granted today become clear. Chapter 4 explores African societies' openness to learning from others about a variety of things, including how to grow food and organize themselves. But they always blended new ideas with old ones, creating new and usually stronger and more resilient cultures. One of the main lessons in this part of the book is to fully appreciate the ingenuity and adaptability that humans have expressed over time and to recognize how much innovations have been shaped by environment and climate.

The second part is titled "African Institutions in the Middle Time Frame." In it models for social, political, and economic organization that are unfamiliar in the Western world, such as matriliny, heterarchy, and the gift economy, are explored. The gift economy is an economy based on social relationships and exchange rather than the market. These kinds of organizations were common in many parts of the world at different places and times and are illuminated well in African history. They also help to explain African participation in the Atlantic slave trade. Heterarchy illuminates a number of characteristics of early African society, including a desire to build effective communities, often with religious and spiritual leaders as the foundation. African religious ideas and institutions used to have a much more prominent place in politics than they do now. These ideas and institutions expand imagination and enrich the sense of what it means to be human.

Part 3 deals with contemporary issues and is titled "Recent History and Politics." This part of the book discusses colonialism and development from both Northern and African perspectives and a variety of ways in which Africans, their institutions, and their actions have had a significant influence on the contemporary world. One example comes from South Africa's experience of trying to build a multiracial state after centuries of racial oppression. Another is from Liberian women who successfully brought a decade-long civil war to an end, and a third is a successful modern nation-state based on institutions and relationships that have been developed in mobile, pastoral societies over millennia in Somaliland. Rather than assuming that African nations need to catch up to more industrialized nations or that they are somehow internally lacking, African pastoralism is a window into a different form of economic, social, and political organization that should have a place in our modern world because it is so well suited to arid landscapes.

Each part has a brief introduction to the time frame under consideration. The chapters in each part have several features in common. Most chapters begin with a specific geographical focus in the hope that the task of describing a whole continent becomes more credible as well as manageable. For example, in chapter 3, the focus is on societies living in the dry land northern regions, often referred to as the Sahel (running between the Sahara to the north and the savanna belt to the south) of the continent, who have adopted a variety of lifestyles in response to climate change. In chapter 4, the history of the kingdom of Buganda, for which the modern-day country Uganda in East Africa is named, is discussed. In chapter 8 on colonialism and development, most of the information is from Tanzania. Map I.1 shows some of the places discussed in the first two parts of the book.

This geographical description is followed by a detailed description of the primary sources used to learn and write about the topic and time period at hand. Thus, in chapter 1, the focus is on paleoanthropology, the backbone of our study of human evolution. Paleoanthropologists and their teams spend years looking for the smallest fragments of ancient human life. In chapter 3, both geology and geography contribute to our understanding of past climate change in Africa. Knowledge of wind and water systems and how they impact vegetation cycles, for example, is crucial to understanding the changes that have taken place in the past and why they have taken place. The reader can find much information about African economies and peacekeeping initiatives, ideas covered in chapters 8 and 9, on the Internet. By the end of the book, readers will have been exposed to a great variety of disciplines and to the ways they are essential to our reconstruction of African history, including historical linguistics, archaeology, and oral traditions, the three most important sources for uncovering early African history. In addition, geography, genetics, geology, anthropology, economics, and political science all feature significantly as well.

Contributions of the Book

This book illuminates our current challenges—ecological, political, social, and economical. Concerns about failing democratic systems considered alongside vigorous heterarchical societies where many feel they have an important role to play suggest that political reform might be considered from the bottom up as much as from the top down. The relatively unstable climate of the Sahel region across Africa suggests that future climate changes will possibly be abrupt (and violent) as well. Viewing African contributions to the global economy, particularly in terms of health care, complicates the view that many students have of the United States as an economic powerhouse. Due to globalization and other factors, the United States does not produce enough medical professionals to adequately

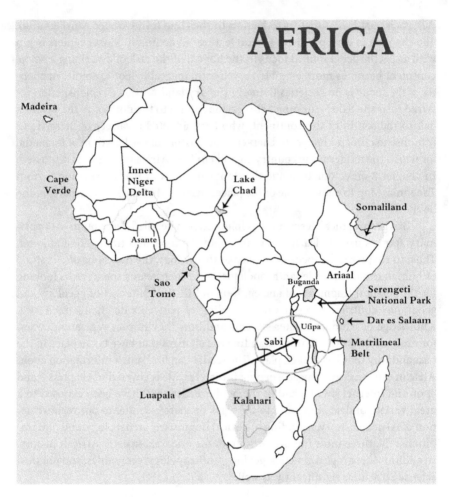

AFRICA

Madeira

Cape Verde

Inner Niger Delta

Lake Chad

Somaliland

Asante

Sao Tome

Buganda

Ariaal

Serengeti National Park

Dar es Salaam

Ufipa

Sabi

Matrilineal Belt

Luapala

Kalahari

Map I.1 Map of Africa depicting some of the areas covered in the first two parts of the book. Courtesy of Jessica Murphy, Xavier University.

care for its population. Instead, North Americans rely on African professionals (and professionals from elsewhere) to keep them healthy.

Second, this book takes African history seriously. It highlights a variety of African historical events, ideas, and institutions as critical human inventions and creations that, while worthy in their own right, also offer a source of illumination for our contemporary situation. Africans have made important and little recognized contributions to our collective past, including restorative justice, societies without political hierarchy, and populating harsh climates with ingenuity and perseverance. By the end, the reader will be better versed in some of the larger contours of African (and world) history and the ways in which an understanding of African history broadens our understanding of Western history, culture, and contemporary times and our thinking about ways to forge different life paths given this knowledge.

Third, it shows how interdisciplinary teaching, reading, and writing are essential to understanding humanity. The multidisciplinary nature of this work is a sign of our times. Interdisciplinary studies are growing in recognition of the fruitful nature of working across traditional academic fields. Archaeologist and anthropologist Chris Gosden argues that economics and science, honed in the modern world, are blunt instruments for understanding prehistory (the subject of the first section of this book). When there were fewer people and more resources to go around, values other than need and utility flourished, and people created complex links between themselves and objects such as metals and food. Thus, the study of African history calls forth intellectual landscapes that are rich and resilient with intellectual variety and raises questions across a wide range of fields.

Fourth, with such far-reaching implications, this book has much to say to the educated reader. This book intersects with public debates in a variety of ways. The study of human evolution has always been subject to the prejudices of human and racial superiority. The relatively recent arrival of *Homo sapiens* as a unique hominin species, forged from dozens of other hominin species' adjustments to a challenging environment, requires us to appreciate the long duration of our humanity and our connection to other early humans as well as other species. Discussion of Africans' earlier adaptations to climate change offers lessons in adaptability over a long time scale, as well as important reminders of the stark choices humans face when confronted with significant climate change. Somaliland's successes at building a new country based on traditional institutions blended with Westphalian ones (about the modern nation-state), with little international aid and almost no international recognition, are important examples of using a different political and social model than the one that has dominated global history over the last several hundred years and that is assumed to be the norm in debates about governance, failed states, and international aid.

Finally, this book suggests that the study of Africa offers more than just academic value. This work shows that history (like other disciplines) has value beyond its rationality, encouraging students to think about African history and our current times as fully sentient beings. As an instructor at a Jesuit institution, with an inclusive academic mission that strives to integrate ethics, spirituality, and intellect, I have come to value whole-person learning. This Jesuit tradition is divergent from the dominant intellectual trend of separating emotion and reason. As archaeologist and anthropologist Chris Gosden has argued, both emotion and reason can be powerful, linear, and controlled or unpredictable and random.

Yet, Europeans have painted human history as the story of gaining control over emotion by reason. Gosden is not so sure that humans can separate emotion from reason, thought from feeling. A state of inspiration, for example, is both an intellectual and an emotional experience. Similarly, this book strives to push our understanding of humanity's past and future both intellectually and emotionally and in particular relation to the reader's past and future. The author's personal life has been deeply influenced by the study of Africa and relationships with Africans. In some small way, hopefully, this text will facilitate such a journey for readers as well.

Suggestions for Further Reading

Paul Ehrlich and Robert Ornstein, *New World, New Mind: Moving toward Conscious Evolution* (Cambridge, Mass.: Malor Books, 1989). This book is a sweeping and fascinating exploration of the causes behind the seemingly human inability to solve many of the intractable problems people face. Ehrlich, a population biologist, and Ornstein, a psychologist, argue that how humans perceive their environment and ourselves developed in our evolutionary past and has to be understood and then altered to cope with the present.

Steven Feierman, "African Histories and the Dissolution of World History," in *Africa and the Disciplines: The Contributions of Research in Africa to the Social Sciences and Humanities*, ed. Robert H. Bates, V. Y. Mudimbe, and Jean F. O'Barr (Chicago: University of Chicago Press, 1993), 167–212. This is an early and comprehensive essay on the ways in which African histories complicate commonplace understandings of world history. For example, research on slaves and African women as historical actors made it clear that they had been excluded from earlier narratives of history. But such information also made it more difficult to sustain the narratives or understanding of world history with which many had become comfortable.

Rhonda Gonzales, *Societies, Religion and History: Central East Tanzanians and the World They Created, c. 200 BCE to 1800 CE*, http://www.gutenberg-e.org/gonzales/. This is one of the most recent works using historical linguistics to reconstruct the cultures of ancient Africans. Gonzales focuses on the Ruvu societies along the central Tanzanian coast and interior, particularly noting the roles of women and religion over the *longue durée*.

Chris Gosden, *Prehistory: A Short Introduction* (Oxford: Oxford University Press, 2003). This is a beautifully written book about a long historical era that is often associated with lack—lack of written documents and lack of civilization. Into this breach steps Gosden, emphasizing the value of archaeology and material objects, the latter for our understanding of the past as well as our present lives.

"Great Acceleration, The," International Geosphere-Biosphere Programme, http://www .igbp.net/globalchange/greatacceleration.4.1b8ae20512db692f2a680001630.html. This website illuminates in a variety of ways how the Earth system has moved outside the range of natural variability as exhibited over the last 800,000 years.

Joseph Henrich, Steven J. Heine, and Ara Norenzayan, "Most People Are Not WEIRD," *Nature* 466 (July 1, 2010): 29. This is a brief summary of Henrich and his colleagues' conclusion that Western, educated, industrialized, rich, and democratic societies have "some of the most psychologically unusual people on Earth."

International Geosphere-Biosphere Programme, The. This program was established to conduct research on global-scale and regional-scale interactions between Earth's systems and human systems. To see the Great Acceleration chart referenced in this chapter, go to http://www.igbp.net/globalchange/greatacceleration .4.1b8ae20512db692f2a680001630.html.

Richard E. Lee, ed., *The* Longue Durée *and World-Systems Analysis* (Albany: State University of New York Press, 2012). Commemorating the fiftieth anniversary of Fernand Braudel's article "History and the Social Sciences: The *Longue Durée*," this book continues Braudel's work through the framework of world systems. The author also demonstrates how much division still remains between disciplines. The final chapter is a new translation of Braudel's French article by Immanuel Wallerstein.

David Orr, *Earth in Mind: On Education, Environment and the Human Prospect* (Washington, D.C.: Island Press, 1994). Orr first argues that changing humanity's future requires changing the way we think about education and then outlines the path to a better education for a better future.

PART I

THE *LONGUE DURÉE*

WHEN A VISITOR stands amidst the Rocky Mountains, he or she cannot escape the feeling that a single human being is very small indeed. And yet, at the same time, many feel a strong sense of connectedness to such majesty. Ideally, the study of history would create a similar sense of relative smallness and concomitant connection. One of the challenges of the teleological narratives of Western history is the assumption that what modern, industrialized nations have achieved is not only meant to be but is the greatest achievement ever. Such audacity is dangerous, as is becoming clear. History, like our planet's grandeur, requires an appreciation for past events, whether awe-inspiring or challenging, that results in monumental ideas and institutions but also an awareness that humanity's role in Earth's evolution is not always benign. To get to this point, a long-term view of history is necessary. Yet, few historians or history classes embrace such a long view, in part because modern society has taken pride in the distance we have come from our ancient roots. Such separation is more apparent than real.

U.S. historian William Cronon points out a parallel between this distancing from long-term history in the human relationship and wilderness in the United States and Europe. For the last 300 years at least, people have demarcated "wilderness" and "civilized society" as oppositional categories, even though our relationship to wilderness has not been stagnant. Prior to the last 100 years, wilderness was frightening and, at the same time, a place of spiritual force. Generally, it was not something humans entered at will. By the late 1800s, many Americans lived in cities and the limits of westward expansion were clear, so a movement to preserve some of the most breathtaking landscapes emerged. Americans began to celebrate the wilderness and preserve it—for example, through the national parks system. Setting aside these areas reserved them for human use, but with the understanding that such use would be brief and have little impact on them. For areas to be worth preserving, human settlement had to be absent. In either period, wilderness reflected human purposes and remained distant from settlement and civilization.

Yet, in the early twentieth century, some began to seek escape from pestilential civilization and polluted and overcrowded cities. They created small, rural utopias in suburban areas, where the lawn was the ideal form of environment. Unfortunately, it was a high-maintenance environment that had to be cut and fertilized to stay attractive. As writer Michael Pollan argues, wilderness and the lawn represent Americans' schizophrenic approach to nature and wilderness: either stay out and let nature run its course so we are not a part of nature (as in the wilderness) or micro-manage the environment for its aesthetic outcomes (as in the lawn). Either way nature is antagonistic. Yet, as Pollan advocates, such divisions are unrealistic. We *are* a part of nature, and it makes sense to explore arenas where human societies and nature both have space for expression, such as gardening. Gardening recognizes the wildness right outside our door, but it tries to put some of that wildness to work for humans.

This long digression into wilderness runs parallel to our tendency to dismiss or distance ourselves from the histories and cultures of other peoples and places as though modern humans are civilized and the "other" or "wilderness" cultures and histories are not somehow part of the human story. Just as gardening requires getting dirty and learning about the limitations of our landscapes, being willing to learn about the broad human past, both "civilized" societies and those that we have distanced ourselves from, will result in more grit and more balance. And these other histories can help guide our future course. Human evolution, the lives of gathering and hunting peoples, the processes of learning how to grow food and keep animals, and a receptivity to new ideas and ways of doing things are all developments of the distant past that scholars and citizens have tended to relegate to the dustbin as lacking meaning for contemporary existence.

Chapter 1 examines early human evolution and emphasizes some of the most recent thinking about the multiplicity of human species from which our ancestors eventually derived. It also takes up the question of what it means to be human. In other words, over the millennia of our development in Africa, what challenges did humans face, and how did those challenges shape people and their capabilities? Chapter 2 deals with the domestication of plants and animals. This is one of the most significant changes that human societies have ever undergone, and it remains the economic foundation of modern societies. Instead of a revolution, this was a slow process and did not necessarily provide distinct advantages to those who practiced it early on. Gathering and hunting as a way of life continued in many places despite knowledge about how to intensively grow food. Chapter 3 looks at climate change over the long term in Africa. This history illuminates the profound impact climate change has had on human populations in the past, as well as the ways in which some environments are more susceptible to drastic change than others. Chapter 3 also examines the practice of pastoralism as an adaptation to a dry climate zone rather than a relic of the past to be dismantled in favor of a more modern sedentary lifestyle. Chapter 4 discusses what some have referred to as cultural "diffusion" as opposed to "conflict"—the mainstay of European history for much of the twentieth century. Most African societies today are a combination of social, economic, and political practices from a variety of cultures. African societies have consistently learned new ideas and incorporated them back into their traditions and institutions, whether in terms of food production, the raising of livestock, various technologies like ironworking and cell phones, or ways to initiate youth into adulthood.

This long-term African history is the figurative majestic landscape against which modern humans build cultures and lives. It is both inspiring and humbling and invites recognition that our past is neither dangerous nor embarrassing but essential in understanding where we have been and the possible choices that lie ahead.

1 Humanity's African Origins

THIS CHAPTER STARTS our journey into African history from the most basic starting point of all human history: human evolution, or the beginning of us. The questions of who we are, how we behave, and how we might face our uncertain future are illuminated by a study of humanity's earliest origins. In contrast, most people take our current state for granted without giving much thought to the millennia of changes and experiences that have accumulated to create the species we belong to today.

There might seem to be little connection between people in the twenty-first century and our earliest ancestors. And certainly, most of our popular descriptions and images of early humans emphasize their differences from us: they are usually drawn as short and hunched over, with primitive weapons in their hands, emphasizing their limited technology. Popular images portray them as cavemen savagely devouring wild animals and don't convey much about their culture, languages, or dreams. Such images and ideas are the products of particular threads in our intellectual past, including classical Greek and Roman scholars who thought our ancestors were more like animals. More recently, the combination of a misreading of Darwin, exposure to people who looked and lived differently than many Europeans, and a developing Western historical sense of progress and hierarchy inspired the belief that people with primitive shelters and technology (such as Africans), including those who lived a very, very long time ago, were not completely human.

The reality, though, is far different. We owe much of who we are and how we behave to our earliest experiences on this planet. Some of these traits include an enhanced ability to cooperate, vulnerable childhoods and a long period of old age, and an instinctive reaction to large, powerful mammals and birds of prey.

An investigation of the ancient past makes it clear that prejudices and other unsubstantiated beliefs hold strong sway over our questions and research. Ideas about race, unique human capabilities, and whether humans are innately violent or peaceful, for example, all deeply color the questions curious people ask and the evidence marshaled for the answers. This study suggests that much of what are considered unique signs of modern humanity, such as some forms of communication, existed in the distant past. Moreover, early human history is far more colorful and varied than many have assumed. Modern humans have many ancestors and cousins who shared some of our abilities but became extinct due to adversity. This history should also make readers appreciate the prominent role Africa has played in human history. Most human species and most human biology and early culture in its broadest sense—artistic expression, social cooperation, and technological development—originated in Africa.

Geographical Place

Because the history of human evolution has been written based on archaeological discoveries across a broad swath of the eastern half of the African continent, there is not a tight geographical focus to this chapter (see map 1.1). In countries where the most work has been done, more discoveries have been made. These include savanna areas in Kenya, Tanzania, Ethiopia, and South Africa. Eight million years ago, the savanna landscapes would have been much wetter, creating a patchwork of trees and grassland when human ancestors developed. Some of the earliest discoveries are shown in map 1.1.

Sources and Methodologies

History is a discipline that marshals evidence and then interprets it. History is not "facts" but interpretation of historical evidence. This is not to say that "anything goes" in history. To the contrary, thoroughly executed research, well-documented use of evidence, and carefully crafted arguments are all necessary for solid historical analysis. Evidence is at the foundation of the historical enterprise. The nature of the evidence for human evolution, as for all facets of human history, plays an important role in what scholars know and how they know it. The information on most of the topics in this book is drawn from scholars who work from a combination of primary sources and secondary sources. Primary sources are forms of direct evidence such as archaeology or historical linguistics. Secondary sources are accounts of a society and its past, often based on primary evidence. Yet, what evidence is available as well as the questions asked at a particular point in time determine much of the interpretation that will follow. This is why there are differing interpretations of historical events, particularly from one era to the next. These different questions help to create a richer, denser understanding of the human past. Similarly, African historians use a wide variety of sources to piece together our understanding of early African history. More available sources and types of evidence help scholars to develop a broader understanding of life millennia ago.

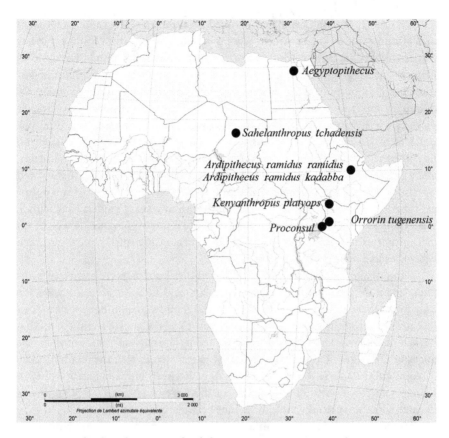

Map 1.1 Sites of earliest discoveries of early human ancestors. Courtesy of Creative Commons, attributed to Kameraad Pjotr and Sting.

In research devoted to early humans, questions about superior species have loomed large for some time. Similarly, in African history, the concern is often with superior civilizations. Because African history, African anthropology, and African studies generally are relatively new fields, having gained legitimacy and wide interest with African independence movements in the middle of the last century, they have formed within the shadow of European history. As a reaction to this, many Africanists sought to justify these fields of study by demonstrating that Africans have just as glorious a past as any other culture. In this view, Africans are just like Europeans: if Europeans had kingdoms, so did Africans; if Europeans had peasants, so did Africans.

There is also the tendency to differentiate Africa from Europe or argue that Africa is the foundation of all that is European, as Afrocentrists, such as Near

Eastern scholar Martin Bernal, have argued. Afrocentrism is an approach to historical study that seeks to correct the long-standing approach to history that has placed Greek, Roman, and other Western civilizations as the foundation of world history, ignoring significant contributions made by many other cultures. Although it is important to investigate Africans' contributions to the foundations of human civilization, as Bernal and others have done, no history of a people or place can neatly be attributed to a narrow set of factors or ideas. For example, much early Afrocentrism, such as Martin Bernal's *Black Athena,* focused on Egypt as the motherland of African culture. Egypt is one of 54 African countries, and although it is home to the longest-lasting civilization in human history and worthy of study as an African civilization, it owes some of its cultural and political inheritance to African societies further south in what is modern-day Sudan. Historian Clarence E. Davis has argued that Afrocentrists have used modern racial categories to understand a distant past, such as ancient Egypt, where such categories had no meaning.

Similarly, for a long time, it was believed that humans were completely different from all other animal species. Scholars assumed that humans were the only toolmakers and were genetically very different from all other species. Then researchers determined that humans were genetically related to the apes and that human characteristics are largely determined by the characteristics of their ape ancestors. Further, it was discovered that chimpanzees in Tanzania and Côte d'Ivoire make and use tools. The distinctions between humans and apes began to fade, and based on studies in which gorillas were taught sign language, it was decided there was actually little difference between apes and humans.

Studies have also shown similarities between humans and ants. Entomologist E. O. Wilson has argued that ants, along with humans, are among the very few highly social animals on Earth. This social capacity in ants is marked by their ability to build complex societies, with individuals acting in specialized capacities and sometimes acting altruistically, such as when nest-weaving worker ants use mature ant larvae as living shuttles to spin thread for the nest. These larvae use all their spinning silk for a communal nest formed between leaves rather than an individual one. Ants are also global, living in every climate on the planet, much like humans. Some ant species practice forms of agriculture. For example, a few species of tropical American ants cultivate mushrooms, creating beds for their growth and weeding out unwanted invasive plants. Other ants "farm" aphids for their nectar.

With such insights, anything unique about humans began to be downplayed. As with most things, scholars are settling somewhere in the middle and finding that there is tremendous genetic continuity among chimpanzees, bonobos (a close relative to the chimpanzee), and early humans. Obviously, other features distinguish us from primates, such as our capacity for language and for thinking about things that are not directly in front of us. All most historical accounts can do is weave another thread into the tapestry of the broader human story, making it more colorful, denser, and stronger than it was before.

In this chapter, the term *hominin* refers to humans and all their extinct bipedal ancestors as one branch of the African apes (gorillas and chimpanzees being the other two branches). In the past, the term *hominid* was used to refer to such species, but today it refers to humans *and* all of the African apes together. Such changes in classification can be confusing, and readers will most likely see both terms used to refer to human and ancestral species, because not all adopt the most recent terminology at the same time. Also, it is important to understand that most of the earlier hominin species numbered in the thousands, so their population size was much smaller than that of most societies today.

Paleoanthropology is the multidisciplinary approach used to reconstruct evolutionary history of the human branch of the tree of life. As the name suggests, it combines paleontology and anthropology. Anthropology is the study of human beings, and paleontology is the study of fossils for evidence about evolution and past ecologies. Paleoanthropology is the study of human ancestors who lived millennia ago, so what we know about them is derived from archaeological or other evidence. The vast majority of our evidence of early human history comes from decades of work by teams of paleontologists uncovering primary evidence, such as Richard and Mary Leakey and their peers working in the 1970s; Maeve Leakey and her "Hominid Gang," both working in Kenya today; and Tim White and his team working now in Ethiopia. Most of these paleontologists have been working for decades in hot, dry landscapes, looking for fossil evidence (usually in the form of bones or tools) of early humans. Paleontologists use many of the same tools as archaeologists (those who study past human cultures). In archaeology, older settlements are usually found below younger ones. Many of the objects found in those layers can be dated, so a succession of societies in one location can be analyzed for change and continuity over time. This is called stratigraphy.

You may already be familiar with the names Leakey and White because they are responsible for some of the most famous hominin discoveries. Tim White's discovery of *Ardipithecus ramidus* in the mid-1990s pushed the oldest hominin fossil back to 4 million years ago or more. Scholars who work in this field usually make a career and name for themselves on the basis of one or two spectacular finds that are subject to their own and their peers' interpretations. The rarity of such finds, their limited nature—partial skeletons if a team is lucky and partial bone fragments more typically—and the tremendous amount of resources (material and human) expended in the search for them all mean it can be a high-stakes game. Thus, perhaps more than other scholars who contribute to African history, paleontologists and affiliated specialists tend to be associated with a particular species or idea and often are in conflict with others over the significance of their finds. This is dramatic history and dramatic interpretation—a fitting start to a continent's fascinating history.

Paleontology might seem like a glamorous job, but it involves difficult, painstaking work, usually in the hot African sun for days on end. Most days, working teams find only a fragment of something—an animal bone, a hominin bone, or a tool. Rarely do they find an entire bone or, even more rarely, multiple bone pieces from the same skeleton. Behind each well-publicized discovery are weeks of excavation by a lead paleontologist and his or her highly skilled African colleagues. The crew that found Lucy, an example of *Australopithecus afarensis,* in Ethiopia in 1974, for example, found about 40 percent of the 206 bones in the human skeleton. One of the reasons the find was so spectacular, however, was that all the bones were from one skeleton. Often celebrated finds are only one or two bones, such as Tim White's discovery of a jawbone in Ethiopia. Thus, our reconstruction of early human history is based on a relatively few bones, numbering only in the hundreds.

Scientists bring their own ideas and presuppositions to their work. For example, in terms of classifying hominins, there are lumpers and splitters. Lumpers tend to group similar finds into one species or genus rather than proliferate genuses and species, whereas splitters believe it is more appropriate to recognize small but influential distinctions with entirely new species and/or genus markers. Thus, the researchers who announced in 2010 the discovery of a new species near Johannesburg, South Africa—*Australopithecus sediba,* which lived 2,000 years ago—are of the latter persuasion. They argue that *A. sediba* has a unique combination of features not seen before in one specimen and that the combination suggests that *A. sediba* might be the most recent ancestor for the genus *Homo.* Others are not so certain and wonder if *A. sediba* belongs to a dead-end branch. Thus, not only are the actual fossil pieces up for interpretation, but how to classify them is as well. The combination of a relatively small number of fossils and human interpretations means that most new finds significantly alter the way scholars think about human evolution. This makes it an exciting field to follow, because in an individual's lifetime, the accepted wisdom about our ancient past might change profoundly.

Paleontologists are also interested in tools associated with hominin sites. The tools are interpreted for the intellectual capacity they represent and the kinds of foods they would have been used to obtain. The *A. sediba* find was accompanied by evidence of saber-tooth cats, mice, wild dogs and cats, hyenas, and horses, providing a broader context for understanding the species and its capabilities.

The best ways to increase our understanding of human evolutionary history are by obtaining more data and improving the analytic methods available for the data already collected. The former occurs when paleontologists find more fossils, and the second occurs when scientists discover ways, such as through

DNA testing, to extract more information from existing fossil evidence. In fact, the combination of genetic testing and morphological categorization is changing some earlier interpretations, including the discovery that Neanderthals and modern humans interbred.

Increasingly, paleontologists incorporate anthropological and other types of evidence into their work in paleoanthropology. For example, physical evidence might be considered alongside oral traditions or linguistic evidence from contemporary societies. Genetics has also become a major contributor to our understanding of early human history. Human genes are the repository for hereditary information, but they are constantly changing. Thus, geneticists can study the changes over time for indications of when certain traits appeared, much like the linguistic evidence African historians use, which is discussed in chapter 4. In his book *Before the Dawn: Recovering the Lost History of Our Ancestors*, Nicholas Wade (2006) states that genetic evidence tells us when parts of the human body became hairless and when the skin turned black. In addition, paleontologists are able to reconstruct early African history using historical linguistics, population genetics, evolutionary psychology, and primatology.

More recently, some of the most exciting genetic news has concerned the Neanderthals. The Neanderthal genome project at the Max Planck Institute for Evolutionary Anthropology involved 57 scientists working over four years to sequence the Neanderthal genome. Using three bones (two bones had dates—38,000 YA and 44,000 YA—and one did not) discovered in a cave in Croatia 20 years ago, the researchers removed half a gram of bone powder for investigation. Using new methods that allow them to improve degraded DNA, separate microbial DNA from nonmicrobial DNA, and quickly and accurately sequence nucleotides, they were able to identify the presence of Neanderthal DNA. Thus, modern humans (mostly non-Africans) do contain a small trace of Neanderthal DNA, which suggests interbreeding between modern humans and Neanderthals.

Another use of genetic data can be seen in studies of human lice. Archaeologists have never been able to determine when clothes were first worn because both fabric and the bone needles used for sewing are highly perishable. After an infestation of head lice at his child's school, Mark Stoneking, an American researcher at the Max Planck Institute for Evolutionary Anthropology, discovered that lice cannot survive longer than 24 hours away from the warmth of the human body. Thus, they must have spread around the globe on humans. His study of lice confirmed the migration pattern implied by human DNA. Lice also can help ascertain the date when humans first wore clothing. When humans lost their body hair, the louse's domain shrank, confining it to the hair on the head. The louse patiently bided its time, however, and many millennia later, when people started to wear clothes, the head louse seized the chance to regain its lost territory by evolving a new variety, the body louse, that could live in clothing. Head and body lice closely resemble each other, except body lice are larger and have claws specialized for grasping material, not strands of hair. Stoneking realized he could date the invention of clothing if he could only figure out from variations in lice DNA the time at which the body louse began to evolve from the head louse.

Using head and body lice from citizens of 12 countries, he analyzed all the variations in a small segment of each head and body louse's genetic material and arranged each population's lice in a family tree. Knowing the rate at which variations accumulate on DNA over the centuries, he could then calculate the dates of the various forks or branch points in the tree. The branch at which the body louse first evolved from the head louse turned out to be around 72,000 years ago. That would be the date when our ancestors began to wear clothing, and it coincides well with other estimates about the flowering of human culture, around 50,000 to 100,000 years ago.

The preceding discussion of the sources used to reconstruct early human history introduced a lot of names and terms. It is now time to sort them out.

An Outline of Human Evolution

Today we know that our earliest ancestors came from Africa, but this information is relatively new. Readers' grandparents would have learned in school that humans developed in Europe. Before the mid-twentieth century, most of the search for human fossils took place in Europe and Asia, not Africa. Until recently, there was much debate about the origins of modern humans. One school of thought—the multiregionalist interpretation—argued that *Homo sapiens,* or modern humans, developed five different times across the globe, roughly corresponding to our current physical differences—what was once considered race. In this interpretation, given recent history and the technological prowess of northern countries, it made sense to look for "origins" and European cultural superiority in Europe.

Despite this focus, Charles Darwin had predicted that early human evolution took place in Africa. Since the 1960s, fieldwork and genetic testing have confirmed that much of the story of human evolution can be found there. The other, newer interpretation (Darwin notwithstanding) is a result of genetic evidence, particularly mitochondrial DNA. This evidence strongly suggests that *H. sapiens* evolved in Africa beginning about 200,000 years ago, and a small band left the continent and eventually colonized the rest of the world, displacing earlier hominin populations. Now much paleoanthropological work is done in eastern and southern Africa.

The long, arduous process that took humans from being small primate-like creatures in a series of new and difficult environments to the dominant species on the planet is not often told. As Stephen Oppenheimer argued, "We were not 'put' here fully formed, thinking, talking, and unique among animals. We were specifically selected and moulded by a fierce, blind, unthinking environment." The appearance of new hominin species coincides with significant climate change. The global climate cooled between 5 and 10 million years ago, with the last 1.5 million years being the coldest. It is likely that our hominin line began to develop during this colder period. During this era, glaciers spread and locked up water that normally would have filled the seas and rained down on the continent. In this cold, dry climate, African equatorial forests diminished, and scattered woodlands developed in some places. In such a habitat, tree dwellers would be forced to spend more time on the ground looking for food, putting them at risk of predation from large animals. As it turns out, the sites of the earliest hominin evidence so far are similar (except for *Sahelanthropus tchadensis*). They are habitat mosaics—made up of a variety of habitats, such as woodlands, grasslands, lakes, and gallery forests along rivers, that are in close proximity. These habitats suggest that early hominins were both tree dwellers (spending some time, including sleeping, in the trees) and ground dwellers (spending some time on the ground). Yet, a more detailed examination of climate change reveals that despite an overall cooling trend, there were sharp fluctuations between warm and cool. These fluctuations became greater starting 6 million years ago, with even greater instability around 2 million years ago (with the advent of *Homo*), and even more instability around 200,000 years ago with the evolution of *H. sapiens*.

Human evolution is outlined through a series of distinct species, identified by the fossils discussed earlier, as you can see in table 1.1. The average fossil mammal species lasts between 1 and 2 million years. During this period, the species will likely change due to random variations and morphological responses to climate change. Because of the limited number of fossils available to us, it is impossible to know with certainty how much variation is reasonable within a species, but researchers have been able to determine typical degrees of variation by looking at variations within living species. What distinctions count varies significantly from one set of researchers to another, as described earlier. Table 1.1 depicts a larger number of species than lumpers would call for.

Our closest relative is the chimpanzee. *Homo sapiens* share 99 percent of genetic material with this species. Over 7 million years ago, one or more species started down a path that led, with multiple twists and turns, to humans, while other species began a journey toward our modern chimpanzees. Paleoanthropologists now believe it is highly unlikely that they will find one species that marks the divide between two species. Archaeologists Robert Foley and Marta Lahr of Cambridge University have argued that speciation, or separation of species, might have taken a million years or more. And genetic evidence indicates that human and chimp ancestors interbred for more than a million years after the original split. Thus, there were likely numerous chimp-like species that possessed some human features.

Table 1.1 A splitting view of early human ancestors. Adapted from Bernard Wood, *Human Evolution: A Very Short Introduction* (Oxford: Oxford University Press, 2005), 47–50. Courtesy of Oxford University Press, www.oup.com.

Category	Species	Dates	Left Africa
Modern *Homo*	*H. sapiens*	200,000 YA–present	c. 50,000 YA
Premodern	*H. ergaster*	1.4–1.9 MYA	c. 1 MYA
Homo	*H. erectus*	300,000 YA–1.8 MYA	
	H. floresiensis	17,000–95,000 YA	
	(probably dead end)	30,000–230,000 YA	
	H. neanderthalensis		
Archaic and	*H. habilis*	1.5–2.4 MYA	
transitional	*P. boisei* (dead end)	1.1–2.1 MYA	
hominins	*A. sediba*	1.97–1.98 MYA	
	A. afarensis	3–3.9 MYA	
Possible early	*A. ramidus*	4.4 MYA	
hominins	*O. tugenensis*	6 MYA	
	S. tchadensis	6–7 MYA	

Distinctions between species are based on differences scholars see between chimpanzee and hominin species, both in physical and cultural forms. They know how modern humans differ from chimpanzees in terms of their body shape, movement, and development. For example, chimpanzees have a low forehead, a projecting face, and small brain size. Humans have a steep forehead, a flat face, and a large brain size. Chimpanzees have a flat hand, long fingers, and a short thumb; humans have a cup-shaped hand and a long thumb. Chimpanzees have a flat foot and an angled big toe, whereas hominins have an arched foot and a straight big toe. Our bone and teeth development is slow, while that of the chimpanzee is fast. Rarely do researchers find all the bones of a skeleton, but one bone from one part of the body can be compared to those of other hominin species and those of panin (or ape) species to help determine where they fit.

Two frameworks will help guide our examination of some of the hominin species uncovered to date. One framework is presented in table 1.1, which classifies species in reference to their date and their relative position to modern humans. The framework in table 1.2 shows hominin species grouped by fossil evidence characteristics as well as by date. Here, brain size and the ability to walk on two feet, bipedalism, are highlighted.

In the possible early hominin category, lumpers would put all the separate species under one genus, *Ardipithecus*. All four have many more traits like those

Table 1.2 Physical characteristics of hominins. From Bernard Wood and Paul Constantino, "Human Origins: Life at the Top of the Tree," in *Assembling the Tree of Life*, ed. Joel Cracraft and Michael J. Donoghue (New York: Oxford University Press, 2004), fig. 29.1. Courtesy of Oxford University Press, www.oup.com.

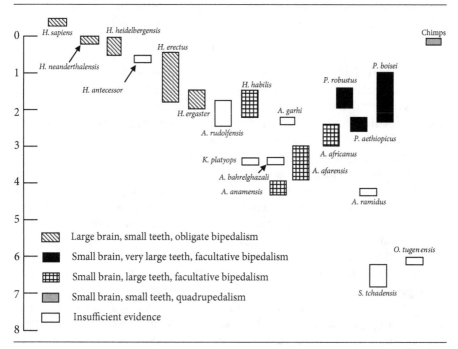

of chimpanzees than any of the species in the latter three categories. Moreover, there is little available evidence for each species at this time. As Wood, a splitter, puts it, the fossil evidence for all four possible species fits into a supermarket cart with much room to spare. More evidence will be needed to make more definitive claims. *Sahelanthropus tchadensis* (found in the Sahel region of Chad) is a particularly important find (a cranium and some bits of mandible) because if it is an early hominin, then our early ancestors occupied a much wider area of Africa than paleoanthropologists previously thought. When *Sahelanthropus* was alive, northern Chad was rainforest, not the mosaic areas where most other hominid fossils have been found. This discovery raises questions about where and how hominids and primates went their separate ways. An upright stance is inferred from the forward position of the foramen magnum, the large hole in the base of the skull through which the spinal column passes. *Orrorin tugenensis* fossils indicate an upright posture. Grooves in femur bones point to places where ligament and muscle attached to the bone, in ways that suggest bipedal capabilities.

Ardipithecus ramidus, like many of the species in the next category and probably both *Sahelanthropus* and *Orrorin,* possessed facultative (or optional) bipedalism, so it could move around effectively in the trees and on the ground. Facultative bipedalism means that moving on two feet was possible but not the typical means of mobility. Wood's second category, archaic and transitional hominins, includes various species within the genus *Australopithecus,* made most famous by "Lucy" (see figure 1.1).

As figure 1.1 illustrates, there is far more fossil evidence for the species in this category than in the former. *Austrolopithecus afarensis*'s brain size is a bit larger than that of an equivalent-sized chimpanzee. The shape and size of the pelvis suggest that this species was able to walk on two feet but probably only for short distances, and thus, like earlier species, possessed facultative bipedalism. Lucy's skeleton still has features suited for arboreal living, such as long hands and feet and narrow shoulders. The latter allowed for easier coordination of the arms above the head. Without tools, they likely still relied on trees and tree cover for protection from predators. *Australopithecus sediba* is a newer find (2008) in this category. The brain is smaller than modern humans but has other modern features. Another genus, *Paranthropus,* is distinguished from *Austrolopithecus* by its projecting face and large chewing teeth that might suggest a largely vegetarian diet. In the same transitional category is *Homo habilis,* the first species known to have made stone tools. One of the interesting things about the species in this category overall is that the basic australopith skeleton remained fairly stable for several million years; even as new species came and went, much stayed the same.

Taking a break from our chronology of hominin species, this juncture, about 2 million years ago, provides some new ideas about human evolution and its similarities to other species. One of the myths of human ancestry is that it was a linear line of human evolution, leading from *Australopithecus* to *Homo erectus* and then on to *H. sapiens,* for example. Due to a tremendous amount of archaeological work over the last few decades, however, scholars now know that *H. sapiens* are the sole surviving species of a multibranched bush. Thus, our species is not the end product of a steady evolution toward superiority but rather the chance outcome of a very messy process, as paleoanthropologist Ian Tatersall has argued. Some paleontologists, like Bernard Wood, argue that what they are uncovering now is just the tip of the iceberg. He believes that in our distant past there were many ape-like creatures, not just the dozen or so specimens we have found thus far. Tatersall argues for an image of a messy bush, rather than a tree, while geneticist Alan Templeton calls for a trellis-like pattern, allowing for change through time while many species were interconnected by gene flow.

Whether a trellis or a bush, *H. sapiens* are not the endpoint of a single trajectory but the lucky descendants of one of many possible evolutionary lines. Earlier hominids formed multiple lines of evolution, some of which were dead ends, like

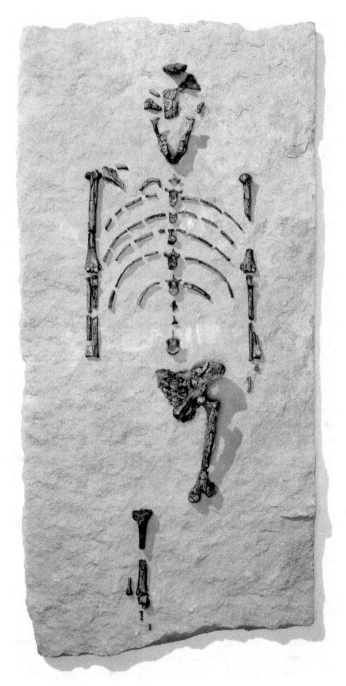

Figure 1.1 "Lucy," an *A. afarensis* fossil, found in Ethiopia in 1974. She is thought to have lived 3.2 million years ago. Courtesy of Houston Museum of Natural Science.

Paranthropus boisei, one of the robust species. A bit less than 2 million years ago, multiple hominid species, such as *H. habilis,* the toolmaker, and *P. boisei,* coexisted and used the same landscape in eastern Africa. We don't know as much as we would like about these species or about their possible interactions, but certainly recent evidence about interbreeding between *Homo neanderthalensis* and *H. sapiens* makes it more likely that they not only coexisted but also interacted. Thus, while *P. boisei* seems to be a dead end, our ancestors might have interacted enough with them to carry their skills, if not their DNA, with them.

Returning to the chronological discussion, premodern *Homo* are larger hominins with larger brain cases and longer legs. They look more like us. *Homo erectus* fossils have been found with evidence of fire use but not of fire-making capabilities. Longer legs meant they were able to travel longer distances more efficiently. This is one of the first hominin species to leave Africa and colonize parts of Europe and Asia. An earlier interpretation credits *H. erectus* with leaving Africa, but it is now believed that the related and earlier *Homo ergaster* left the continent. *Homo neanderthalensis* is the best-known species in this category and lived not in Africa but in Europe. They lived from 30,000 to 230,000 years ago and are distinctive in a number of ways. Physically, they have a large nasal opening, a large cranial cavity, and thick limb bones, likely adjustments to the cold European climate. Culturally, they were one of the first hominins to bury their dead, so paleoarchaeologists have found many more fossil remains of them than of other species. For some time, scholars thought they were our closest ancestors, but they now know this is not the case.

One of the more recent paleoanthropological finds, *Homo floresiensis,* is a miniature-sized human, sometimes called "The Hobbit." It was found on the island of Flores, Indonesia, in 2003 and likely shrunk in size due to island geography. Island geography often encourages change in species size: enlargement of small species and shrinking of larger ones. The island of Flores was home to a giant rat as well as pygmy elephants and perhaps pygmy humans. The youngest specimen of this species found so far is 13,000 years old.

Modern humans, *H. sapiens,* are present in Africa by 200,000 years ago and are marked physically by smaller teeth, face, and jaws; a high, round cranium; a pronounced chin; brow ridges; a mixed diet; and sophisticated toolmaking. Not only did they make stone tools from a prepared core so a single blow would create a finished point, but they began to attach these stone tools to spears. The first evidence of *H. sapiens* outside of Africa begins about 50,000 years ago. Most likely at that time, a small band of 150 people or so walked from Ethiopia and Somalia across the southern end of the Red Sea, when the water was much lower. They and their ancestors came to populate the rest of the world; we are all descendants of this small band from the area of present-day Ethiopia and Somalia.

One question that remains is why it took so long for *H. sapiens* to leave Africa if they had our modern capabilities. One reason might be that they faced other hominins, such as descendants of *H. ergaster*, who had adapted to their environments in the Middle East. Another might be that catastrophic climate change led to a significant decrease in the *H. sapiens* population, reducing the chances of discovering new territories. Genetic studies point to the near demise of our own species about 100,000 years ago, when our population likely dwindled to a few thousand adults.

Another mystery of our early history is whether or not *H. sapiens* displaced all previous hominins during the last dispersal or if there was interbreeding between resident hominins and the newer ones who moved in. It was long thought that interbreeding was highly unlikely, even though a few fossils did demonstrate mixing of anatomical features. Examples of such mixed heritage can be found in the early Cro-Magnons from the Czech Republic. These individuals have modern skeletons with Neanderthal cranial features, as anthropologist Pamela Willoughby reports.

As noted above, researchers have evidence that modern humans interbred with Neanderthals. One to 4 percent of the genes non-Africans carry are Neanderthal in origin. The interbreeding took place after modern humans left Africa. Thus, modern-day Africans' DNA does not show traces of Neanderthal DNA, as do the genes of Chinese, French, and North Americans. This evidence confirms that there was something different about *H. sapiens* that eventually allowed them to become more successful than all previous hominin species, including Neanderthals.

Another question that arises when we study this history is "Why aren't humans still evolving?" The answer is that we are. Modern humans have not escaped the long-term history of genetic shaping. A group of Europeans who occupied north-central Europe (the area that now includes the Netherlands, northern Germany, Denmark, and southern Norway) demonstrate recent evolutionary developments. The adults of this European culture were able to digest milk throughout adulthood. They kept cattle and relied on their milk for part of their diet. Most of them were lactose tolerant, while the frequency of lactose tolerance decreased in populations outside the core area.

Thus, these European cattle keepers show a human population evolving, in recent times (within the last 10,000 years), in response to a change created by human culture. Lactose is a special sugar contained in mother's milk. The gene for the enzyme that digests lactose is switched on just before birth and, in most people, switched off after weaning. Because lactose does not occur naturally in most people's diets after childhood, the lactase gene is not needed after that and the body switches it off because it would be a waste of the body's resources to continue making the lactase enzyme. But in people of mostly northern European extraction, and to some extent in African and Bedouin tribes who drink raw milk, the lactase gene remains active for decades or throughout life.

Lactose tolerance illustrates three things. First, evolution did not stop 50,000 years ago with the departure of modern humans from Africa. Second, human genes respond differently in different populations to the same stimulus, as in the cattle-keeping peoples of Europe and Africa. Third, cultural changes can cause genetic changes, just as the drinking of milk caused genetic change in cattle-keeping populations.

Another possible way in which humans are evolving is through diminution of our physical stature. Since 40,000 years ago, in multiple places, our skull size has been decreasing. This trait often accompanies domestication or taming. Wade argues that *H. sapiens* have become tamer than our ancestors—*H. neanderthalensis,* for example—and our smaller heads reflect that. Other animals have demonstrated diminution of head size as a result of domestication as well, such as recent experiments with silver foxes, Wade notes.

Human Evolution and Race

Studying early human history challenges one of the common ways scholars differentiate people: by race. Many students assume that race is a biological reality, but this is not what recent genetic and anthropological work demonstrates. Our current understanding, the "Out of Africa" interpretation, is that modern humans, or *H. sapiens,* originated in Africa about 200,000 years ago; therefore, we are all African.

But the significant physical differences between Africans and Europeans and between Africans and Asians that have occupied the multiregionalists deserve an explanation. The physical characteristics associated with race for so long, such as skin color, are the result of more recent adaptations to various climates, but they do not connote innate differences in intellectual or social capabilities. All *Homo* species were darkly pigmented at one time, and today, darkly pigmented peoples are found near the equator and lighter ones are found closer to the poles, as anthropologist Nina Jablonski argues in her book on human skin. Greater exposure to ultraviolet radiation near the equator requires darker skin to protect the body from too much radiation but also to safeguard the body's folate stores against degradation. Folate plays a critical role in maintaining and expressing DNA. Without healthy amounts of folate, developmental disorders and degenerative diseases occur. As early *Homo* moved out of the tropics, however, their exposure to ultraviolet rays, and thus vitamin D, decreased. Vitamin D is essential for skeletal growth and maintenance and the normal functioning of the immune system, among other things. In the north, lighter skin could afford some ultraviolet protection, while also speeding the absorption of vitamin D in less ultraviolet ray–intensive areas.

Our physical differences are just that: they tell us about our adaptation to climate, not about our cultural or intellectual capabilities. Yet, there are some biological or genetic differences between human communities; the greatest genetic differences between humans are between continents, largely due to lack of interbreeding between continental populations for the last 15,000 years or so. Our continental communities showed marked genetic continuity from about 14,000 years ago, as the last Ice Age ended, until the last 500 years.

Becoming Human

One of the more important ideas about our early existence suggests that hominins struggled to stay alive and reproduce in challenging environments without the intellectual and technological superiority possessed today. As the examples of more recent human evolution demonstrate, the physical characteristics outlined above are only the beginning of understanding who we are. Archaeologist Chris Gosden puts it nicely when he says, "Human history is about the extension of the inherent capacities of the body through actual use, and because various cultures have different needs and values, human bodies are given different skills and develop various capacities." Here the interest is in some of the general ways in which humans have extended the inherent capacities of the body.

The existence of a certain size of tooth or cranium in and of itself does not prove a particular trait or culture. In fact, many paleoanthropologists believe that much of what makes us human is a result of exaptation rather than adaptation. Exaptation means that the species already possessed the physical infrastructure for some skill or capability but only started to use it in a certain way after some time. The trait might or might not have been the result of previous natural selection. Our language capabilities are quite possibly the result of exaptation, for example. Another way of saying this is that earlier humans might have had the same capacity for culture as modern humans have but did not need to exercise it.

When our ancestors came to develop human culture and why are unclear. For a long time, as anthropologist Willoughby argues, scholars assumed that once hominins dispersed out of Africa, they became modern behaviorally and undertook the cultural innovation and change that are associated with our technological species. Here, the assumption was that modern humans became culturally so in Europe. But Willoughby cautions that the kinds of prejudices and assumptions that were at the root of colonialism have also led scholars to research and investigate human innovation and culture in Europe at a far faster rate than in Africa until recently.

Specialists in African prehistory increasingly believe that anatomically modern humans also possessed modern culture—that is, that our modern culture developed in Africa. Modern culture is not a checklist, and it did not spring full-blown in all its characteristics. It involves technological, social, ecological, and cognitive dimensions. The technology aspect involves innovation and responding to surroundings in a variety of ways. Decorative art is one feature of technological culture that archaeologists look for. Grindstones used for processing pigment as old as 250,000 years have been found in eastern Africa. The evidence for modern culture in Africa includes 135,000-year-old shell beads from Algeria and 76,000-year-old shell beads from southern Africa. Ochre pieces with crosshatched sketches on them date to the same time period and suggest deliberate symbolic intention. The wearer would have been conveying identity and status symbolically. Barbed bone fish points were found in Zaire in strata about 100,000 years old. But the date for these is not confirmed and could even be much later. Socially, modern culture includes forming networks to allow for exchange of information and resources. Wade argues that our unique form of sociality involves four institutions: the nuclear family, which gave all men a chance to procreate and a reason to cooperate with others; fairness and reciprocity, marked by exchange and trade; language; and religion. Such institutions eventually (in the last few thousand years) enabled human societies to transcend the basic social unit of 50 to 100 members that is commonly found in earlier human societies.

Also lending weight to cultural development in Africa is increasing evidence from a variety of sources that our ancestors were profoundly shaped by the savanna environment in which they evolved. Coexisting with lions, cheetahs, and hyenas; frequent climate change; and vulnerable babies, among other things, all distinctly shaped us. Paleontologists Donna Hart and Robert Sussman argue in *Man the Hunted* that early humans were prey rather than predators. This is a total reversal of the image that most of us have of "cavemen" with primitive weapons bringing down wild game. The assumption has been that as soon as humans came on the scene, they were strong and fierce hunters. It turns out that is not the case at all. Certainly, hominins eventually developed the skills to hunt, including the necessary tools. But Hart and Sussman argue that for most of hominin history, people were prey rather than predators and that this reality has deeply shaped who we are and why we behave the way we do. They probably take their argument too far, trying to paint our ancestors as peace-loving, vegetable-eating, cooperative folk, but much of their data reflect our early challenging environment.

They started by looking at how our closest relatives—gorillas, orangutans, and chimpanzees—were affected by predation. They found that predation was a fact of life for primates, and our earliest ancestors would have been just as attractive targets for wild cats, hyenas and wild dogs, and eagles. The Taung child, a 2.5 million–year–old australopithecine, had two keyhole-shaped incisions in the back of the skull from an eagle's talons. The eye sockets were chipped and scratched where the eagle tore out the eyeballs.

How did early humans cope with such dangers? Forming social groups was an adaptation to predation. They were safer in larger groups than individually or in smaller groups. A group of proto-humans could scan the landscape more effectively than an individual. They also used their larger body size, vocalizations, bipedalism, increasing complexity of the brain, and defensive behaviors.

How cooperative humans might have been in the past is one of those deeply biased questions, because most who ask it want to find out if, at our root, humans are predominantly violent or cooperative. Curator emeritus at the Field Museum of Natural History in Chicago, William Burger has concerns about the undue emphasis on cooperation, though he does not doubt that cooperation played an important role in our evolution. But he finds no satisfactory explanation for our significant brain expansion over millennia. As he notes, brains are costly "in lives lost during birthing, extended period of maturation, and continuous energy demand." Given such high costs, there must have been a continuous and severe selective force for increasing brain size. And this selective force, he argues, was intergroup warfare. The increased needs of our brains made us more susceptible to starvation and made defending our resource territories imperative. We were in competition with one another, or, to use his words, we were "being stalked by an increasingly clever predator that operated in small packs." It may be that we got smart because of the trouble we caused one another. Another possible explanation for brain expansion is climate change. But, Burger argues, the effects of the ice ages were different in different places of hominin occupation, but the "effect of nasty neighbors was identical."

Yet, other researchers suggest a more complex picture. Nicholas Wade notes that human social behavior has developed from modified chimpanzee behavior. Chimpanzees possess both strong territorial defense and violence against fellow chimpanzees, as well as cooperation with others, particularly males with males and females with females. Chimps and humans are the only two species who violently defend territory. Yet, *H. sapiens* also share altruism with bonobos, also close relatives and far less studied than their chimp cousins. Bonobos, according to researcher Vanessa Woods, demonstrate high levels of trust, tolerance, and altruism, all traits that human communities share as well. Humans can be more aggressive than chimps and more conciliatory than bonobos, making our societies combinations of both impulses.

Ardipithecus, with a limited tool kit and probably no ability to run, was possibly more cooperative than *H. erectus,* who had more sophisticated tools and the ability to run for long distances. Early hominins found they had to cooperate within their own species against other species in order to survive. The interspecies rivalry that so marks chimpanzees, for example, would not have benefited early hominins as they became accustomed to the mixed forest and grassland environments in which they found themselves. There they would have had to escape predation and find a way to gain access to their own supply of food. They would have initially done so by scavenging, because they did not have the tools to compete with lions, for example. Yet, they had to compete with a wide range of scavengers, including hyenas, wild dogs, and vultures. Once these scavengers were through, all that remained were the bones with the marrow still intact. Bones with cut marks on top of scavenger tooth marks indicate that hominins were coming in after the other scavengers and breaking open the bones for the rich marrow. Linguist Derek Bickerton agrees that hominins developed a type and degree of cooperation unknown in any other primate species, save bonobos. Bickerton argues that the niche our ancestors came to occupy and that drove our language evolution was as scavengers of large herbivores: elephants, rhinoceros, and hippopotamus. These animals were too large for predators to kill and had thick hides that predators' teeth could not penetrate. Hominin stone tool users, however, could cut through the hide.

After 2 million years, the markings on the bones frequently showed stone tool cut marks below animal teeth marks, indicating that our ancestors had moved to the top of the scavenging pyramid. At the same time, hominins started ranging over far wider territories and consuming animals and their meat on the spot. Rather than relying on bones of already picked-over animals, now early humans were able to eat both meat and marrow from dead animals. Such scavenging would be risky, however, and would no doubt attract other predators, like lions. Thus, scavenging could only be successful if a large number of people were involved, and the only way to recruit them would have been if our ancestors were able to communicate with others about an object they couldn't see, much as ants and bees do. Almost all other species, including primates, are able to get their food without any help from kin. Thus, the roles of cooperation and competition in early human history are debated, as is the prominence of a vegetarian- or meat-based diet and many other features. The important point, however, is that there is evidence of each in our inheritance and a compelling case for its significance early in our evolution.

So far it is clear that our enhanced ability for cooperation is an important part of human culture and that our environment played a critical role in its development. Similarly, many cite our ability to walk upright, our bipedalism, as a uniquely hominin trait. Many primates are preadapted and predisposed to bipedality. Why early hominins became two-legged creatures is still debated. Certainly, it served numerous advantages. It was easier to keep our energy-intensive brains cool under the African sun as upright primates, because the amount of surface area exposed to the sun decreased. It was also 40 to 50 percent more efficient than the four-limbed gait of a chimpanzee. Standing upright made it possible to see greater distances across the savanna and would have helped in defense against the large predators who made their home there. Finally, walking left our hands free to wield tools. But as Lucy's skeleton demonstrates, our ancestors were able to walk upright long before they came to depend on it full time.

The size of the brain compared to body size is also a unique human feature, but as with so many of the traits discussed, it is not unique to modern humans. Between *H. habilis,* less than 2 million years ago, and *Homo rhodesiensis,* about 1.3 million years ago, brain volume increased about two and a half times. During the next 1.2 million years (500,000 years longer than the previous interval), brain size increased and then decreased a little, for a net increase of 6 percent. Thus, most of the growth in brain size that is associated with modern humans occurred before the more modern hominin species. As Oppenheimer puts it, the earliest period of the human tree was the most dramatic in terms of our physical features. It is worth noting here that size and capability are not directly correlated, so it is not fair to assume greater capacity due to increased brain size alone. The most important measurement is brain size relative to body weight. Using this ratio, humans have the largest brain of any living organism.

Our relatively large brains brought along a whole host of traits that mark us as human, including long, dependent childhoods; long periods of old age; increased attention to offspring by fathers; and a focus on household survival. As humans developed a bipedal gait, the pelvic bones came closer together, necessitating a smaller baby's head for safe passage through the birth canal. For this to happen, much brain development had to take place outside the mother's body rather than inside. Thus, human babies require a decade or more of close attention. Grandparents would have been an essential component in ensuring maximum child survival. They possess an accumulated body of knowledge that would have been very useful. Fathers would have been as well. Chimp fathers do not spend much time providing food or shelter for protection to their mates or their offspring. In contrast, human fathers do.

Scholars think this change in attention can be seen in the archaeological record. The change is one from separate male and female hierarchies of the chimpanzees to the male–female bond of human societies. Such a change might indicate males taking greater interest in protecting and feeding the mothers of their children. The teeth of male chimps and hominins can tell us about differences in male–female relationships. The chief male primate weapon, large canines that could be sharpened, is not a feature of hominin males. Small canine teeth appear as far back as *S. tchadensis.* By *A. ramidus,* both male and female canines were the same size. Thus, hominin males must have gained some benefit by cooperating with females rather than fighting other males for occasional access. Similarly, the skeletons of male and female *A. ramidus* are nearly equal, suggesting greater interaction and cooperation. By caring for their offspring, males could make a decisive difference in the survival of their offspring. And their offspring needed more care than chimpanzee babies because the smaller birth canal (an adjustment that resulted from bipedalism) required infants' brains to continue to grow outside the womb for some time, just as ours do.

Mothers' families were likely central to hominin early survival. The earliest Africans who practiced foraging and hunting more often lived with their mothers after marriage than with their husbands' families, at least initially. And many think that for these societies, as well as even earlier hominin societies, that such a residence choice made it more likely that her children would survive. Matrilocality, or living with one's mother's family, meant that a mother had access both to the work and care of the children's father as well as her female relatives, whereas if she lived with her husband, she would lose the benefit of her female relatives' care. Some studies of *H. erectus* (about 2 million years ago), in fact, argue that if female *H. erectus* were to successfully raise enough children to replace the population, their children would have needed the care and provisioning of both their fathers' and mothers' families. As anthropologist Chris Knight has argued, there is some evidence that the *H. sapiens* population was at one point very small. To recover from this small number and go on to populate the globe, they had to have exceptional child care. The optimal solution to ensuring such care would have included mothers cooperatively resisting male sexual control, relying on their male kin for support, encouraging multiple suitors to work hard to provide for them, and taking advantage of every available child care resource.

Thus, the emphasis on connection through the mother's family and the practice of husbands maintaining links both to their natal and consanguineal family (family by marriage) lent a fair amount of balance and stability to these otherwise relatively mobile societies, whether *H. erectus* or later *H. sapiens,* and ensured successful reproduction. These societies were mobile not in our sense of mobility but in an earlier sense as second and third generations moved out beyond their natal region, though not necessarily too far away. As these societies diversified and split into different groups and eventually began speaking different languages than their predecessors, they continued to adjust to their surroundings and changing needs.

There remains one qualitative difference between modern humans and chimps we must discuss, and that is speech. For many who study early human history, the supposition is that the key innovation in the evolution of modern humans was the development of symbolically based language and culture. By creating mental symbols and combining them in new ways, modern humans can recreate the world in their heads. Oppenheimer and many paleoanthropologists argue that our ancestors likely possessed the ability for speech 2.5 million years ago and that this capability drove our larger brain size (as opposed to Burger's argument about intrahuman rivalry driving brain size). Linguist Derek

Bickerton argues that our capacity for language developed first and then led to a more complex brain, not vice versa. Brains, he contends, do not grow larger of their own volition; they grow because animals need more brain cells and connections to do new things. Greater reliance on meat by early hominins likely contributed to increased brain size but would not account for all of it. Human language is unique. Thus, our ancestors must have experienced some very strong and unique need that pushed them toward language that no other animal species possesses.

Human language differs from the ways in which animals communicate because it is not tied to individual fitness (or survival) or to situations in the here and now, as a monkey's alert call for an approaching eagle is. Until humans could talk, we could not even think. Animals can react to situations but not think about them in advance. Animals can solve complex problems but not complex problems that are not facing them. Humans can think and speculate about objects and ideas that are not within our immediate purview. Thus, our language and our creativity are intricately linked and differentiate us from all other animals. *Homo sapiens* have both habit and thought, while animals have just the former. The two together make up our consciousness. Gosden provides the example of riding a bike. We can think about how we ride a bike and come up with better ways of doing so, but we can also ride our bikes and think about the day ahead or the discussion of the last few hours (as I do on my commute to work), while only occasionally being aware of the bike and its movement through traffic.

The first linguistic feats had to have benefited the speaker as much as the hearer, from the point of view of fitness. Bickerton sees language evolution as an essential element in human evolution and not as a separate development. In other words, the environments our early ancestors lived in, including the animals they shared them with and the work they had to do to survive and procreate, all elaborated above, are very important pieces of the puzzle and are often overlooked in discussions of language evolution.

Using niche construction theory from biology, Bickerton demonstrates that there must have been something particular in our environment, or niche, in the past that selected for the ability to develop language. And in niche construction theory, then, once these traits are in place, organisms modify the environment still further, which in turn leads to more changes in the organism. Cattle herders developing a genetic change that enabled them to drink milk as a result of intensive cattle keeping is such an example. The species makes the niche and the niche makes the species. Similarly, the niche creates the intelligence—not some generalized cleverness, but whatever specialized intelligence the niche needs. It is far more likely that something in our niche drove our language evolution than something in our genes, because our genes are nearly identical to those of chimpanzees and other primates.

Bickerton argues that pressed to find food in the savanna, our ancestors moved from typical animal communications to a protolanguage that used signals and sounds that were not about the here and now. For example, one member of an early human band might have imitated the sound of an animal that was dying or dead on the other side of a hill, encouraging the group to follow her. Bickerton believes that all premodern *Homo* used a protolanguage. Pidgin language with little syntax (prescribed word order) followed protolanguage. He then surmises that *H. sapiens* developed full-flowered language. Language, like niche construction, is an autocatalytic process. Once it is started, it drives itself, creating and fulfilling its own demands. Bickerton believes that an early start to language (about 2 million years ago) was followed by a painfully slow development of language over the next two millennia. Thus, over millennia, our ancestors moved from simple language to much more complex language with words that stood for concepts.

Still other reasons have been put forward for the development of speech. Anthropologist Robin Dunbar argues that language is a far more efficient means for establishing and maintaining social bonds than the time-consuming grooming of chimps. In this view, language developed because of a need to belong to larger social groups for safety and effective reproduction. Evolutionary psychologist Geoffrey Miller, on the other hand, has argued that sexual selection has driven the evolution of language. Just as a peacock's tail indicates health, speech signals intelligence. Like so many other aspects of human evolution, there are still many questions about the development of human language.

Finally, genetic and linguistic research converge to shed light on who might have spoken the first human languages and what the languages might have been like. Southern Africa might be the home of modern human language. The two oldest populations in the world are the Hadzabe in Tanzania, East Africa, and the !Kung San of southern Africa, and they both speak click languages. They are the oldest in the sense that they are the most genetically diverse of all populations and thus more closely related to our common ancestors than any other peoples. Based on examination of mitochondrial DNA, the Khoisan people have the most diversity and thus are likely the oldest of the ethnic groups today. Genetic evidence suggests that the Hadzabe split off from the San before any other peoples, so it is very possible that the first human language had clicks in it. Using the same principle that decreasing genetic diversity occurs farther from the point of origin, Quentin Atkinson has studied the phonemes of a variety of languages. Phonemes are the subunits of words—the consonants, vowels, and tones that make them. His conclusion is that the farther early humans who spoke that language traveled from Africa, the fewer phonemes the language used. The click-using languages of Africa have more than 100 phonemes, while Hawaiian has 13 and English has 45. Research anthropologist Alec Knight and his team speculate that about 60,000 years ago, clicks were widespread in human language. Thus, both mitochondrial DNA and phoneme research support the idea that Khoisan represent the oldest human species alive and quite possibly were speakers of the earliest full-blown human language as well.

Current Issues

One final way in which our big brains have defined us as humans is through our technological capacity. Motorization, mechanization, and industrialization have made cars, trains, airplanes, ships, and a variety of health, household, agricultural, and communication technologies possible. The use of fossil fuels to replace wind, water, solar, human, and animal power has created a major problem: global climate destabilization. This, too, is part of our human inheritance. More than any other species, *H. sapiens* create technology and solve problems and often use the former to cope with the latter. It is this technological prowess, combined with our population of the entire globe, that has led us to some of the serious economic and environmental concerns raised in the introduction. Now that we know such proclivities are part of our human inheritance, as students, teachers, and citizens, we must use this information to make wiser choices moving forward. Modern humans are not likely to change millennia of biological inheritance and to become an antitechnological species. But we can use our other unique capacities in service toward more balanced ends. Our language and resulting culture can be shaped to take into account both the human past and the challenges we currently face. Perhaps our linguistic and social capacities should be used to set limits on the use of energy and technology to preserve both our species and our planet.

Our study of human evolution also reminds us of the ways in which modern humans are more closely related to the animal world than we might commonly think. Barbara Natterson-Horowitz and Kathryn Bowers argue in *Zoobiquity: What Animals Can Teach Us about Health and the Science of Healing* that the illnesses and diseases that afflict humans are found in animals as well and that veterinarians and physicians have much to learn from each other about treatments and causes. A variety of animals, for example, get a variety of cancers, including feline leukemia, breast cancer in jaguars, and melanoma in penguins. As David Abram reminds us, our bonds to the community of plants and animals, wind, soil, sun, and water are part of our inheritance as well. They are, however, bonds that our technological prowess tends to minimize. There is far more to learn about human evolutionary inheritance in terms of medicine and much else.

Homo sapiens are a marvelous and complex species, and what scholars know now is probably the tip of the iceberg in terms of what they may still learn from new evidence. Much of our genetic and cultural traits are from our African ancestors, both ape (panin) and hominin. To understand what makes us uniquely human and the genetic and cultural constraints within which our species has and will continue to operate, a clear understanding of the African environments in which humans evolved is important. Our earliest history is African, and the capabilities humans express today, whether it is hip-hop music, race car driving, or derivative financial trading, all result from capacities with deep roots.

Even though scholars can't know specific names of our early ancestors or what their family lives were like or if they had any form of leadership, we can still identify with some of their challenges and struggles: keeping children safe from danger, the importance of caring adults for a young child, the significance and complexity of communication, and the desire to create a better tool for the task at hand. We also know that we carry their genes, even if, in some cases, they are not direct ancestors.

Humility is in order not only because of the long distance humans have come but also because of the clear evidence that it will take all of our inheritance and all of our species-specific creativity to face our future. Our journey began 8 million years ago. Only 200,000 years ago, our ancestors began to behave in ways that are familiar today. Early steps in human evolution were followed by increasing adaptations to a variety of environments and increasing cultural complexity, as we will see in the upcoming chapters.

Suggestions for Further Reading and Viewing

David Abram, *The Spell of the Sensuous: Perception and Language in a More-than-Human World* (New York: Vintage Books, 1996). In his own words, the premise of this book is that "we are human only in contact, and conviviality, with what is not human."

Derek Bickerton, *Adam's Tongue: How Humans Made Language, How Language Made Humans* (New York: Hill and Wang, 2009). As one reviewer noted, this book is the first one to treat the evolution of human language alongside the evolution of humans. Bickerton argues that previous theories for how human language evolved are not adequate and suggests his own.

Abdeljalil Bouzouggar et al., "82,000-Year-Old Shell Beads from North Africa and Implications for the Origins of Modern Human Behaviour," *PNAS* 104, no. 24 (2007): 9964–9969. This is a recent contribution to the debate about the origins of culturally modern humans. This scientific article describes their archaeological site, the shell bead findings, and the authors' interpretations of their significance. This is the kind of primary research necessary to build a more complete picture of the role of Africa in human evolution.

William Burger, *Perfect Planet, Clever Species: How Unique Are We?* (Amherst, N.Y.: Prometheus Books, 2003). This book explores the remarkable coincidences, in terms of both our planet's attributes and our evolution, that have brought us to the present.

Coincidence in Paradise (2000), a film by Matthias von Gunten, presents some of the most influential scholars in the field of human evolution, such as paleontologist

Tim White and biologist Christophe Boesch. Through interviews and footage of them in their field and research sites, viewers get an unusually broad and intimate view of the wide range of scholarship and research that informs our understanding of early human evolution.

Bert Holldobler and Edward O. Wilson, *The Ants* (Cambridge, Mass.: Belknap, 1990). This is a landmark work in the study of ants. Holldobler and Wilson celebrate ants as the dominant insect species, similar to humans as the dominant vertebrate species. Much like humans, ants are social insects and profoundly alter their environments.

Nina G. Jablonski, *Skin: A Natural History* (Berkeley: University of California Press, 2006). Anthropologist Jablonski investigates multiple aspects of human skin such as the link between hairlessness and sweat glands, as well as the origins of the variety of colors.

Chris Knight, "Early Human Kinship Was Matrilineal," in *Early Human Kinship,* ed. Nicholas J. Allen, Hilary Callan, Robin Dunbar, and Wendy James (Oxford: Blackwell, 2008), 61–82. Knight explores aspects of matrilineal kinship both in terms of the anthropological evidence and the ways in which that evidence has been interpreted over time.

Barbara Natterson-Horowitz and Kathryn Bowers, *Zoobiquity: What Animals Can Teach Us about Health and the Science of Healing* (New York: Knopf, 2012). Written out of an encounter between a physician and a veterinarian and their ongoing conversations and research, this book investigates how much there is to learn across the species divide about health.

Ian Tatersall, "Once We Were Not Alone," *Scientific American* (January 2000): 56–62, http://www.ucd.ie/artspgs/langevo/earlyhominids.pdf. This is an easily read interpretation of fossil evidence in East Africa and its implications for our understanding of human history.

Nicholas Wade, *Before the Dawn: Recovering the Lost History of Our Ancestors* (New York: Penguin, 2006). Wade's focus is on what DNA evidence has taught us about human evolution, both in the distant and near past. He also covers Stoneking's discovery about lice and clothing.

Pamela Willoughby, *The Evolution of Modern Humans in Africa: A Comprehensive Guide* (Lanham, Md.: AltaMira, 2007). Willoughby is an African archaeologist. In this book she explains clearly the varied evidence for the evolution of modern humans in Africa despite long-held assumptions that modern human traits developed in Europe. Her current research in Tanzania is fascinating and worth reading. You can find her and her work at the University of Alberta.

Bernard Wood, *Human Evolution: A Very Short Introduction* (Oxford: Oxford University Press, 2005). This is part of the Very Short Introduction series and is a great place to start. Wood gives an authoritative overview of human evolution.

Vanessa Woods, *Bonobo Handshake: A Memoir of Love and Adventure in the Congo* (New York: Penguin, 2010). Woods is a scientist and journalist, and this book is part love story, part zoological exploration of bonobos.

2　Early Subsistence

Gathering-Hunting and Agriculture

AFRICA IS NOT only the home of human evolution, but it is also one place where humans have practiced the full continuum of economic subsistence, first developing a gathering-hunting lifestyle and then different forms of agriculture. How societies obtain food is one of the most important aspects of history, but historians give it scant attention. One of the reasons is that in industrialized countries, like the United States, there is easy access to a great variety of food and usually little contact with the farmers who produce it, so it is easy to take this characteristic of societies for granted. But disconnection from the source of one's food is relatively new and not universal. Throughout history, most civilizations relied on either gathering and hunting or farming to feed themselves.

Gathering and hunting was the longest-lasting lifestyle in human history. Since the dawn of *Homo sapiens,* about 200,000 years ago, humans were gatherer-hunters for all but the last 10,000 years. To put this in perspective, if the 200,000 years after modern humans first came into existence were condensed into one hour, then humans began to farm only in the last four minutes. And only within the last minute or so did farming become their primary means of subsistence.

Africa is also home to many agricultural innovations, and it has contributed several food crops to global agriculture. In an older view of history, a series of revolutions brought us to the present time. The first of these—the agricultural revolution—occurred in Mesopotamia (what is now Iraq) about 12,000 years ago. The second was the Industrial Revolution, which was launched in Great Britain in the eighteenth century, and you could consider the current information revolution as the third. Other, smaller, revolutions also took place, such as the green revolution of the 1960s and 1970s, where military technology was applied to agriculture, resulting in modified seeds and food crops.

This view of history is important for many reasons. First, although human societies have had several revolutions since the agricultural one, almost all societies still rely on agriculture for sustenance (though no longer subsistence). The distinction is that until the last few hundred years, the majority of people in most places in the world grew their own food for a large part of their needs, or subsistence. Today, in some countries, like the United States, less than 2 percent of the population grows food, and even then they sell what they grow. North Americans, however, still buy food that was grown on a farm or in someone's garden. And globally, food production remains humanity's primary occupation. Approximately 40 percent of the world's population farms for a living, and farming occupies 40 percent of the world's land area. Thus, subsequent revolutions have not erased the significance of agriculture in our history and current circumstances. Subsequent revolutions have, however, altered our relationship to agriculture.

Second, while these revolutions acknowledge fundamental transformations that took place in the societies affected, they tend to discourage seeing history as a process. In other words, not everyone adopted agriculture at the same time, for the same reasons, and with the same technology, as current gatherer-hunter peoples illustrate. Many of the fruits of the agricultural revolution are only clear in hindsight. So people did not adopt agriculture in linear fashion. Some tried it and abandoned it after a while, whereas some continued to rely on gathering and hunting while slowly learning to farm.

Third, the agricultural revolution tends to mask an attendant significant economic change: that of the domestication and keeping of animals like cattle, sheep, and goats for human use. Animal domestication took place at much the same time as plant domestication, but it did not always follow from or accompany it, as pastoralists living in eastern and southern Africa today can testify.

Fourth, rarely does Africa get much consideration when it comes to global agricultural change. Mesopotamia was not the only place where agriculture developed. People began domestication independently in many areas, including several parts of Africa. For example, probably the best-read account of this process, Jared Diamond's *Guns, Germs and Steel,* barely mentions agricultural innovation in Africa, even though three independent cases of crop and animal domestication took place there. Tom Standage's *Edible History of Humanity* doesn't mention domestication of crops or animals in Africa either. The work of domesticating plants and animals was particularly arduous on the African continent. It involved adapting techniques and ideas to different ecosystems at multiple times, as journalist Jared Diamond notes. What grew in one of the early centers of agriculture, Egypt and Sudan, did not grow in the highlands of Ethiopia or the savannas of western Africa. Thus, one of the unavoidable lessons of domestication in Africa is the hard work and ingenuity that were involved in figuring out which foods to rely on more heavily and to cultivate toward human preferences. In addition, agriculture in Africa attests to the ways Africans learned from one another about skills and techniques for various agricultural practices. This type of communication is a common African trait of openness to new ideas that are often incorporated into older systems.

Geographical Place

This chapter examines events related to subsistence lifestyles across the African continent. Most early agricultural developments took place in the northern half of the continent, while gathering-hunting lifestyles were practiced throughout the continent for millennia. The few peoples who remain gatherer-hunters today live mostly in southern Africa, where agriculture is not possible. Plant and animal domestication began in the Nile River Valley, the highlands of Ethiopia, and the Sudan and savanna regions of West and Central Africa between 10,000 and 2000 BCE. The crops developed in these localized regions, however, eventually were cultivated by peoples in similar climates throughout the continent in the years that followed.

Sources and Methodology

Most of the information scholars have about gatherer-hunters comes from anthropology, the study of contemporary peoples and their cultures. The field of anthropology was born with imperialism in the nineteenth century in an attempt to study those who were being ruled by Europeans. Europeans believed they could create more effective rules and institutions if they learned how Africans did it. Thus, effective rule was tied to cultural understanding for European colonialists. Information about gatherer-hunter societies has mostly been collected in the twentieth century from the few small societies that still practice this lifestyle in South America, Africa, and Asia. Anthropologists have been interested in how many hours gatherer-hunters worked in a week; the variety and nutritive content of their diet; their family relationships, including marriage and sexual relationships; and their relationships with their neighbors, like farmers. Yet, contemporary anthropology cannot be used as direct evidence for previous lifestyles.

Evidence of domestication comes largely from archaeology. For plants, archaeologists work with seeds, plant fragments, and pollen. Pollen is sometimes preserved in caves, bogs, and lakebeds. Seeds may be embedded in the earth, and plant material or imprints may be present in pottery. Archaeologists can distinguish differences between the size of a seed and the size of a grain stalk to determine whether a plant is wild or domesticated. Sorghum, domesticated first in northeastern Africa, differs from its wild ancestor in that its seed stays on the stalk rather than falls off, and the seeds are larger. Sometimes the plant from which the domesticated variety derived still grows in the wild and can be compared with the domesticated version.

In the case of animals, their bones usually survive. Though there is some disagreement, many believe that domesticated animals are generally smaller than their wilder ancestors, so their bones would be relatively smaller. Also, the horns of goats and the tusks of domesticated animals are smaller than those of wild ones. In addition, many young and diseased animals are found at these sites, suggesting that herding spread diseases among them. Many other features of animals would change with domestication, such as the size of the udder or changes in hair or wool, but these parts of animals' bodies are lost to decay.

Domestication involves growing a plant or breeding an animal so it changes genetically from its wild ancestor in ways that make it more useful to human consumers. The definition might sound easy enough, but, as Jared Diamond ably shows, it is not that simple. Certain characteristics of a plant, for example, would make it more attractive to humans. The goal was to pick plants that consistently have those traits. Thus, humans often bred plants for larger grains or seeds (in the case of wheat or oats), good taste (in almost all cases), high oil content (in olives, castor, and sesame), more flesh (on fruits), and long fibers for making cloth (such as cotton). In addition, to successfully cultivate seed plants, they needed seeds that stayed on the plant at least throughout their maturation or, even better, during transport once harvested. Grains that matured at the same time would also be valued. Domesticated animals, on the other hand, were chosen for their docility and social structure (ability to follow humans' lead), their ability to breed in captivity, and the ease of replicating their diet in captivity.

Domesticated plants and animals are weaker than their wild cousins. Most domestic animals, for example, have poorer sight and hearing. Thus, domestication is a compromise that has increased utility for humans at the cost of the hardiness and resilience of the plants and animals on which people depend. This dependence is no small outcome of the process. Writer Tom Standage argues that plant and animal domestication has domesticated people just as much as the animals and plants. In other words, *H. sapiens* are a weaker species than our gatherer-hunter ancestors because of our dependence on a small number of plants and animals compared to the great number of wild varieties available to our ancestors.

Two fascinating aspects of our domestication history are how few plants and animals have been domesticated over the last 10,000 years and how most of those were domesticated thousands of years ago. We have our ancestors to thank for the entire food source on which the planet relies. Modern humans owe them a debt for their work and perseverance. For example, it took over 200 years to turn wild wheat into the grain we grow, harvest, and eat today.

Gathering and Hunting

Scholars do not know as much as they would like to about the gathering and hunting lifestyle because gathering and hunting people left no written records and only scant materials in the archaeological record. Much like human evolution, humanity's ideas about foragers have changed over the course of the last hundred years. Some of these changes are the result of new information, such as interviews with women in the 1970s, and some are from changes in how research-ers view the world around them and the questions they have about it, such as who provides the bulk of the nutrients for a family. Many speak of hunter-gatherers as those who foraged for a living before (and after) the dawn of agriculture, but the term *gatherer-hunters* more accurately reflects the primary economic activ-ity: gathering. Women were the gatherers and generally were responsible for a majority of the caloric needs of their families. In a study of San in the Kalahari in the 1960s, for example, women provided two and a half times more food than men. When anthropologists first began studying gatherer-hunter societies, they assumed that the way nineteenth- and early-twentieth-century Europeans ar-ranged their societies was the way others did as well, so males were assumed to be the primary breadwinners, and they assumed that gathering and hunting was hard work. Researchers know now that neither was true.

Gatherer-hunters have rarely been understood on their own terms. Prior to the 1800s, many Europeans just assumed that gatherer-hunters were not as civi-lized as Europeans. Thomas Hobbes (1588–1679) said gatherer-hunters' lives were "nasty, brutish, and short." In contrast, centuries later, Marshall Sahlins's post–World War II study of gatherer-hunters, based on a compilation of anthropologi-cal data, suggested a people to be envied. He titled his work *The Original Affluent Society,* seeking to recast the way Europeans thought about wealth and leisure through the lens of the gathering-hunting lifestyle. Elizabeth Marshall Thomas's book *The Old Way,* about her family's experiences with the San in Namibia in the 1950s, has a similar tone, praising a cooperative and simple lifestyle that began to change irrevocably in the decades to come. Since Sahlins and the experiences of the Marshall family, others have studied gatherer-hunter societies from other perspectives, such as a focus on women's experiences. These researchers have dis-covered traits to be envied or marveled at and others that are concerning. Some studies, such as those by Marjorie Shostak, emphasize the freedom, sexual and otherwise, that !Kung women experienced, and others, like Nancy Howell, em-phasized nutritional health challenges. Even more recently, some observers of the Okiek in Kenya have noted the close relationship these gatherer-hunters have with the animals upon which they depend. As farming and pastoralism (raising livestock for a living) increased across the continent, gatherer-hunters were of-ten pushed to marginal environments where they probably struggled more than in earlier times to gain access to a sufficient quantity and quality of food. Few gatherer-hunters remain in Africa today.

Agriculture—A Mixed Blessing

Farming, or agriculture, is a much more recent form of subsistence and is linked to many changes associated with our current lifestyle, including sedentary living, class distinctions, and economic specialization. One obvious reason why humans eventually adopted agriculture over gathering and hunting is that it is far more intensive. A small group of gatherer-hunters would need tens of thousands of acres for their survival, while the same number of farmers could subsist on 25 acres. Yet, there are many other factors to consider besides sheer productivity. While farming is more productive than gathering and hunting, it carries other consequences. It is also increasingly linked with significant ecological disturbances as agriculture began to manipulate the environment in ways and to an extent that had not been possible previously, as biologist Duncan Brown has argued. Specifically, agriculture began to redirect the flow of nutrients in our biosphere (our air, water, and soil) in ways that interrupted ecological cycles.

Agriculture did not instantly supply the benefits now associated with it: increased population or increased wealth and economic stratification, among others. Think about how risky it was to rely on seeds that took months to turn into food when you were used to going out into the surrounding area to dig up food and eat it the same day. Too little or too much rain could spell disaster for a crop that a community planned to eat over the next several months. In addition, it was more work to rely on farming and livestock than to gather and hunt. The studies that anthropologist Marshall Sahlins relied on indicate that gatherer-hunters in southern Africa and Australia both worked on average about 4 to 5 hours per day. Farmers during the growing season had to work 8 to 12 hours per day. During the off-season, they repaired fences, houses, and equipment and tended livestock.

Agriculture also meant reliance on fewer kinds of food than gatherer and hunters were used to. For example, gatherer-hunters in southern Africa eat about 75 different wild plants. How many different foods do you eat over the course of a day? A week? As a result, early agriculturalists were often less healthy than gatherer-hunters. Paleoanthropologists can study the bones of ancient people for signs of tooth enamel defects and scars that indicate disease such as anemia and leprosy. According to anthropologist George Armelagos, a review of more than 20 studies of stature and health (based on ancient skeletons) in societies transitioning from foraging to farming revealed that people's height decreased and their health worsened during the transition. One study of Native American skeletons from mounds in Illinois and Ohio demonstrated that life expectancy was 26 years before agriculture and 19 years after.

Given all the negative consequences of farming, why would people have turned to it in the first place? First, it is important to recognize that no one ever made a conscious choice to significantly change economic ways. Instead, it was a gradual process and one that was encouraged by a number of factors. Consider sedentism, or living in one place. Many of the settled African communities in what is now the savanna and Sahel made a living from fishing long before the introduction of cultivation. They settled down but still foraged. Fishing could be very productive, so it made sense to stay in one location for the fishing and to forage as a secondary means of providing subsistence. Thus, sedentary living did not always lead to farming, but it did make the switch to farming more likely for a number of reasons. Once settled, there would be greater inclination to plant some seeds close to home for extra insurance. Grains would have become preferred foods because they could be stored for future use, unlike many vegetables and fruits.

Each small decision or choice, like greater reliance on grains, was a step to becoming primarily dependent on domesticated plants and animals. Grinding seeds required large, heavy grindstones that were not practical for mobile populations. Beyond sedentism, other factors were at work after 11,000 BCE, such as cumulative development of food production technologies, like grinding stones. Once people had grinding stones, baskets, and pottery for collecting and cooking, farming made more sense. When our ancestors made grains a major part of their diet, growing more of them and living in one place year round became their major way of life.

Second, as people started producing more food, they would have been able to support slightly larger populations, which, in turn, would have required increasing reliance on agricultural production. Mobility was key to the gatherer-hunter way of life, allowing them to follow sources of food as the seasons changed. Needing to walk distances to gather food and to move camp meant that women could not afford to have a lot of young children who needed to be carried and supervised. As a result, they had fewer children than those in agricultural societies. When societies became big enough that the surrounding environment was no longer sufficient for their subsistence, they had to move elsewhere or stay put and rely on their own efforts at cultivation, leaving behind gathering and hunting.

Finally, the transition to an agricultural way of life began as human populations came out of the last ice age. After a brief return to cold conditions between 11,600 and 12,800 years ago, world climate began to stabilize. Over the past 8,000 to 10,000 years, Earth's climate system has been unusually calm, with only minor fluctuations documented in climate records from the deep-sea and Greenland ice cores. This era is referred to as the Holocene, and our chief form of sustenance is a result of this remarkable climatic episode. This episode has ended, and a different climate regime has begun. About a decade ago, scientists began calling this new era the Anthropocene, because its most notable feature, and the one that will endure in the geologic record, is the control that humans are exerting over the environment and the climate.

Nobel Prize–winning Dutch chemist Paul Crutzen first used the term *Anthropocene* at a scientific conference when discussing the serious impact that humans had exerted on the planet by the turn of the millennium. It is a term now widely used but that derives from geology and the accompanying study of stratigraphy. As Elizabeth Kolbert wrote in a recent *National Geographic* article, the job of stratigraphers is "to piece together Earth's history from clues that can be coaxed out of layers of rock millions of years after the fact. They take the long view—the extremely long view—of events, only the most violent of which are likely to leave behind clear, lasting signals. It's those events that mark the crucial episodes in the planet's 4.5-billion-year story."

British stratigrapher Jan Zalasiewicz and others have determined that our current era will leave its mark in the geological record and thus deserves a separate identity from the Holocene, the era when agriculture was born. And many of the changes that will be clear to future scientists will be due to agriculture. Some obvious changes include the traces of corn, wheat, and soy pollen that will extend for acres in place of the varied pollen record left by rainforests, prairies, and savannas. The deforestation that accompanies the growth of population and the need for more food, including richer foods like beef and other animal-based protein, will also be visible in the stratigraphic record through increased soil sedimentation in rivers and dams and in the extinctions caused by such disruptions. Probably the most distinctive change will be in the composition of the atmosphere, most commonly noted by an increasing accumulation of carbon dioxide. Modern agriculture contributes to increasing levels of greenhouse gases by its reliance on fossil fuels for fertilizers, herbicides, and pesticides; for plowing, planting, harvesting, processing, and transporting food; and for livestock (which produce more potent greenhouse gases, like methane, than carbon dioxide).

One last important point about the Anthropocene is that it can be traced to the invention of agriculture, according to paleoclimatologist (someone who studies changes in climate throughout Earth's history) William Ruddiman. Deforestation linked to agriculture would have increased the amount of carbon dioxide in the atmosphere just enough to hold off what would have been another ice age. Others disagree and put the beginning much later, when carbon dioxide levels began to rise without interruption in the late eighteenth century or in the mid-twentieth century, when rates of population growth, industrial production, and consumption accelerated rapidly.

Like many events in human history, the adoption of agriculture by Africans at various times and in various places had a great variety of unforeseen consequences, including significant impact on cultures, trade across cultures, and the environment. Africans grew a variety of crops that were native to the continent and, over time, adopted new crops from places as far away as Central America and southeastern Asia.

Agriculture in Africa—The Earliest Crops and Animals

Africans contributed to the earliest stages of plant and animal domestication. Before Africans could rely on agriculture exclusively, they experimented with various forms of plant manipulation in the form of watering plants, removing undesirable plants from the area, and burning fields prior to full-scale participation in plant domestication. John Reader states that the earliest evidence of this kind of deliberate manipulation of food resources comes from Klasies River cave studies in South Africa. A soil-poor region, the people there ate tubers and roots as part of their diet. Evidence of burning inedible parts of plants has been found there, dating to 70,000 years ago. When the surface vegetation was burned, the seed cases would burst and release their seeds over the cleared ground, resulting in greater concentrations of tubers in the following years. Without this burning, some seeds might have lain dormant for decades. Such evidence suggests that humans experimented with manipulating food sources for tens of thousands of years prior to more intensive and extensive dependence on such sources. It also suggests that gatherer-hunters were more sophisticated than stereotypes allow.

Another site that offers early evidence of cultivation and more intensive food collection comes from the Nile Valley, prior to the formation of ancient Egypt. More than 20,000 years ago, the people there collected tubers and seeds from plants along the Nile River and fished its waters. They used grinding stones and blades for cutting and grinding wild grains. Archaeological evidence indicates a growing population marked by larger and more numerous settlements. Increased rainfall and flooding brought this way of life to an end by about 11,000 BCE.

Historical linguist Christopher Ehret conceptualizes early African history in terms of major linguistic groups, identifying four such groups that laid the foundation for all contemporary African societies. Map 2.1 depicts the four language groups around 9000 BCE, when the first evidence of African agriculture exists. In this next phase of African agriculture, three African societies domesticated plants and animals between 9000 and 3500 BCE: the Afrasan, located in northeastern Africa (and descendants of those early seed collectors); the Nilo-Saharan (the parent language group for the Sudanic peoples, the name used on the map), located in north-central Africa; and the Niger-Congo, located in northwestern Africa.

Different Afrasan peoples domesticated a number of food crops, including ensete, finger millet, and t'eff. Ensete is a plant that looks like a banana tree, but instead of eating the fruit, Africans ate the stem and bulb of the plant. They dried and pounded it to make flour, which they used for porridge. This development alone is worth more consideration. Think of the work involved in first contemplating eating a different part of a plant than usual and then trying out each part (testing for taste, toxicity, energy provided, and other factors) before finally discovering that the bulbs tasted the best and had the most benefits. After deciding to grow it intentionally, the process of choosing plants with bigger, tastier stalks would have begun. Finger millet, a grain, became an important food crop throughout much of eastern Africa, while ensete and t'eff have remained important in the highlands climate of Ethiopia. T'eff is a staple grain in Ethiopia and

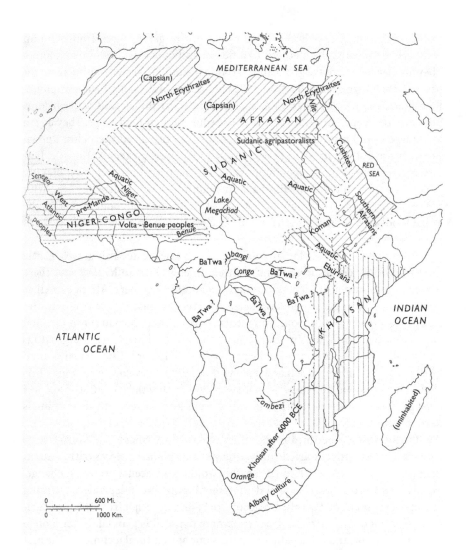

Map 2.1 Four major African civilizations, c. 9000 BCE. From Christopher Ehret, *The Civilizations of Africa: A History to 1800* (Charlottesville: University of Virginia Press, 2002), 63. Courtesy of University of Virginia Press.

is used to make *injera*, a staple food in much of Ethiopia and perhaps familiar to those who have eaten the fermented pancake-like bread served in Ethiopian restaurants.

Over three centuries from the eleventh millennium, Nilo-Saharans were in contact with Afrasan speakers, learning much about agriculture from them, as suggested by adopted words (or *loan words*, as historical linguists call them) in Nilo-Saharan. Nilo-Saharan societies learned to gather grain from Afrasan speakers but adapted the methods to different crops such as sorghum and fonio. They also learned to make grindstones from Afrasan speakers, adapting them for use with their own grains. By 7000 BCE, Nilo-Saharans began growing sorghum, then gourds and calabashes, and then cotton, pearl millet, and watermelons. They also developed innovative ways to use some of their food crops. They began weaving cotton by 5000 BCE. Nilo-Saharans also produced the oldest-known earthenware pottery in Africa, second only to Japanese pottery worldwide. Pottery made some forms of cooking possible for the first time, including making porridge, soups, and stews. Nilo-Saharans enjoyed a more varied cuisine with pottery. Porridge is still an important way of cooking throughout Africa, as the staple foods of *fufu* in West Africa and *ugali* and *sadza* in eastern and southern Africa attest.

Around 8000 BCE, Nilo-Saharans began to domesticate cattle as well. Cattle were likely only domesticated two to three times in human history, and there is evidence to support independent domestication in northern Africa as well as Turkey. Cattle keeping would have been attractive because it gave communities ready access to dense nutrition. It might also have allowed them to control animal damage to their crops. Raising animals was also a logical way to use marginal agricultural land. Livestock can eat the grass of a savanna or hillside when rainfall or labor and technology are inadequate to maintain or develop agriculture. This change led to population growth and new ways of using the land. Cattle keepers need land for grazing rather than growing crops and moved with their animals to sources of food.

By 8000 BCE, the third group of early African farmers, the Niger-Congo peoples of West Africa, started cultivating yams by planting pieces of the yam in the ground. Like the switch to ensete, this would have been a profound change. This is a significant technological development requiring independent thinking and experimentation; it is called vegeculture to distinguish it from the seed agriculture developed by Afrasan speakers, where the seed is planted. Niger-Congo also cultivated oil and raffia palm using the same agricultural technique. The first was used for cooking, and the second for clothing.

After 3500 BCE, in response to a drying climate, Niger-Congo–speaking Africans domesticated rice in the Inner Niger River Delta. The earliest available dates for its domestication are at the turn of the Common Era. Rice growing diffused from there to a number of places in West Africa, especially the Upper Guinea Coast (modern-day Guinea-Bissau, Guinea, Sierra Leone, and Liberia). Africans learned how to grow rice in both dry and wet environments in 18 distinct microenvironments, including mangrove swamps, according to historian Edda Fields-Black's account of rice farming. They created a variety of rice-planting methods and developed sophisticated water management techniques and tools for growing rice in a variety of challenging environments. These techniques became important in rice-growing regions such as Georgia and South Carolina during the era of the Atlantic slave trade. Slaves cleared acres of land and prepared plantations for tidewater rice production.

Bananas were introduced from Asia to Africa millennia ago through long-distance trade, but exactly when is not certain. The earliest written evidence of bananas in Africa comes from the sixth century CE. Then, more than a decade ago, banana remains were found in the archaeological record in Cameroon dating to 500 BCE. Anthropologist Peter Robertshaw explains that direct evidence of ancient agriculture is usually in the form of charred seeds. Since banana seeds are so small, archaeologists rely on phytoliths (which means "plant stones"), which are microscopic silica bodies found in the stems and leaves of plants that don't decay. Such phytoliths have been found more recently in Uganda dating to 5,000 years ago, much, much earlier than anyone thought bananas or agriculture existed in Central Africa. Bananas are highly productive because they are perennial plants. Once they have matured, after three years or so, and bear fruit, they require little care for pounds of bananas each year. Bananas are ten times more productive than grains like sorghum or millet. Thus, for the same amount of labor, bananas can support larger, denser populations. Like many Africans, farmers in Buganda often interplanted ground crops, such as beans, with their bananas. Intercropping allowed African farmers to rely on a variety of crops and to reduce the risk of famine due to the failure of one crop.

Both grain and banana farming in parts of western and eastern Africa and in Central Africa involved cutting down forest to plant crops. Tropical forest has dense vegetation that does not permit enough sunlight to reach the forest floor for agriculture. With the development of ironworking around the first millennium BCE, probably in Central Africa, it became possible to forge axes and hoes that made both the felling of trees and the working of the ground much easier. Iron smelting, the process of heating iron-bearing rock so the iron separates from the rest of the rock, requires very high temperatures. These temperatures are achieved in a furnace by burning charcoal. It is a scientifically complex process, so much so that it was probably only invented a few times in human history. Archaeologist Peter Schmidt believes, based on furnace shape and possible internal furnace temperatures, that one of those places was in Central Africa.

One region remained somewhat isolated from these developments: southern Africa. In fact, by the 1920s, researchers had ceased to use terms referring to agriculture in reference to southern African peoples, assuming that until Bantu-speaking peoples (originally from the Niger-Congo area of West Africa) arrived from the north in the early centuries of the first millennium CE, the gatherer-hunters of the region did not adopt herding or cultivating. Thus, what we knew about agriculture in southern Africa came from an interpretation of southern

African history that made it easy for South Africans of European descent to justify their occupation and dominance after the seventeenth century. Dutch merchants arriving in the seventeenth century encountered Khoisan speakers who
practiced both livestock keeping and gathering and hunting but they saw no evidence of farming. Khoisan are the fourth major language group in Africa and the
one with the greatest genetic and linguistic diversity, making them the language
group with the deepest roots on the continent.

There is clear evidence that domesticated food production was practiced in
southern Africa long before the arrival of Bantu speakers or Europeans. It has
long been assumed that sheep are evidence of Khoekhoe pastoralists (descendants of the Khoisan language family shown in East Africa in map 2.1) arriving
from the north. South African archaeologist Karim Sadr argues that despite four
decades of research that has turned up sheep bones in gatherer-hunter sites, this
view has changed little because it challenges long-standing assumptions that San
gatherer-hunters (also descendants of the Khoisan language family shown in East
Africa in map 2.1) remained untouched by economic developments elsewhere.
With little evidence of Khoekhoe settlements and the existence of many San sites
with small numbers of sheep, Sadr argues that there is plenty of evidence for the
keeping of sheep by San gatherer-hunters. Some sites with large numbers of sheep
might indicate the presence of Khoe speakers, but most sites likely do not. Thus,
by including animal domestication in our study of early African societies, as in
this chapter, South Africa has its own history of herding and thus domesticated
food production prior to the Common Era.

Africans developed multiple forms of agriculture and animal keeping over
the last 10,000 years. Many of the crops mentioned above, and others that have
been introduced more recently, continue to play an important part in African diets. As Africans populated the continent, slowly grew in numbers, and developed
more stratified societies, some people, like artisans and medical and religious
practitioners, did not grow food for themselves but relied on others to grow it for
them; often it was used as payment for services rendered.

Agriculture in Africa—A Case Study

When Europeans arrived in Africa in the fifteenth century and after, they found
an astonishing variety of cultures, languages, and economic systems that had
been honed by Africans over the last several millennia and adapted to particular
climate and soil conditions. They also found that both men and women participated in agricultural tasks, often dividing them up so men performed the more
laborious, short-term tasks (such as preparing fields for sowing) and women the
more repetitive tasks (such as weeding and harvesting). But there was and is tremendous variation across the continent. One widespread aspect, though, is that
farming was not gendered in the way it came to be in Europe. For example, in

southwestern Tanzania lies the Fipa plateau, sandwiched between Lakes Tanganyika and Rukwa. By the time Europeans arrived, it was largely grassland, probably caused by deforestation due to farming and iron smelting. The soil was poor, and in response, Fipa had devised multiple methods of soil enrichment, including *ntemele,* a local form of shifting agriculture that involved cutting down trees and branches, arranging them in a circle, and setting fire to them just before the rains started in October. Men usually performed this work. Millet was then sown on the remaining ash, and at harvest time, both men and women threshed the millet.

Another response that was unique to the Fipa plateau and much more complicated and labor-intensive was forming *intumba.* Toward the end of the rainy season, the ground was broken into rough chunks of sod and piled into mounds with the grass and weeds facing inside. Both men and women performed these tasks. The mounds were initially planted with a quick-growing crop, like beans, that could be harvested in June. Then, when the rains started again in October, the mounds were broken up, and millet or maize was planted in the soil that had been mulched and enriched with nitrogen from the beans. Many Europeans noted that Fipa divided farmwork more or less equally by gender. In addition to these systems, Fipa practiced crop rotation and intercropping to increase productivity.

With increasing integration into the colonial economy after the 1950s and Tanzanian policy after the 1960s, Fipa agriculture was simplified. Colonial officials in Tanzania and elsewhere feared shifting agriculture because of the burning involved and the potential for soil erosion; it was banned in 1957. As a result, *ntemele* field production came to an end. Greater access to the colonial economy was also a factor. A railway to the north and mines both north and south of Ufipa provided market opportunities in the 1950s, and Fipa responded by growing more grain for sale. Maize became increasingly popular and was grown in rows in flat fields, with outside inputs, if they could be afforded. This method was far less labor-intensive than using *intumba,* but it was also less productive because the soil was not as enriched. Social differentiation occurred as a class of large-scale producers emerged. By the 1970s, there was evidence, such as using sloped land for farming and cultivating land continuously without allowing it to lie fallow, that Fipa were seeking greater production than the regularly farmed land would yield. In Ufipa, older methods of building soil fertility had been abandoned by the 1970s in favor of larger-scale grain agriculture, a trend worldwide.

American and Asian Plant Domestication Comes to Africa

Another factor that changed African agriculture significantly was the introduction of new crops to the continent, like bananas. This occurred over millennia, some coming from Asia via the east and others coming from the Atlantic Ocean and the West. Through what Alfred Crosby calls "ecological imperialism," domesticated plants, once grown only in certain geographical areas, had spread to various parts of the globe. Two of those plants, sugarcane and maize, have had a profound effect on African history in more recent times.

Maize

Maize (called corn in the United States) probably comes from southern Mexico. The domesticated plant has a different reproductive biology, maturation time, height, and kernel size than its wild ancestors (likely teosinte). Archaeologists have debated how long it must have taken to go from a puny plant with almost negligible nutrition (half an inch long or less) to a larger plant with a cob the size of a human thumb, but it was likely centuries, if not a millennium—much longer than it took to domesticate wheat or barley. By the early sixteenth century, Mexican Indians were growing corn with 6-inch ears. Today, the ears of corn grown in the fields of Iowa and Indiana are 12 to 18 inches long.

Maize was brought to Africa beginning in the fifteenth century in a variety of ways: through sea-borne trade across the Atlantic and Indian Oceans and long-distance trade across the Sahara; it is now one of the most widely grown foods on the continent. For centuries, in most places in Africa, maize was a vegetable crop grown alongside a wide variety of older crops. As such, it complemented a wide variety of foods but was not consumed daily. Africans preferred to eat it at its green stage—either boiled or roasted. Several varieties of maize species were grown in different areas of the continent, depending on the soil, the climate, and taste preferences. It was only in the late twentieth century that maize became a staple grain in Africans' diets, grew in only a few varieties, and in some places in southern Africa came to be grown on an industrial scale. James McCann, in a book on the history of maize in Africa, noted that prior to the twentieth century, "maize . . . was an element of biodiversity and farming as an eclectic art, which would give way to homogenization and an expansion of global scale." In most countries, including southern Africa, most of the maize that is grown today is for urban human consumption (as opposed to our maize production, which is mostly for animal feed). In Malawi, for example, maize is grown on 90 percent of cultivated land and makes up 54 percent of a Malawian's caloric intake. Thus, Malawians and many other Africans are very dependent on this one food for their survival in a way that is new in African history.

This expansion of maize production and dependence has brought a train of effects, one of which is increased risk of malaria, McCann shows. Researchers in Ethiopia have found that mosquito larvae that feed on maize pollen have a higher survival rate to the adult stage and also live longer in the adult stage, so they are able to transmit malaria more effectively. Maize has supported significant population growth and urbanization in Africa but also reflects negative consequences of such developments, such as overreliance on a small number of food crops and increased vulnerability to malaria.

Sugar

Early in the second millennium CE, Arabs introduced sugarcane to Europeans, among a wide variety of Asian crops. It was domesticated in New Guinea and began to spread to other parts of the world around 8000 BCE. Sugarcane would become one of the primary agricultural commodities worldwide over the next millennium. By 1650, in England, the wealthy classes relied heavily on sugar in their diets and their medicines. The ability to consume sugar became an integral part of rank and status. By the early nineteenth century, sugar was consumed at all levels of society, and by 1900, sugar provided almost 20 percent of the calories in the English diet. Africans would provide much of the labor for its production between 1450 and 1850.

In the second half of the fifteenth century, the Portuguese established sugar plantations on the islands of Madeira, Cape Verde, and Sao Tome. In 1490, Madeira was the major sugar producer for Europe, followed by the Canary Islands under Spanish production, and then by 1550, Sao Tome was the top producer. These Atlantic islands soon diminished in significance, though, as sugar production in Brazil began. By 1580, there were more than 100 sugar plantations in northeastern Brazil. From the seventeenth to the nineteenth centuries, however, Caribbean islands, such as Barbados and Cuba, dominated sugar production. Though the production of sugar occurred in many places over the centuries, the use of African slaves in that production remained constant. The best estimates are that 12 million slaves left Africa between the fifteenth and nineteenth centuries to work in various enterprises in the New World, including the production of sugar in Brazil and the Caribbean. Between 1811 and 1870, about 32,000 slaves per year were imported to the Caribbean. The Atlantic slave trade, probably the best-known aspect of African history, was driven in part by increasing demand for sugar in Europe.

Agriculture, Development, and Modern Economies

While maize and sugar are examples of agricultural crops that spread to many parts of the world, most agricultural history, including that of Africa, involves local crops being grown for local consumption. Marcel Mazoyer and Laurence Roudart argue in their book, *A History of World Agriculture: From the Neolithic Age to the Current Crisis,* that over thousands of years, a variety of agriculture systems developed in a number of regions of the world, of which the African systems mentioned above were just a few. By the end of the nineteenth century, the productivity of the systems varied widely, mostly between those practices that relied on rainfall and those that were irrigated, the latter being ten times more productive than the former. The vast majority of African agricultural practice at the end of the nineteenth century was rain-fed and thus of lower productivity than irrigated systems. But then, in less than a century, the industrialization of agriculture, including the mechanization of farming (through tractors and other farm equipment), the use of engineered seeds, and manufactured fertilizers, as well as government support for such systems, meant that much of the industrialized world, including the United States, had agricultural systems that were 1,000 times more productive than those in Africa.

What made these differences important was the transportation revolution of the nineteenth and twentieth centuries that brought these very disparate systems into competition for the first time in history. Increasing productivity in industrialized agriculture led to continually falling food prices. It is possible that this trend that dominated the twentieth century will not continue into the twenty-first, as decreasing availability of oil and interest in biofuels and global climate destabilization have already contributed to a rise in agricultural prices.

For the latter decades of the twentieth century, at least, food and agricultural prices fell, squeezing less-mechanized farmers from the global market. For example, farmers in West Africa compete with Texas cotton growers on the world market. And though the West African farmers are generally more efficient cotton growers—that is, for the same amount of energy, they produce more cotton—they do not grow on the same scale as Texas farmers or with the government support they receive; therefore, they must charge more for their cotton than U.S. cotton farmers. As a result, West African cotton is not as attractive on the world market, and West African cotton farmers do not receive as much income as they might from their efforts.

The result of falling agricultural prices has been a significant net difference in income between industrialized agricultural countries and small-scale agricultural countries. Industrialized agricultural countries export their cheap grain around the world now. Faced with low-priced imported grain, Africans have begun to grow crops that cannot be grown in the temperate zones of the United States, Canada, and Russia, such as coffee, cotton, tea, and peanuts. Often, they must sacrifice their subsistence crops in the process. Along the way, most African countries became food dependent, importing cheap grains to feed their population. And even export crops have faced increased competition from more mechanized production and synthetic substitutes. Without sufficient income from agricultural products, African farmers cannot reinvest in tools and seed for the following year. To do so, they must cut into their capital stock (sell livestock or use the same old tools) or skimp on clothing, health care, and other goods and services purchased in the marketplace. As the situation for many African farmers has grown more tenuous over the last few decades, more and more have left their rural lifestyle for the potential opportunities available in the city. Because of the low price of food in the industrialized world, wages in African countries are kept low and the prices of goods and services are low, leaving Africans in a vulnerable and weak situation vis-à-vis citizens of industrialized countries. African subsistence agriculture and its related poverty are also deeply gendered. Since the colonial era when officials focused their agricultural extension efforts on men, women became the key subsistence providers in rural areas as men sought to become cash crop farmers or to earn wages in urban areas. Thus, African women have particularly felt the burden of falling agricultural prices worldwide.

Historical and Future Implications of Agriculture

Though domestication of plants and animals was a slow, halting process, in evolutionary terms the change has been fast. In the blink of an evolutionary eye, our species shifted to a dependency on cultivated food. Shortly after that, most people were fed, reliant on food grown by a small percentage of the human population. Most textbooks and studies of early agriculture concentrate on the ways humans learned to manipulate the environment. But many scholars now point out that this process of plant and animal domestication also domesticated us. As humans changed their environments and the food they ate, the environments also changed human beings. This altered environment in turn shaped and continues to shape humans. Archaeologist Chris Gosden, quoting fellow archaeologist Ian Hodder, argues that society itself was the main thing domesticated during the development of agriculture. Gosden uses the term "commensualism" to explain this phenomenon. Commensualism is a process of living together in mutual support and dependency. Agriculture brought us into commensualism with a host of plants and animals and material objects in an unprecedented way. *H. sapiens* now depend on corn and cows for food, and these animals and plants depend on us for propagation, nurture, and survival. Domesticated grain seeds, for example, usually can't penetrate the ground without human assistance, and the sweet, large apples we buy are the result of grafting, not growth from a seed.

Throughout these changes, human population has exploded. Jared Diamond, in fact, argues that the worst mistake in human history was the adoption of agriculture because it freed us from some very real limits on human population growth. As the ice ages came to an end and populations of gatherer-hunters slowly increased, they would have needed to find new ways to feed their larger families or to limit population growth. Those that chose the former eventually came to dominate. Diamond argues that when our ancestors faced a likely unconscious choice to limit population or increase food production, they chose food production. The result has been starvation for some and tyranny as a result of class division for many. Added to this explosive population growth has been the unusual climate stability of the past 10,000 years or so. As noted in chapter

1, evolution over the long haul instilled in humans a suite of adaptations that enabled our lineage to adjust to or recover from climatic perturbations; yet, over the past several thousand years, these capacities have been expressed in a peculiar time of remarkable stability.

Biologist Duncan Brown argues that the two most important biological events in the history of our planet have been the accumulation of elementary oxygen in the atmosphere, beginning perhaps 3.5 billion years ago, and the development of agriculture. Brown shares Diamond's concern with population growth and the large human population on the planet, but he is also concerned about soil loss and depletion. For every hamburger consumed, the land where the wheat grew and the land where the cow grazed gave up nutrients for someone else's eventual consumption and energy. Those nutrients get cycled through our bodies and then dumped into a sewage system, where often they flow out to sea and are never returned to the soil again. In this way, nutrients are transferred from the soil to our food and lost for agricultural purposes forever. The combination of increased population and decreasing soil fertility is a concern of Brown's.

What this means for our future is difficult to know, but all of us face it more realistically with an acceptance of several things: our mutual dependence on all life forms, particularly those with whom humans have coevolved over the last 10,000 years; our relative luck in terms of climate stability for what many would call the entire length of human civilization—that is, since the dawn of agriculture; and the fact that societies are now millennia out from an unconscious choice not to limit population growth. If anything, human beings will likely have to make conscious and large-scale decisions about population growth and size to adjust agricultural ways to meet new challenges.

Africa has given us a wide variety of sustainable agricultural practices that were adapted to particular ecological environments, such as the Fipa plateau or the highlands of eastern Africa. These methods allowed people to sustain themselves for generations largely on the resources available in their environments. Domesticating a variety of plants, eating a variety of plant parts, intercropping, using rainfall and irrigation, and integrating livestock into farming all helped Africans survive in a challenging set of environments. Their long-term, sustainable solutions are part of our human inheritance.

Suggestions for Further Reading

Duncan Brown, *Feed or Feedback: Agriculture, Population Dynamics and the State of the Planet* (Utrecht: International Books, 2003). This is a strongly ecological account of the impacts of agriculture on soil and its nutrients. Brown argues that for centuries societies have been moving soil nutrients from farm fields to urban waste fields and sewers, resulting in depleted soil health worldwide.

Mark N. Cohen and George J. Armelagos, *Paleopathology at the Origins of Agriculture* (New York: Academic, 1984). This continues to be a highly cited reference regarding the early transition to farming in a variety of societies. The scientists included in the volume relied on skeletal pathology to interpret the health of transitional societies.

Jared Diamond, *Guns, Germs and Steel: The Fates of Human Societies* (New York: Norton, 1999). This is a popular and widely read account of how some societies came to be more powerful than others based on a geographical argument that early access to domesticated animals and plants created societies that developed immunities and technology that served as a long-term advantage for Eurasian societies. There is not much coverage of Africa.

Jared Diamond, "The Worst Mistake in the History of the Human Race," *Discover* (May 1987): 64–66. Turning the more common narrative of the benefits of agriculture to human societies on its head, Diamond examines the poor quality of early farming diets and the inequality and division of labor that resulted. The mistake was not consciously made, but it was the consequence of choosing to increase food production instead of limiting population growth.

Edda L. Fields-Black, *Deep Roots: Rice Farmers in West Africa and the African Diaspora* (Bloomington: Indiana University Press, 2008). Fields-Black uses historical linguistics to write a history of rice farming in West Africa and its impact on the New World.

Elizabeth Kolbert, "Enter the Anthropocene—The Age of Man," *National Geographic* (March 2011), http://ngm.nationalgeographic.com/2011/03/age-of-man/kolbert -text. This is a straightforward introduction to the Anthropocene, as well as some of the evidence that will mark this new geological era.

Marcel Mazoyer and Laurence Roudart, *A History of World Agriculture: From the Neolithic Age to the Current Crisis,* trans. James H. Membrez (New York: Monthly Review Press, 2006). This is a magisterial treatment of major agricultural developments, particularly in terms of productivity of agriculture. The focus is mostly on Europe, with a few examples from other early agricultural societies, such as Peru and Egypt. The authors argue that the current economic crisis has its roots in the integration of modern, mechanized industrial agriculture and subsistence agriculture, mostly in the developing world.

James McCann, *Maize and Grace: Africa's Encounter with a New World Crop, 1500–2000* (Cambridge, Mass.: Harvard University Press, 2005). This is a local and continental account of maize's journey to Africa, first as an introduced crop and then to become the primary staple crop in most of Africa.

John Reader, *Africa: A Biography of the Continent* (New York: Knopf, 1997). This is a sweeping, synthetic work of geological, environmental, social, and political history. The information about gathering-hunting women in this chapter comes from this book.

Peter Robertshaw, "Africa's Earliest Bananas," *Archaeology* 59, no. 5 (2006): 25–29. Robertshaw, an African archaeologist, reports on evidence from Uganda that indicates that bananas have been cultivated there for 5,000 years.

William F. Ruddiman, *Plows, Plagues and Petroleum: How Humans Took Control of Climate* (Princeton, N.J.: Princeton University Press, 2005). Ruddiman, a paleoclimatologist, traces human impact on the climate back to the discovery of agriculture, a second stage in human history when we began to control the environment. The third stage is the more recent extensive and intensive human impact on the environment.

Marshall Sahlins, *Stone Age Economics* (Chicago: Aldine-Atherton, 1972). This widely cited and influential anthropological work focuses on gatherer-hunter societies' production, distribution, and exchange. The first section, "The Original Affluent Society," is the one referred to in this chapter.

3 Early Adaptation
Climate Change and Pastoralism

Although global climate change is much in the news recently, rarely is mention made of the significant ways the changing climate impacted human history in the past. Early African history demonstrates how peoples of the past have responded to drastic climate changes and, particularly, drying environments. Many of the major developments in early African history, such as important advancements in early human evolution, and the creation of a variety of domesticated food sources, were likely driven by climatic shifts. Even more recent dramatic examples of climatic change have longer histories than commonly thought, such as the shrinking of Lake Chad. Peoples of the Sahel and Sudan region of Africa have been responding to dramatic climate changes for millennia due in part to their geographic location.

In the United States, discussion of climate change tends to focus on changes in temperature, because that is what differentiates our seasons. Yet, in Africa, it is the presence or absence of rain that determines seasons and climates. As primarily farmers and livestock keepers, rainfall is the most relevant climatic variable of food production and the growth of pasture.

Africa can help us understand the drying of our planet. James Workman writes in *The Heart of Dryness* that population growth and climate change have led to half the planet's terrestrial surface being classified as dry lands—arid landscapes inhabited by a third of humankind. Increasingly, arid nations such as India, Mexico, China, Egypt, Yemen, Israel, Australia, and Botswana lack sufficient water to efficiently grow enough food to feed their populations. Thus, it is particularly apt in this chapter to focus on the drier parts of the continent, because they offer vital information that pertains to a significant fraction of our global landscape.

Geographical Focus

This chapter focuses on the Sahel region (see map 3.1), a dry land area that runs across Africa just south of the Sahara. Climate change has impacted many

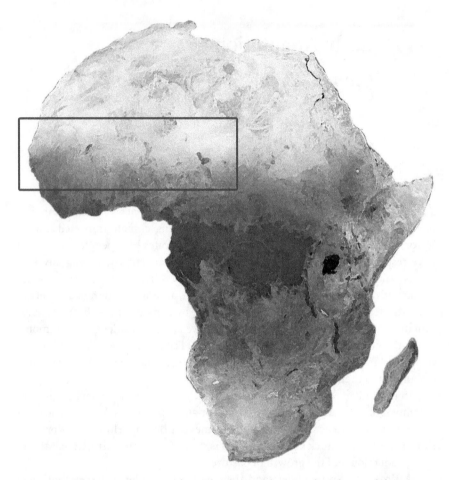

Map 3.1 The Sahel zone of western Africa. The transition between the Sahara and the savannas to the south is the Sahel zone, outlined by the black box. Courtesy of Jessica Murphy, Xavier University.

regions in Africa, but there is evidence that the Sahel and savanna to the south have been prone to dramatic shifts over both the short and long terms. Similar areas exist elsewhere in the world. In fact, they make up about one-third of the world's land area.

Sources and Methodologies

To reconstruct the role of climate in African history, African historians must rely on the work of scientists in a number of disciplines, such as geography, earth sciences, and oceanography. Geographers use place-based reasoning to solve a variety of problems relating to human-environment relations. Mike Hulme of the School of Environmental Sciences at the University of East Anglia argues that geographers' skills are exactly what are needed to study climate change because they have experience working on the boundaries between nature and culture, and they understand how knowledge, power, and scale work together. Oceanographers are important because the ocean influences the distribution of rainfall, droughts, floods, regional climate, and the development of storms, hurricanes, and typhoons. In addition, oceanographers work on air-sea interactions, such as those of the Sahel. In addition, the work of anthropologists and paleontologists contributes to our understanding of the role of climate change in early human evolution. Paleoanthropologist Rick Potts digs for fossil traces in the Rift Valley of East Africa, hoping to reconstruct ancient worlds, not just ancient humans. He believes we are who we are and we do what we do because of the changing environmental conditions to which our forebears had to adjust.

Climate Change in Ancient African History

Dramatic changes in the climate of North Africa have led to some dramatic developments in ancient African history. Climate changes have been important factors in human evolution, though not likely the driver of bipedalism, as previously thought. During the Plio-Pleistocene (about 2.8 million years ago), drier and cooler conditions changed the East African landscape from closed canopy to open savanna vegetation. An ability to forage on the savanna may have been beneficial as the forests shrank. One study identifies adaptations for running that are 2 million years old. This capability would have made Australopithecines far more successful on the savanna than species that could not run on two feet. At the same time, there is evidence of at least two Australopithecine lineages coexisting. And later, during another drying phase about 1.9 million years ago, the earliest evidence of the *Homo* species appeared. In both cases, scientist Peter B. deMenocal surmises that a more arid climate led to adaptations that resulted in speciation. Mark Maslin, a geographer in England, is an expert on regional and global climate change. Maslin has argued that three unusually abrupt wet periods (lasting approximately 200,000 years) that occurred between 1 and 2.7 million years ago were rapid swings that forced hominids to quickly adapt to the new environmental conditions. Maslin observes a correlation between increased brain size during these wet periods, suggesting adaptation.

Lake Chad: A Case Study—Part 1

Not only has the climate dried in many places, but one of the long-term characteristics of the Sahel is the erratic nature of its climate. Droughts occur in two out of five years, so what is considered "normal" rainfall might not be relevant. Evidence suggests that the Sahel is prone to either a desert or a green state, as it did over 5,500 years ago. In the late Pleistocene and early Holocene (5,500 to

14,500 years ago) periods, an ancient lake, Megachad, covered over 150,000 square miles. At the time, Lake Megachad sat at 1,100 feet above sea level and drained into the Atlantic Ocean through the Benue River. For the sake of comparison, a lake of over 150,000 square miles is slightly smaller than the state of California at 167,000 square miles and slightly bigger than the largest inland water body, the Caspian Sea, at 143,000 square miles. During this green state, it was the largest of many lakes in the present-day Sahara. Sedimentary deposits such as coastal sand ridges; remains of aquatic animals, such as the bones of fish and crocodiles; and human artifacts, such as fishing tools, are evidence of this previous wetter era when people made a living from the lake's resources, according to a study by paleoenvironmental scholar Mathieu Schuster in 2009. During this time period, inhabitants around the lake would have been gatherer-hunters and fishers, some at least practicing sedentism due to the rich resources of the lake.

Jonathan Foley, director of the Institute on the Environment at the University of Minnesota, discovered that at the end of the Holocene Climatic Optimum (over 5,500 years ago), the climate in northern Africa changed from wet to desert conditions (see table 3.1). This fits with more recent interpretations that climate changes have occurred and can occur rather rapidly—over a few centuries, a few decades, and sometimes a few years. Scientists Jonathan Adams and Randy Foote, for example, have noted that evidence is mounting that in the past, climate has changed very suddenly—within a decade—on a number of occasions, with drastic consequences for human cultures. Yet, its implication for history and our future is only now being seriously investigated according to climatologists. Climatologists, says British science writer Fred Pearce, now believe that the climate system is more delicately balanced than was previously thought. They believe that the system is linked by a cascade of powerful mechanisms that can amplify a small initial change into a much larger qualitative shift in temperature

Table 3.1 Regime shifts

Era	Lake size	State
5,500–14,500 years ago Late Pleistocene and early Holocene	Lake Megachad 150,000 square miles	Green
2,500–5,500 years ago	Close to current size Roughly 9,000 square miles	Desert
1931–1960	Highly variable with a maximum of roughly 9,000 square miles	Desert
1968–1997	Highly variable from less than 1,000 square miles to 9,000 square miles	Desert

and aridity. While it appears that changes in Lake Chad's size have been slow in coming, looking back over 5,000 years, the evidence is mounting that the climate of the Sahel (and likely Earth more generally) does not change in gentle rhythms. Instead of thinking about the slow effects of climate change, Adams and Foote argue that the model should be that of plate tectonics, where stress surfaces as earthquakes rather than gradual shifting of plates. Pearce notes that the past is a better indicator of how climate systems work than computer models. And the past suggests that climates go through periods of stability broken by sudden drastic changes.

Though the surface area (and thus volume) of the lake has varied and continues to vary significantly from season to season and from year to year, over the last 5,000 years, the lake has been constantly shrinking, with some evidence that it nearly dried out altogether in 1908 and 1984. It reached close to its current dimensions about 2,500 years ago, averaging 200 feet lower than before and covering only 5 percent of its original surface area (about 9,000 square miles). This change, like all climate changes, required human adaptation. Three thousand years ago, Chadic peoples who lived in the area and whose ancestors had come from northeastern Africa and belonged to the Afrasan language family left fishing and turned to cultivating sorghum and other crops on land that had previously been underwater. Some moved beyond the old lakebed, where they also grew sorghum and millet and kept livestock on landscapes that were becoming more like savannas alongside Sudanic peoples.

Ancient Egypt's existence is largely due to a drying climate at the end of the Holocene Climatic Optimum that drove Afrasan-speaking peoples who had been living in the grasslands that once occupied the area of the Sahara toward the narrow strip of the fertile Nile River Valley. The civilization of ancient Egypt was born out of a fusion of southern Sudanese cultures, which spread from the south to the north of the country, and Afrasan cultures. For example, images on clay pottery from this time bear an astonishing resemblance to the pictograms in rock drawings in the Sahara, according to historian Wolfgang Behringer. As Christopher Ehret shows in his linguistic work on African history, ideas of sacral leadership, including burying servants with the dead in preparation for the afterlife, come from Sudanese cultures. The subsequent dense populations that grew there led to the developments of economic and political stratification, a royal class with access to enough labor to build monumental stone pyramids and the longest-lasting kingdom in history. The royal class helped to maintain the irrigation infrastructure that was essential to the prosperity and longevity of the kingdom. Periods of bad weather and poor crop production are associated with a decline in centralized control, indicating the strong link between agricultural production and power. But such an outcome was initiated by an inability to make a living elsewhere in northwestern Africa.

Just as Africans began to live along the Nile River to produce food, many others discovered new ways to obtain food in a changing climate. Some West Africans who had collected and domesticated yams had to learn how to use seed agriculture. West Africans domesticated African rice during this period as well.

It is possible that the changing climate encouraged people to more directly control this food in an effort to ensure a steadier supply. Others began to rely more heavily on pastoralism, or the keeping of livestock. Jonathan Foley and colleagues, for example, note that archaeological evidence also shows that highly mobile pastoralist cultures began to dominate the region at this time—between 5000 and 2000 BCE—replacing the more sedentary lake-dwellers.

More recently, historian James Webb notes that in 1600, the Sahel zone all across north-central Africa began a long-term and dramatic shift toward increasing aridity. Over the course of 250 years, the desert frontier moved as much as 300 kilometers south. As a result of this significant change in northern Africa, pastoral peoples (many of Arab culture) increased and strengthened in numbers, and new identities were forged. One result of shifting ethnic relations was an increase in predatory and raiding activity and enslavement of agricultural peoples by pastoral and nomadic peoples. Webb claims that desert peoples were increasingly able to enforce their claims to part of the agricultural production of sedentary farmers.

In addition, between the 1300s and the 1600s, a new ethnic identity emerged along the desert edge as a result of Arab immigration south of the western Sahara. This identity grew out of cultural change and assimilation among the Berber peoples, Arab nomads, and Africans south of the Sahara, such as the Wolof and Soninke (Niger-Congo speakers). Because of their proximity to and interrelatedness with the black Africans below the Sahara, Sahelian pastoralists (both Berber and Arab) came to refer to themselves as *Bidan,* which in desert Arabic means "the whites." Webb also states that this new Sahelian ethnicity was a response to both Arab immigrants' pressure for assimilation into Berber society as well as rapid climate change. White warriors could exploit these new ethnic distinctions by raiding black communities across the Sahel for slaves and material goods. Climate change reinforced ethnic distinctions based on the keeping of livestock and farming, distinctions that still impact politics in countries like Mali.

Pastoralism

Africans' adjustment to a tremendous variety of climates is one of their contributions to human civilization, just as it is a marker of the human species more generally. Adaptation to the Sahel is among those environments. Where and when lakes and rivers are not abundant, the most obvious choice for subsistence living is pastoralism. Livestock pastoralism is a food production system in which a human community relies on domestic livestock for their basic subsistence. For example, for most pastoralists of East Africa, milk makes up 70 percent of their diet, supplemented by meat and cash items such as grains, sugar, and tea. Pastoralists take their animals to pasture and water rather than bring food and water to them as ranchers do. Only about 5 to 10 percent of a family's herd is sold annually. Thus, it is an economic system that has only limited interactions with a transaction or market economy. Beyond relying on their animals for food (milk, meat, and blood), they also try to build their stock of breeding females and to produce enough animals for trade and social obligations such as bride wealth and ritual consumption.

Pastoralists might not engage the market economy as much as modern politicians would like, but they have always had significant interactions with gatherer-hunter peoples in their vicinity, who could supply them with gathered foods, such as honey, while pastoralists supplied gatherer-hunters with skins and other livestock products. While pastoralists often view such gatherer-hunters as poor in comparison to them, most who live in close proximity to Maasai (Nilo-Saharan speakers), such as the Okiek and Dorobo, have a long technical and cultural tradition of their own. Some of them, however, speak the Maasai language, attesting to the significance of their social and economic interactions in the past. Clearly, there have been complex, interdependent, and differing relationships between pastoralists and others who make a living on the same landscape.

Exchange and interdependence have long been parts of the pastoralist lifestyle. Jan Shetler demonstrates in her study of northwestern Tanzania near and in Serengeti National Park that for at least two millennia, gatherer-hunters, pastoralists, and agropastoralists (farmers who also kept livestock) lived in the area. Each group occupied a certain ecological niche and became associated with a different ethnicity, while maintaining movement among the three groups as well. Hunters could become pastoralists or farmers if they raised livestock, and farmers and herders could become hunters during difficult times. Gatherer-hunters eventually were limited to the montane forests, agropastoralists to the forest-savanna region, and pastoralists to the savanna grasslands. This kind of interdependence is a key part of Africans' adaptability to the landscape.

Just as those around a receding Lake Chad have sometimes chosen pastoralism for thousands of years, so too have many in northern Kenya. There, pastoralism is the only viable way of making a living and has been relatively successful for a variety of societies that focused on keeping a number of different animals. The approximately 7,000 Ariaal who live in Kenya's largest and most arid region near Lake Turkana are masters at this latter strategy and have been able to withstand a variety of challenges over the last 50 years (see map 3.2). Ariaal ancestors were refugees from Samburu and Rendille societies during drought, famine, and war in the nineteenth century. Over time, the refugees created a hybrid society, now known as the Ariaal.

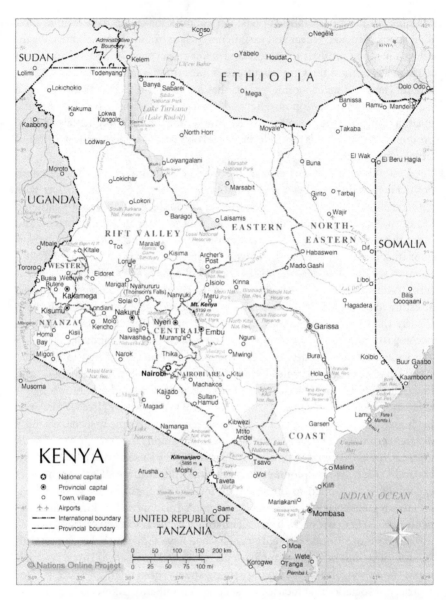

Map 3.2 The pastoralist Ariaal of Kenya are located in north central Kenya, just southeast of Lake Turkana in Kenya. Courtesy of Central Intelligence Agency, en.wikipedia.org/wiki /File:Kenya-relief-map-towns.jpg.

The Ariaal keep camels, cattle, and small livestock to take advantage of the benefits of each kind of animal, as well as the diversification necessary to survive the too common droughts and violent raids that are part of the pastoral life in northern Kenya as of late. Camels produce more milk than cattle but don't fetch as much in the marketplace. Camels graze in hot deserts, while cattle prefer wet highlands. Sheep and goats can graze in dry lands but need access to water every two to three days, so they must be near springs and wells. Thus, Ariaal families deploy members in different parts of their homeland to manage their livestock. In addition, to raising multiple kinds of livestock, the Ariaal rely on interhousehold cooperation and ties with other societies for grazing and other functions. Cooperative herding groups are necessary when a household has insufficient stock to feed its members or insufficient labor to manage its livestock. Having different kinds of livestock is one solution to a challenging environment. Mobility is another, as is maintenance of extensive social ties to people in distant areas. In this way, the Ariaal have much in common with those living around Lake Chad, who over generations, as well as annually, have to adjust to a changing lake level. The lake-dwellers deal with such variability through mobility and diversity of food resources and economic activities, like the Ariaal. These include fishing, soda mining, pastoralism (including the raising of cattle, camels, sheep, and goats), and farming in recessional lands.

Over the past several decades, as the population increases, the government establishes game reserves, and development occurs near important water sources, access to enough land has been an increasing challenge for the Ariaal. For example, Korr was a seasonal watering hole before a Catholic mission was built there in the early 1970s. At Ngurunit, the river provided dry-season water for Ariaal cattle and had an outlet for cattle sales. Then, in 1971, the African Inland Church established a mission there, and the first missionary on the site did not want the Ariaal to water their cattle in the catchment area, even though he had built several water tanks for his own use.

More recently, scholars and African pastoralists have demonstrated the value and wisdom of African pastoralism. For example, according to Fred Nelson, long-time development worker in northern Tanzania, tourism in northern Tanzania accounts for at least 5 percent of the country's gross domestic product. The area boasts a number of national parks and game reserves that used to be home to pastoralists, such as the Maasai. In fact, part of the rationale for creating Serengeti National Park was to preserve it from overgrazing and environmental degradation. Yet, the wildlife in these parks continue to pass through and rely on lands occupied by pastoralists. Also, the abundance and variety of wildlife in northern Tanzania are likely, according to Nelson, a "result of pastoralist land management practices such as grazing and the use of fire" over the past 3,000 to 4,000 years. Thus, the Maasai and their pastoralist peers have contributed to the biodiversity of the savanna landscape in northern Tanzania and thus shape a valuable asset for the Tanzanian government. Yet, despite this, the Tanzanian government continues to pursue policies that would privatize grazing land and promote ranching, rather than maintain the long-term lifestyle of pastoralism and the valuable ecosystems' services they provide for the tourist industry.

Old Ideas about the Sahel and Its Climate

Not only do pastoralists, like the Maasai and the Ariaal, live in a challenging climate, but they also face large outside forces, such as the modern nation of Kenya and international organizations, like the United Nations, that have a narrow view about how to make a living. These more recent institutions were preceded by British colonialism in the late nineteenth century. British colonists had their own ideas about indigenous peoples' destruction of the environment as well as ways to make a living. Anthropologist Jeremy Swift has uncovered several colonial land studies that argued that the Sahara was "advancing at an alarming and measurable rate," mostly due to human activity. The term *desertification* originated from this era to describe this process. Desertification is a degradation of dry land ecosystems. According to Swift, blaming African farmers and pastoralists suited colonial desires for central planning and control of natural resources. The colonial government believed that traditional pastoralism was not economical in that it emphasized the display and accumulation of wealth rather than production for market. Such thinking was carried forward into the postcolonial era as the Sahel experienced another dry phase punctuated by a series of droughts. James McCann argues that in the 1970s, a combination of leftover colonial assertions, embryonic scientific hypotheses, and popular assumptions linked African farmers and pastoralists with the advancing desert in the popular press. Such ideas resonated with others about African crises. Both sets of ideas reinforced popular conceptions of ill-informed Africans. In truth, as geographer Thomas Bassett and historian Donald Crummey argue, African farmers and herders are "knowledgeable and responsible environmental managers."

Similarly, anthropologists James Fairhead and Melissa Leach have demonstrated in Guinea, West Africa, that forest patches in the savanna are a result of deliberate planting and tending by peoples nearby, not remnants of a wetter era. Both colonial and modern interpretations of the landscape were that humans had degraded the landscape and that the forest islands with villages in the middle were what remained from a larger, forested region. Instead, evidence exists that human settlement has encouraged forestation.

The Ariaal have been deeply impacted by these ideas about their lifestyle and climate. One outcome of desertification fears was a United Nations International Conference on Desertification in Nairobi in 1976, where pastoralists were blamed for turning arid lands into deserts by maximizing herd size, overgrazing an already fragile environment, and rarely selling their animals. The underlying assumption was an old one: the "tragedy of the commons." In the late 1960s, Garrett Hardin argued that people will overuse a shared resource out of selfishness, even if they know they are destroying it by such actions. Yet, his essay was not based on any empirical evidence, and many other scholars, including institutional economist Elinor Ostrom, have shown through historical and anthropological research that many common resources are protected by societal rules, norms, and institutions to ensure their sustainability. For example, the Maasai of northern Tanzania and southern Kenya, according to Fred Nelson, use different wet- and dry-season grazing areas and to increase livestock numbers to be able to withstand common periods of drought. Instead, the destruction of commons, at least in more recent times, is often due to outsiders, not those who have lived on the land for centuries.

Similarly, in the Sahel, during the colonial era and in independent Kenya, little account was taken of political or economic causes of famine in these areas, such as government support of game reserves for tourism or the promotion of cash cropping in marginal agricultural areas. Also, little account was taken of climate variations that had changed the climate in the past. Missionaries and UN projects have operated in Ariaal lands with the goal of changing them from mobile societies to sedentary societies that rely on agriculture, or at least rely more on the market economy than they do now. Such projects and ideas assume that the pastoral way of life is not sustainable and that those who practice it must be shown new ways to make a living that are not harmful to the land.

These projects, however, have taken little account of the histories, cultures, and values of the Ariaal and others in the area who know that stewardship of their grasslands is essential to their survival. Westerners, instead, have assumed that leading Ariaal and other pastoralists to market their livestock rather than invest in it would decrease pressure on the land and allow some of their society to settle in urban areas. The Integrated Project on Arid Lands that began in Kenya in 1976, for example, had little contact with pastoralists themselves and believed that the reorganization of pastoralist societies and, ultimately, their removal from the grasslands were the best ways to save the desert ecosystems.

The Ariaal and their way of life are also deeply impacted by the teleological narratives of Western history, where the assumption is that pastoralism (and the mobility that often accompanies it) is at best antiquated and at worst an uncivilized way of life that should be modernized. Elliot Fratkin argues that "the Ariaal represent a possibility for African societies, the possibility that a pastoralist people living in the dry margins of the Sahara can feed themselves and maintain their socio-cultural systems, even in the face of ecologic, economic, and political dislocations." Of course, the idea that such people cannot (or should not) maintain themselves was essential to pursuing the colonial, and now the postcolonial, agenda of collecting taxes and creating a population with easy access to modern education and health care. But it is not necessarily true that such a settled way of life is possible in many of the drier areas of the African continent. Fratkin also found that sedentary life resulted in poorer health and nutrition in children than the mobile lifestyle. This is another reason why a long view of history is so important. It makes no sense to expect the dry areas in Africa to support agricultural populations, although that is exactly what foreigners, like missionaries and development workers, and national governments have been trying to do in many areas, not just Kenya.

Africans' history and contemporary societies that have not completely sedentarized also demonstrate another important lesson: the value of human adaptation to the environment rather than vice versa. James Workman has written about the Khoisan of the Kalahari, particularly a band associated with the deceased matriarch, Qoroxloo, and their recent battle for survival with the government of Botswana. He noted that Qoroxloo's fundamental rule of adaptation was not to organize and mobilize physical resources to meet expanding human wants but rather to organize human behavior and society around the limits imposed by diminishing physical resources. It is fortunate to have both living and ancient peoples to study. One of the long-term consequences of the agricultural revolution was that human society entered into a positive feedback cycle, with the ability to produce food encouraging an increasing population and an increasing population requiring the production of more food, more land, better technology, and so on. Pastoralists, on the other hand, experience a negative feedback loop such that the population and health of their societies are limited by ecological factors such as available rainfall, plants, and animals. When these fail to produce as much as usual, a reduction in fertility and frequent deaths ensue. It makes little sense to innovate out of such a system because mobility is the key to its success.

Though this chapter focuses on the Sahel region of Africa, many other areas of the continent have been facing more recent human-induced climate change for several decades now. In eastern and southern Africa, for example, changing ocean temperatures are contributing to a drying trend. In 2008, a study published in the *Proceedings of the National Academy of Sciences* demonstrated that a warming Indian Ocean is leading to decreased rainfall across Ethiopia, Kenya, Tanzania, Zambia, and Zimbabwe. Rainfall in that region has decreased by 15 percent over the last 20 years because the rain is falling on the ocean instead. Predictions are that rain-fed agriculture will be deeply impacted by these changes, leading to new agricultural techniques, new crops, or greater migration of people to more fertile areas. Others are studying climate change and disease and predicting an increase in the risk of malaria as the climate warms and mosquitoes are able to spread to previously cool, highland areas. The impacts of climate change continent-wide are vast, ranging from disease to economics to politics.

Lake Chad: A Case Study—Part 2

A more recent climate shift around Lake Chad particularly illustrates how global climatic changes can alter a specific region and how these changes, in turn, create feedback loops that reinforce the original impact. This shift began in the late 1960s after a wetter era. This was one of the longest and most severe climate shifts in recent history. Between 1968 and 1997, precipitation over the Sahel was 25 to 40 percent lower than it was between 1931 and 1960. In the 1970s alone, almost half of domestic livestock in the region died, and nearly a million people had starved to death, according to Jonathan Foley. Now, Lake Chad covers between 115 and 200 square miles (1,000 times smaller than it was 5,000 years ago), and the fish yield is six times less than it was 50 years ago—about 50,000 tons a day (see map 3.3).

The land that is exposed by a drying Lake Chad is subject to the powerful jet stream that blows over the area, creating several hundred million tons of atmospheric dust. In fact, according to oceanographer Robert Stewart, the Bodele Depression in the Sahel where Lake Chad is located is the dustiest place on Earth. As the wind blows westerly, it deposits minerals needed by phytoplankton, such as calcium and potassium, in the Atlantic Ocean and fertilizes the Amazon Basin. According to geologist Gene Shinn, Sahelian dust is also the likely cause of the decline in coral reefs as well, due to the bacteria, among other things, that are carried in the dust masses. Peak dust production years coincide with peak coral

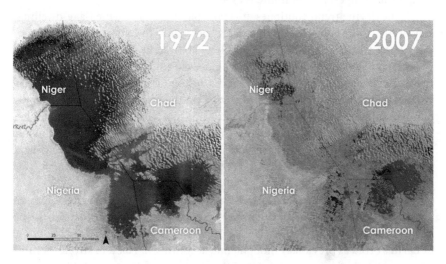

Map 3.3 Changes in the size of Lake Chad from 1972 to 2007. Former lakebed with fertile soil surrounding it. Courtesy of UNEP Atlas of Our Changing Environment, http://ourworld .unu.edu/en/sucking-dry-an-african-giant.

decline years. Also, the drier and colder the climate gets, the more desert there is, and the more dust there is in the atmosphere, reinforcing the dry regime.

These more recent changes are impacting the lives of those around the lake in significant ways. The water and fish resources are no longer enough for the 30 million people in the region—in neighboring Chad, Cameroon, Niger, and Nigeria—who depend on the lake. Another four countries—the Central African Republic, Algeria, Sudan, and Libya—share the lake's hydrological basin as well and are impacted by the lake's changes. One fisherman noted a 75 percent decline in catch in recent years, from $200 per day to $50 per day, according to a newspaper report in 2010. Thus, some fishermen are choosing to migrate to different regions within their own and neighboring countries in an attempt to find a way to make a living. Many of them move to already job-poor urban areas, where the likelihood of finding labor beyond petty trading is limited. One way to think of those displaced is as *environmental refugees*—a relatively new term for those who can no longer gain a secure livelihood in their home area due to drought, soil erosion, desertification, deforestation, or other ecological problems. By some estimates, as of 1995, there were 25 million such refugees.

Others who live around the much smaller Lake Chad have turned to farming the soil exposed by the drying of the lake in recent years, much as ancient Chadians did years ago. Although the soil in these areas is extremely fertile, farmers complain of desert sands encroaching on their fields as access to water becomes more limited. Conflicts between livestock owners and farmers are increasing as well due to competition for limited resources.

If the drying trend continues, it is possible that a lacustrine (lake-dwelling) way of life in the Sahel region that dates back 9,000 to 10,000 years will disappear in the area of Lake Chad. The peoples who lived near Lake Chad thousands of years ago contributed to a distinct Nilo-Saharan civilization, from which a number of contemporary African societies descend. They developed a sedentary village lifestyle without agriculture, relying on the steady and abundant supply of fish to support denser populations, according to African historian Christopher Ehret. But it may not be the end of humans' habitation of the area. Some scholars, including anthropologist Richard Potts, argue that many adaptations to abrupt changes in climate over a long period of time have made humans more adaptable than almost any other creature.

The explanation for these sudden shifts is important for students of human civilization, because we are part of a very complex set of global ecosystems. The suddenness of the shifts responsible for Lake Chad's changes is a result not only of Earth's orbit, as previously thought, but, according to Foley, of strong, nonlinear exchanges between vegetation and the atmosphere. These feedback loops are the result of changes in incoming solar radiation, the temperature of ocean surfaces, or the degree of land degradation, and they can amplify or buffer changes

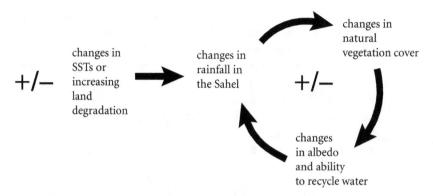

changes in
natural
vegetation cover

changes in
SSTs or
+/− increasing
land
degradation

changes in
rainfall in
the Sahel

+/−

changes
in albedo
and ability
to recycle water

Figure 3.1 Feedback between vegetation and the atmosphere over the Sahel, leading to a
dry and wet Sahel. This diagram shows feedback loops among vegetation cover, albedo
(reflectivity of sunlight off a surface), and evapotranspiration and monsoon rainfall. From
Jonathan A. Foley, Michael T. Coe, Marten Scheffer, and Guiling Wang, "Regime Shifts in the
Sahara and Sahel," *Ecosystems* 6, no. 6 (2003): 534. Courtesy of Rightslink.

in a system. Positive feedback loops associated with climate change are the result
of increasing global temperatures, as figure 3.1 shows. As soon as one factor increases or decreases, the other factors change as well, encouraging the cycle to
continue in a positive feedback loop. Scientists have speculated about feedback
loops that would exacerbate heating or cooling of the planet for a hundred years,
and now there is significant evidence of such feedback.

This feedback explains the tendency for a "green Sahara" or a "desert Sahara"
for at least 6,000 years. A small shift in Earth's orbit will cause a decrease or an
increase in monsoon rains and, in turn, lead to changes in vegetation that will
reinforce a cycle of rain or drought. Others working on the more recent regime
shift suggest that complex interactions among the atmosphere, the earth, and the
ocean led to a drying of the Sahel beginning in the 1960s, as figure 3.1 illustrates.
Changes in sea surface temperatures (SSTs) impact how much rain falls on the
Sahel of West Africa, and the amount of rainfall in turn influences the types
and quantities of plants that are able to grow. And the plants or vegetation cover
impacts the ability of the ground to retain rain when it falls, as well as how much
sunlight is reflected off the surface of the Sahel (albedo). Fewer plants and vegetation means less water retention and more of the sun's radiation reflected off the
surface rather than absorbed.

If the North Atlantic is relatively warmer than the South Atlantic, rainfall
will fall on the Sahel, but if southern waters are relatively warmer than northern
waters, the rain will fall south of the Sahel. Increases in sea surface temperatures
have altered monsoon patterns and thus seasonal rainfall patterns. Similarly, as

the climate dries, drier plants replace moisture-loving plants and then promote the conditions for drier plants, reinforcing the cycle. Large lakes can create their own precipitation patterns due to water evaporation. Small lakes, like the current Lake Chad, cannot. As the lake shrinks, the temperature of the remaining water rises, and it evaporates faster, as well. Thus, both 5,500 years ago and in the last century, what might have begun as a small change in the monsoon rains, sea surface temperatures, or vegetation has accelerated a drying phase set in motion by small shifts in the planet's orbit.

Humans have also impacted this most recent drying regime, particularly contributing to a warming North Atlantic. According to scientists at the National Oceanic and Atmospheric Administration (NOAA), human-induced global climate change is expected to exacerbate differences between North and South Atlantic temperatures. It is quite likely that the most recent shift, which has accelerated the drying trend started millennia ago, is a result of much greater concentrations of greenhouse gases in the air and sea than ever before. These greenhouse gases are largely due to emissions in the industrialized northern part of the world (Europe, the United States, Japan, and increasingly China and India). Africans produce about 4 percent of global greenhouse gas emissions. These gases, in turn, increase ocean temperatures. And as rainfall decreases, communities upstream from the lake build irrigation dams to maintain their crops in a drying climate, which further decreases the water reaching Lake Chad. Thus, it is not clear whether or not the current desert state caused by planetary changes is reversible, as it is now being exacerbated by human activity both locally and globally. Current climate studies suggest that causes beyond local resource use are the cause of the Sahel's drastic climate change. Desertification in the Sahel and the shrinking of Lake Chad are attributable to global climatic processes (some of them human-induced) rather than African actions.

Africans millennia ago adjusted to significant climate change by domesticating new crops, moving to other areas, or adopting different economic lifestyles. In hindsight, the outcome was sometimes very impressive cultural and economic changes. Of course, what is not as well recorded is the massive displacement and death that resulted from such changes. The historical record does not leave such data. The lesson from these examples is not that climate change will not be a problem and may, in fact, produce unforeseen positive consequences. Instead, the lessons are twofold. First, the long-term outcome is unknown. Second, and just as important, the planet has experienced plenty of major climate changes prior to the current one. The difference is that humans are now impacting changes that are already underway, thus enhancing our inability to predict the outcome. Science writer Fred Pearce notes that past climate will not provide a blueprint for our future because past climate events will not necessarily repeat themselves. Just as Africans were part of the important developments in early history as they built kingdoms and worked out new ways to obtain food, they can possibly show others how to make the best of a rapidly changing climate. Africans will be heavily impacted by the results of unprecedented levels of greenhouse gases in the atmosphere and likely have as much to teach us now as in the past about successful responses to such changes.

Africans' adaptation to unexpected and dramatic climate changes is remarkable and is part of the larger story of human adaptation generally. As Rick Potts says, that such a harsh, indifferent world "has happened to preserve us as part of its rich living fabric is extraordinary." The difference is that Africans have been adapting to the environment longer than any other humans. Altogether, our understanding of ourselves as a species with a history of important and long-term adaptations leads to a greater appreciation of our past and a bit less bravado about predicting the future. It will, no doubt, require humans to be just as adaptive and ingenious as our forebears. And this will include being willing to consider sedentary lifestyles as more than a stepping-stone on a linear progression to civilized, urban life. As the climate warms, openness to all forms of adaptation to various climates will provide greater flexibility and resilience for our livelihoods and future.

Suggestions for Further Reading

Jonathan Adams, Mark Maslin, and Ellen Thomas, "Sudden Climate Transitions during the Quaternary," *Progress in Physical Geography* 23, no. 1 (1999): 1–36. One of the most surprising outcomes of a recent study of Earth's history has been the discovery that climate has changed rapidly in the past. Adams and his team examine some of those transitions over the past 130,000 years.

Thomas J. Bassett and Donald Crummey, eds., *African Savannas: Global Narratives and Local Knowledge of Environmental Change* (Oxford: James Currey, 2003). This collection of environmental research on the savanna climate zone just south of the Sahel in many regions of Africa links the biophysical sciences and the social sciences. The researchers argue that Africans have a more intensive knowledge about the savanna landscape than colonial officials, development officials, or contemporary African politicians acknowledge.

Jonathan A. Foley, Michael T. Coe, Marten Scheffer, and Guiling Wang, "Shifts in the Sahara and Sahel: Interactions between Ecological and Climatic Systems in Northern Africa," *Ecosystems* 6, no. 6 (2003): 524–532. This article focuses on the causes and consequences of two dramatic climate changes in the Sahel about 5,500 years ago and again starting in 1969. Due to nonlinear feedback among the vegetation, the ocean, and the atmosphere, two alternative stable systems are predicted: green and desert.

Elliot Fratkin, *Ariaal Pastoralists of Kenya: Surviving Drought and Development in Africa's Arid Lands* (Boston: Allyn and Bacon, 1998). This is one of several books by Fratkin on the Ariaal pastoralists of northern Kenya. It is accessible and gives good, detailed descriptions of Ariaal culture and economy, as well as the challenges they currently face.

Peter Little, "Pastoralism, Biodiversity, and the Shaping of Savanna Landscapes in East Africa," *Africa* 66, no. 1 (1996): 37–51. Little demonstrates that rather than promoting grassland degradation, the pastoralists of northern Kenya contribute to biodiversity.

James McCann, "Climate and Causation in African History," *International Journal of African Historical Studies* 32, no. 2–3 (1999): 261–279. This is one of the first historical treatments of climate change in African history. McCann is a well-known historian of Africa who has written about environmental topics on the continent for decades.

Fred Nelson, "Natural Conservationists? Evaluating the Impact of Pastoralist Land Use Practices on Tanzania's Wildlife Economy," *Pastoralism: Research, Policy and Practice* 2, no. 15 (2012): 1–19. Nelson demonstrates that Maasai pastoralists' conservation of grasslands contribute to the Tanzanian economy by ensuring the well-being of the wildlife that attract foreign tourists to the country. Thus, pastoralism is in the interest of the Tanzanian nation-state.

Fred Pearce, *With Speed and Violence: Why Scientists Fear Tipping Points in Climate Change* (Boston: Beacon, 2007). A science writer for *The Guardian,* Pearce amasses mounting evidence that past climate changes have been abrupt and that we, too, likely face abrupt changes due to triggering tipping points, such as melting permafrost in Siberia and changes in the "ocean conveyor belt" system.

Rick Potts, *Humanity's Descent: The Consequences of Ecological Instability* (New York: William Morrow, 1996). Paleoanthropologist Potts seeks to explain our evolutionary past as a time when the Earth fashioned our existence—when we were ecological beings. He sees this work as an essential underpinning to making sense of the current situation of humans' ecological dominance.

Mathieu Schuster et al., "Chad Basin: Paleoenvironments of the Sahara since the Late Miocene," *Comptes Rendus Geosciences* 341 (2009): 612–620. This is a multidisciplinary scientific approach to understanding changes in the Lake Megachad environment and the ways in which humans interacted with the environment.

Jan Bender Shetler, *Imagining Serengeti: A History of Landscape Memory in Tanzania from Earliest Times to the Present* (Athens: Ohio University Press, 2007). Shetler uses oral traditions and oral history to allow western Serengeti peoples to demonstrate their long history in the area and the ways the landscape preserves their history and how they adapted to and changed the landscape.

Jeremy Swift, "Desertification: Narratives, Winners and Losers," in *The Lie of the Land: Challenging Received Wisdom on the African Environment,* ed. Melissa Leach and Robin Mearns (Oxford: Oxford University Press, 1996), 73–90. Using colonial documents, Swift uncovers a general attitude of fear of desertification and a series of measures implemented to try to combat it.

James Workman, *Heart of Dryness: How the Last Bushmen Can Help Us Endure the Coming Age of Permanent Drought* (New York: Walker, 2009). While not seeking to glorify the Bushmen of the Kalahari Desert, Workman illuminates their strategies for living in an arid landscape and narrates their battle for access to scarce water resources with the government of Botswana and its key economic interests: diamonds and tourism.

4 New Ideas and Tradition

THE BLENDING of new ideas with old ones is an important theme in early African history. Such a declaration might contrast with what many readers have heard about Africa: that it is a continent full of peoples who hold fast to tradition and are not interested in new, modern ways. And, in some coverage, such traditions are one reason for Africans' lack of modernity and poverty. Often, for example, ethnic identities or long-standing cultural loyalties are blamed for conflict on the continent.

African historian Jan Vansina wrote about traditions in Central Africa among Bantu speakers (who belonged to the Niger-Congo language family) that had not changed for millennia. In this interpretation, a constellation of ideas is associated with a word or term. Which terms are important or what they relate to changes with time. It is this more flexible notion of tradition that is explored here. Most societies, African or otherwise, are constituted of traditions that, although rooted in the distant past, have been influenced by ideas and changes from both within and outside the society. Particularly, many contemporary African cultural norms are syntheses derived from long-standing interactions with peoples of different economic and cultural backgrounds.

In an era of globalization, it might be difficult to imagine the world millennia ago when contact with those who were different would have been less frequent, when the ideas developed by one society over centuries, if not millennia, were significantly different from what another society had experienced up to that point. But it is easy to imagine how those contacts might have been peaceful when resources were plentiful and not so peaceful when resources were scarce. It is important to study the adoption of ideas because it helps us to understand why certain cultures might have interacted with others and the benefits they gained from it.

Geographical Focus

This chapter focuses on the heart of Africa, including Central, East, and South Africa. It is in this area that one major language group—the Bantu speakers of the larger Niger-Congo language family—predominate (see map 4.1). The first examples we examine are from the last millennium BCE and the first millennium CE, when these Bantu speakers traveled from West Africa to Central and East Africa and eventually outnumbered the original inhabitants. One of the best examples of the adoption of new ideas and integration of them into older ones occurred in East Africa during these years.

Two thousand years ago, speakers of the four main continental language families (Niger-Congo, Nilo-Saharan, Afrasan [Afro-Asiatic in map 4.1], and Khoisan) populated the interior of East Africa (including modern-day Uganda, Rwanda, Burundi, Kenya, and Tanzania), making it by far the most linguistically diverse area on the continent. In contrast to this early diversity, from 1500 CE on, Bantu speakers and Nilotic speakers (belonging in the larger Nilo-Saharan language family) became dominant. What happened to the speakers of Afrasan and Khoisan languages in the area? Why did they disappear? How might they have disappeared? These are some of the questions that historians have been trying to answer and that will be considered in this chapter.

Sources and Methodologies

Reconstructing the events of the early years CE to about 1500 CE has been challenging. The region is totally devoid of written evidence before the mid-1800s. Scholars in the past characterized this lacuna as a serious problem that could only be partially overcome with the use of other evidence. Yet, as is often the case, exploring nontraditional evidence has yielded unforeseen rewards. Some historians have mastered the techniques of historical linguistics and learned to interpret archaeological reports in order to write a history of the East African interior. How all four language groups shaped East Africa and how these many distinct peoples interacted has enormous consequences for understanding cultural contact throughout world history.

African historians have used this evidence much more effectively than scholars of other regional histories. Linguistic scholars study word lists of contemporary societies and the subsequent reconstruction of precursor or parent languages and then compare the presence of a word in older societies to its use and distribution in contemporary societies. Christopher Ehret is one African history scholar who has worked extensively with historical linguistics and whose ideas about African history have influenced the contents of this book. Language evidence, he argues, forms the most comprehensive and dense documentation available to us; it reflects the ideas and cultures of ordinary Africans and is thus more democratic than other sources for early African history, such as archaeology.

Languages, by their nature as vehicles of social communication, contain immense vocabulary resources that express and label the full range of cultural,

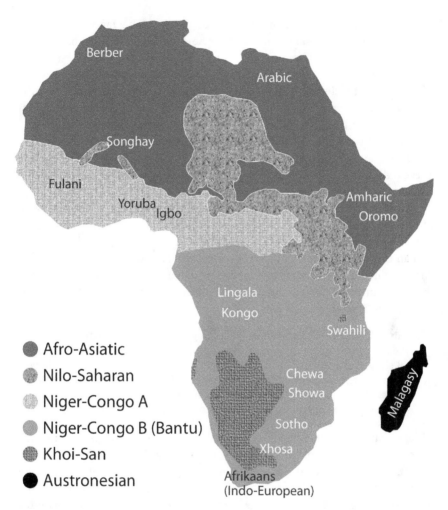

Map 4.1 Current distribution of major language families in Africa. Afro-Asiatic is referred to as Afrasan in this text, following Christopher Ehret's terminology. The Bantu group of the Niger-Congo is marked separately here. The final group, the Austronesian, who are found in Madagascar, is not covered in this book. Courtesy of Wikimedia Commons, http://en.wikipedia.org/wiki/File:African_language_families_en.svg.

economic, and environmental information available to their speakers. With care and perseverance, the scholar trained in historical-comparative linguistics can use the data available in a set of related modern languages to reconstruct their relationships and earlier histories. The first task is to create a family tree of languages that serves as a history of the family—say, that of the Niger-Congo language family. Then, by comparing words in newer languages with those in older languages, historians can begin to see how an idea or tradition has endured in that culture.

When vocabulary or grammatical structures do not continue over the long term or are not included in an ancestral language, it may be because a new, distinct language developed, possibly marked by economic, social, or political differentiation. Historical linguists also look for new words that were not used in an ancestral language. Borrowed words signal the meeting of discrete groups of peoples, and one group borrowed activities, ideas, or beliefs from the other. These indicate a new idea or skill, possibly learned from another group, such as the word for "finger millet" (*-lo) discussed below.

In his essay "World History and the Rise and Fall of the West," William McNeill argues that the role of linguistic and cultural contact in world history has been one of the primary change agents in human history. Most differences in human community until about 10,000 years ago, he contends, would have been due to adjustment to climate and landscape. After that, rather than changes in the environment, "relations with neighboring human bands" were the "principal occasion for innovation." He continues:

> This, in turn, made connections with strangers, who possessed different skills and ideas, critically important. Communities that reacted by borrowing useful skills and ideas, and then knitting new and old ways together by suitable invention, tended to expand their ecological niche, increasing both power and wealth. Those that clung fast to familiar routines tended to be left behind and survived only by retreating to marginal environments.

What scholars have pieced together of early East African history is a testament to the success that comes of embracing new ideas, as McNeill suggests.

The linguistic record, in particular, can demonstrate relatively peaceful cultural interaction or the adoption of new ideas from a different culture into longer-standing traditions or ideas, such as those regarding social organization or political authority. Some ideas, such as the domestication of the cow, are put into practice only a few times in human history, eventually spreading to other parts of the world. Other ideas are generated independently numerous times, such as clothing and hunting implements, and they take on their own cultural identity. But even in this latter case, these ideas spread from one society to another, and that diffusion can be traced in the linguistic record. The result is a history rich in ideas and interactions. While the linguistic record does not inform us about the possible violence associated with adopting new ideas from another culture, it does suggest, at least, an openness to new ways of doing things, either out of curiosity, a mark of *Homo sapiens,* or out of necessity, or both.

New Ideas and Traditions in East African History

East Africa is the site of some of the earliest evidence for human history; different hominids and humans have occupied much of the region for millennia. Significant linguistic evidence, though, is only available for the last 4,000 years or so and it has been carefully investigated by Christopher Ehret. His research is the foundation of the discussion over the next few pages. At the beginning of this period, hunters and gatherers from one or more linguistic groups (Khoisan and possibly Nilo-Saharan) occupied the region. Southern Cushitic speakers (belonging to the Afrasan language family) began moving into northern Kenya (from Ethiopia) about 3000 BCE. And Nilo-Saharan language speakers, particularly Central Sudanic and eastern Sahelian, began to occupy the Western Rift Valley and Great Lakes area (today this area is part of eastern Democratic Republic of Congo, Uganda, Rwanda, and Burundi) by 2000 BCE. Bantu speakers were the last to arrive after 1000 BCE.

By examining loan words in Bantu languages that are spoken in East Africa today, scholars conclude that Central Sudanic speakers brought with them knowledge of sorghum and millet cultivation. The word for "finger millet"— *-lo*—found in Bantu languages around the Great Lakes region of East Africa is not in ancestral Bantu languages, nor is there evidence that it was internally innovated from Bantu words in use at the time. A similar term—*do*—is found in Central Sudanic languages spoken today, indicating that Bantu speakers learned the word *-lo* and the knowledge associated with growing finger millet from their Sudanic neighbors. Similar linguistic evidence demonstrates that the word for "sorghum"—*-pu*—came from Central Sudanic languages. These crops would not have been suitable to the rainforest climate that the Bantu speakers came from in Central Africa, so as they encountered either natural or human-made savanna areas in eastern Africa, they would have needed a crop more suited to these environments than their forest-derived yam. Millet and sorghum became the staple crops for many Bantu speakers and remained so for centuries until the twentieth century, when maize began to replace it.

Nilo-Saharan and Afrasan speakers taught disparate groups of Bantu speakers how to raise and care for cattle. Eastern Sahelian speakers introduced Lakes Bantu speakers to cattle with the accompanying word *-ka*. Earlier, eastern Sahelian speakers introduced another branch of Bantu speakers, Mashariki Bantu, to new ideas regarding livestock, as witnessed by words for "livestock fence" and "pen." In other areas of the Great Lakes, southern Cushitic speakers introduced Bantu speakers to cattle keeping and the breeding of cattle. Thus, Bantu speakers came to be mixed farmers, practicing both agriculture and livestock keeping, thanks to their new neighbors in East Africa.

The second dominant group in East Africa today comes from the Nilo-Saharan language family. Southern Nilotic speakers, who came to dominate western

Kenya and northwestern Tanzania, moved into Kenya in the ninth century BCE. They were keepers of livestock and farmers of millet and sorghum. It is probable that eastern Cushites (coming from Ethiopia and belonging to the Afrasan language family) introduced circumcision and clitoridectomy as rites of passage. The Nilotic terms for "to circumcise" and "circumcised boy," among others, demonstrate Cushitic origin. Southern Nilotic speakers developed cycling age sets based on initiation with the accompanying surgical procedure. Age sets were groups of youths and men who were given a name when they were circumcised and initiated together and then belonged to the youngest age grade. Their particular name was part of a cycle of names that recurred after several generations. Originally there were eight age-set names.

Age grades are stages of life with ascribed tasks, such as cattle herding. Boys of approximately the same age (in this case, an age set) moved together from one stage of life to another, or one age grade to another, while assuming joint responsibility for their duties. Circumcision and the accompanying initiation ceremony brought together boys from multiple kin groups, linking together people from a wide area—an example of heterarchy. Having experienced significant psychological, emotional, and physical challenges as a group, these adolescents would have bonds with one another and be expected to remain loyal to one another for the remainder of their lives. To this day, Nilotic initiations and age grades are one of the distinguishing characteristics of contemporary East Africa in contrast to the rest of the continent.

Scholars who work with historical linguistics in both East and Central Africa argue that the eventual dominance of Nilotic speakers in East Africa and Bantu speakers in both areas was due to newcomers absorbing earlier settlers. Bantu speakers hunted and gathered, cultivated yams, and kept goats as they moved from Central Africa to East Africa in the first millennium BCE. In East Africa, they adopted both cattle keeping and grain agriculture, the former from contact with Cushitic and eastern Sahelian speakers, and the latter from contact with Central Sudanian and eastern Sahelian speakers. In addition, from at least 900 BCE on, Bantu speakers worked iron, a skill they possibly learned from Nilo-Saharan speakers. Some Bantu speakers, neighbors to Nilotic speakers in southwestern Kenya and northwestern Tanzania, gave age sets a more prominent cultural role than previously as a means of facilitating cooperation between more distant peoples. Developing a combination of economic strategies enabled them to live successfully in almost any environment and eventually to carry their successful economic package to southern Africa. Moreover, their diverse economic tool kit led to population growth that was likely augmented by strangers moving to their settlements and marrying there.

Because Bantu speakers were able to effectively maintain stable population settlements in contrast to the more mobile communities of gatherer-hunters or pastoralists, they likely absorbed the latter into their communities over time. Bantu population centers would have been attractive to peoples who were cattle keepers moving seasonally with livestock between one or more camps or gatherer-hunters because they could be places of refuge in times of trouble or attractive places to seek a spouse. Nilotic speakers' adoption of age sets and age grades with accompanying initiation ceremonies and surgical operations, such as male circumcision, produced alliances with people outside of their kin networks and mobilized youth for defensive or ritual purposes. In this way, they would have had an advantage over transhumant cattle keepers who did not employ these forms of organization.

What is worth emphasizing is that the process by which Bantu speakers and Nilotic speakers became dominant was a long one, occurring over several millennia, and not initially marked by significant inequality. The oral traditions maintained by Bantu-speaking peoples in Central Africa, for example, attest to the essential role gatherer-hunters played as teachers in the new environment. Gatherer-hunters were considered the original inhabitants and extolled as teachers and healers who possessed knowledge of local medicines. Gatherer-hunters also would have been considered the best ones to intercede with the spirits associated with the land. Bantu speakers, as newcomers, would have recognized that the gatherer-hunters' ancestors were buried on the land they now sought to use and thus were more legitimately connected to it. Historian Kairn Klieman notes that French ethnographies of the Aka gatherer-hunters and their Niger-Congo–speaking agricultural neighbors (in this case from the Ubangian subgroup) indicate that the farmers credit the gatherer-hunters with introducing them to fire, cooked food, ironworking, and the domestication of plants. This is a very powerful set of ideas, both spiritually and economically, and all but ironworking remain essential to making a living for most in Central Africa. Oral traditions told by both Aka and their Bantu-speaking neighbors in the 1970s recall Aka inviting the Bantu speakers to live among them and teaching them how to live in that environment. One day, though, after returning from a hunting expedition, the Aka found that the immigrants had taken over the village and the iron forge. Oral tradition captures what the linguistic record illuminates as well: that initially gatherer-hunters were the ones with the necessary skills for survival and Bantu speakers were their inferiors and learned everything from them.

Anthropologist Igor Kopytoff has argued that when peoples settled a new area or frontier, they often incorporated some of the original residents to ensure the success of the new village. The original settlers, however, would have little reason to join an immigrant population, and too many of them would threaten the immigrants' cultural identity. So incorporation was usually done through real or fictive family ties. In this light, early Bantu and Nilotic speakers were not in any way inherently superior as they entered these new environments but dependent on the earlier inhabitants as they adapted. Their survival initially depended on the peoples settled there and the skills and knowledge they possessed.

Historian Jan Shetler's study of East Nyanza Bantu speakers near Lake Victoria demonstrates a similar process of Bantu speakers learning from residents the skills necessary to survive and thrive in the landscape. By 1000 CE, Bantu speakers were the dominant people on the landscape, and 500 years later, they had differentiated into a half dozen or more group, each with a distinct language and associated with a particular location and natural resources. Even after the newcomers made up the larger part of the population, they continued to interact with the original residents in ways that allowed them to have access to a wide variety of resources to ensure the best chances for survival and success.

Bantu speakers were not the only ones who learned new skills. African historians Jan Vansina, John Robertson, and Rebecca Bradley argue that it is likely that the original inhabitants learned technologies from Bantu speakers and adopted their language, becoming Bantu in the process. This adoption of the language and culture explains the growth and diffusion of these skills and languages. In time, the combination of skills of grain farming, livestock keeping, and ironworking, as well as novel forms of social organization, allowed Bantu speakers to live in more compact and permanent villages than the autochthons, or original inhabitants. Therefore, their languages and rituals eventually dominated the region as their numbers and prosperity grew.

Intercultural borrowing contrasts with earlier notions that Bantu speakers invaded Central and East Africa by wielding superior iron weapons. Using new linguistic evidence, Vansina and colleagues posit that the popular idea of the "Bantu expansion," which held that Bantu success was due to "a vast technological differential," including farming and metallurgy, is no longer credible. Because of flawed linguistic data, they argue, authors assumed the migration took place in one wave over several hundred years. Due largely to linguistic evidence and some oral traditions, historians now know that the migrations were slow and piecemeal and involved adoption of new ideas, by both the original settlers and the newcomers, rather than innate cultural dominance.

Instead of crossing the continent with an appreciable technological advantage compared to those they encountered, Bantu and Nilotic speakers entered East Africa lacking the necessary tool kit to thrive. They adapted and learned from gatherer-hunters (probably the descendants of Khoisan speakers), Central Sudanic, eastern Sahelian, and Cushitic speakers. Even though the populations of Central Sudanic and Cushitic speakers in East Africa are currently quite small, their historical legacy is large and can be traced through the words modern-day speakers use to describe some of their most important economic and social activities. Thus, East African history before 1500 CE is not a story of conquest but of communicating with, relying on, learning from, and intermarrying with those from other cultural and linguistic groups in order to better adapt over the long run. Historical linguistics research in East Africa has yielded a rich picture of interaction over 3,000 years.

Not only are Central and East Africa the sites of complex cultural borrowing over thousands of years, but they are also home to a highly skilled and technological process of iron smelting. Iron smelting involves heating iron-bearing rocks to temperatures beyond the melting point of iron in the presence of carbon so that the metal is separated from the ore. Due to its complexity, this is an idea invented likely only twice in world history. One confirmed site of invention is in modern-day Turkey, about 1500 BCE. A second possible site is in Central Africa, according to Ehret. By 1000 BCE, there is archaeological evidence of iron smelting north of Lake Tanganyika in East Africa and near Lake Chad in West Africa even earlier than dates in northeastern Africa, where Asian ironworking first spread. It is highly unlikely that it developed twice in Africa, so there must have been a central point of origin not yet identified by scholars, possibly in the Central African Republic.

Early Africans used iron to make hoes for farming and axes for cutting down trees to clear land and build boats. They also used iron for bodily ornamentation. Like other rare and valuable commodities, iron was an item of trade. Ironworking required the presence of both iron-bearing rock and large forests to create the charcoal necessary for the high temperatures of the smelt, so not every society could work iron. Ethnoarchaeologist Peter Schmidt works among the Haya in Tanzania and has demonstrated that Africans achieved higher temperatures and thus a different quality of iron than Asians and Europeans at the same time. For Africans, achieving such quality was both technical and cultural, requiring specific behaviors on the part of ironworkers and their family members. Particularly, they linked the fertility of the iron smelting process with human fertility. In an agricultural society, successful human reproduction meant enough people to perform the necessary labor. Successful iron production meant the creation of tools that increased productivity of the laborers. Societies that adopted ironworking had an additional advantage that enabled them to produce more food and thus increase the number of people their societies could support.

This evidence of borrowing ideas in eastern Africa can be compared with other regions in world history. One example is the current rethinking of Indian-Aryan interaction between 1500 and 500 BCE on the Indian subcontinent. Instead of viewing Aryans as violent conquerors, scholars today emphasize their interactions with local peoples and their borrowing of local cultural ideas. Indian loan words found in the language of the Aryan speakers and in their adoption of certain religious practices, such as *yoga,* indicate this learning and interaction. Similarly, recent scholarship on religious interactions along the Silk Road (linking the Middle East and India with China) suggests that for 2,000 years, Silk

Road traders transmitted multiple religious traditions such as Zoroastrianism, Judaism, and various forms of Christianity to inhabitants of the region. Central Asia during this period, much like eastern Africa, was an area of cultural fluidity in which multiple religious traditions coexisted, building on earlier cultural and religious elements, creating new syntheses.

Returning to Africa, another example of cultural diffusion comes from southern Africa. The ancestors of the peoples now referred to as San (of the Khoisan language family) were likely the earliest inhabitants of southern Africa. They practiced gathering and hunting and had a rich cultural tradition that included rock art, efficient poison arrows, and ritual specialists who could heal through trance dancing. As other Africans, such as Bantu speakers, moved into the area in the first centuries CE, San were valued for their spiritual powers.

Later arrivals from Europe, however, were not so appreciative of San culture. Geoffrey Blundell, curator of the Origins Center in Witwatersrand, South Africa, recounts how the San suffered after the arrival of Europeans in the seventeenth century. On the eastern Cape frontier, raiding parties went out regularly to abduct San children for slaves. These raids were conducted with tremendous violence. One farmer claimed to have killed 2,700 San personally and another 3,200. As a result, by the end of the nineteenth century, San communities almost entirely disappeared as distinctly recognizable groups with their own language. But they also might have adopted other identities, including that of Khoi or Coloured (a more favorable designation under the apartheid regime of South Africa in the twentieth century). Interestingly, modern economic forces continue to impact San identity. In Botswana, for example, the government did not allow San to work in South African gold mines, so San often claimed a Bantu identity in order to become eligible for this work. Today in South Africa, there are only a handful of speakers left in northern South Africa, and some San speakers remain in Botswana and Namibia.

But just like the gatherer-hunters of Central Africa, San culture lives on in a variety of ways. Those San who survived prior to the twentieth century merged with their Bantu-speaking and Khoe (also of the Khoisan) neighbors. Bantu speakers from East Africa, where they had achieved the suite of characteristics discussed above, traveled to southern Africa about 2,000 years ago. Origins of the Khoe are not as certain. They either have been in southern Africa (what is now Botswana likely) for a very long time or they came from Central Africa, bringing sheep and pottery with them.

A variety of evidence demonstrates that San impact on these communities was significant. First, there is a high percentage of San genes in some Bantu-speaking communities. Just like the gatherer-hunters of Central Africa, the San intermarried with the sedentary Bantu speakers. Second, Nguni languages (a subset of Bantu languages) have "click" sounds that were adopted from the

San. Third, elements of San religion and beliefs can be seen in the rituals of a number of Bantu-speaking communities. As Blundell notes, "While they have disappeared as independent communities with their own distinctive languages, San culture thus lives on through the Bantu-speaking peoples."

In eastern and southern Africa, both archaeological and linguistic evidence reveal different models of historical processes that can fruitfully illuminate the history of other regions. In the interior of eastern and southern Africa, peoples of distinct backgrounds came together over several thousands of years, learned from and lived with one another, and created new economic and social syntheses, utilized by Bantu and Nilotic speakers, who carry their debt to these other societies in their vocabularies and genes.

What these two examples demonstrate is that our historical research, to date, has been unnecessarily impoverished by an overreliance not only on Western history but also on concepts of Western history as constructed by nineteenth- and twentieth-century Western historians who relied on written evidence and paradigms based on centralized states, organized warfare, and narrow concepts of progress and technology. Instead, armed with historical linguistics, researchers can see that knowledge of a particular landscape and religious power, for example, was as important for survival as a productive economy or new forms of technology. Just as earlier hominids live on in our genetic structure, gatherer-hunters' knowledge, ideas, and genetics live on in modern-day Africans as well.

New Ideas and Traditions in Recent Times

Of course, cultural diffusion continued to occur in African history in the colonial and postcolonial periods. A few brief examples will suffice to illustrate the ways Africans continue to embrace cultural change. Returning to South Africa, one of the minority populations is of Indian origin, largely due to forced labor migration starting in the late nineteenth century. Between 1860 and 1911, more than 150,000 Indian workers traveled from India to Natal in South Africa to work on sugar plantations and in other economic ventures. Merchant Indians followed soon thereafter, seeking commercial opportunities within the Indian community in South Africa. These migrations resulted in a variety of Indian cultures and languages within Natal, where the Zulu dominated. Indians became one of the most multilingual communities in South Africa between 1900 and 1950. They spoke their native language, often another Indian language; used a pidgin for communicating with the Zulu and white population; and increasingly started to speak English. Others might have known some Zulu and Afrikaans as well.

But between the 1950s and 1980s, Indian languages were spoken less frequently as English became more popular. Linguistics professor Rajend Mesthrie notes a number of reasons for this shift. The first is that the Indian population itself was divided linguistically and culturally, so it was unlikely that a dominant

Indian language would emerge. Instead, English came to play that role. In addition, Indian languages did not hold much prestige in wider South Africa. They were not taught in schools in the area, and they suffered competition from Afrikaans, recognized as an official language of the government. The result has been a South African Indian population that now uses English both in school and the workplace, as well as at home, while maintaining an Indian cultural identity. For future historians using historical linguistics, what will appear in the record is the loss of these Indian languages, and without other evidence—archaeological, written, or otherwise—one might assume that cultural change accompanied this language shift as well.

One last point about the role of intermarriage in this language shift is relevant. Before the 1980s, intermarriage among Indians across linguistics groups was rare. Rajend Mesthrie argues that intermarriage did not quicken the pace of the loss of Indian languages in South Africa, but rather the process of indigenous language loss, already underway through educational and economic changes, made it easier for Indians from different cultural backgrounds to interact and, thus, marry. Therefore, looking back in history at the ways in which gatherer-hunters were absorbed by farmers and pastoralists, it is important to realize that only part of the story is clear and that changes in culture and language do not necessarily follow in tandem and that marriage across linguistic divides might occur after other changes have taken place to make communication and attraction easier.

A second example illustrates cultural change due to ideas of global significance rather than local significance, as our earlier examples indicated. In many African societies, chiefs were the primary leader in a community. In Ghana, for example, for the past 500 years or so, several linguistic and cultural groups have recognized a chief as their leader and protector, the best known of which is the Asante. During the colonial period, often traditional political authority was weakened, and this was also the case in Ghana as well.

After independence, Ghanaian presidents considered chiefly authority both threatening and beneficial. Depending on the area of the country the president and particular chief came from, they could either be allies or rivals for authority. But in 1992, the position of the chiefs within the modern nation-state was enshrined in the constitution, and they now have a role to play within the national government. Through the House of Chiefs, Ghanaian chiefs advise all government bodies and work to codify customary law, among other things. Most Ghanaians today would consider themselves both citizens of Ghana and subjects of a particular chief—the latter representing authority for hundreds of years, the former representing a shorter term of authority and power.

Increasingly, Ghanaian chiefs have lived and studied abroad before being asked to return home to take up the chieftancy in their home communities.

When they are asked to become chief after such an experience, they are being called upon in their capacity as an educated Ghanaian and as one who has foreign connections and ideas that might facilitate development. Thus, in the span of 100 years or so, Ghanaian chiefs' responsibilities have broadened from ensuring that tradition is honored through ceremonies, land rights, and customary laws to also being responsible to the nation and to the increasing popular demands for economic development. A form of authority, developed over centuries in a particular location and influenced by other societies in the area, is now influenced by ideas from abroad as to how best to lead a community.

A third example illuminates the attraction and impact of some forms of technology. Africans have embraced the cell phone with astonishing speed. According to Sebastiana Etzo and Guy Collender, the first cell phone was used in 1987. In 2009, there were about 350 million mobile phone subscribers on the continent, according to a *Guardian* article. This means that on average one in every three Africans has a mobile phone, but usage is distributed unevenly. In some countries, like Ethiopia, fewer than one in every ten people has a phone, and in Gabon, almost everyone does. Mobile phone usage is growing faster in Africa than anywhere else in the world. Many places on the continent never had landline phones and likely never will, as investment in cell phone infrastructure has overtaken the previous technology. Thus, despite the economic challenges that many African countries face, their citizens and entrepreneurs are embracing cell phone usage and sometimes creating their own cell phone companies, as did Sudanese businessman Ibrahim Mo, who founded Celtel (now Zain). A newswire article from 1998 featured a picture of a Mossi chief (from Burkina Faso) dressed in robes and speaking on a cell phone. The article noted that chiefly authority remained strong in the area even though the Mossi were embracing changes, like cell phones, associated with the modern era. Clearly, Africans continue to seek ways to exchange ideas and learn from one another.

Evolution and Cultural Change

These processes of cultural evolution or cultural change provide us a window into human nature and human evolution that is very important. For a long time, scholars assumed that the only determining factor in human behavior was biological—that humans did what they did because it promoted the success of our offspring. Then it was believed that it was because it promoted the replication of our genes. In both cases, the biological and environmental factors seemed most salient. But there is much in human cultures that does not necessarily promote genetic replication, such as the choice increasingly made by men and women in Europe and the United States not to have children. One way of explaining human culture, and of explaining why it is so different from chimpanzees or bonobos (beyond the reasons already covered in chapter 1), is that memes, or ideas that can be passed from one person (one brain) to another, have taken hold of our evolution.

Our genetics and our evolutionary past remain important; they can explain our desire for high-calorie foods or sex, but they cannot explain why Americans eat pizza with beer and not with orange juice or shake hands when they greet. Much of what humans now do does not seem designed for survival, psychologist Susan Blackmore argues. This, according to evolutionist Jonnie Hughes, is due to memes—the rule of ideas in our human world. People now solve problems not by adapting our biology to fit the problem but by adapting our culture. And memes, like genes, seek to be copied or replicated and are alive and ever-changing.

Thus, in this view, hominins and now humans are addicted to ideas—learning about them, talking about them, and spreading them. Bantu speakers in eastern and southern Africa managed to share a wider variety of ideas and ways of living on the landscape than did others with whom they came into contact, such as the Cushites. Indians in South Africa seek to belong to the world of ideas even if it means abandoning a language that previous generations have used. Modern Africans, of course, want a cell phone if they can obtain one because it can expand their capacity for sharing ideas and networking—important values for Africans. And it makes sense that in Ghana, if an institution like the chieftaincy, a meme as well, has survived alongside other ideas of political authority for decades, it has remained relevant to the wants and needs of Ghanaians and thus continues to find a way to compete in the idea sphere of political authority in modern-day Ghana.

Whether or not one accepts the concept of memes, Africans in both the distant and recent past demonstrate clearly the changing nature of culture and the ways in which humans rely on the ideas and practices of others. In the end, not all ideas are equal, but the embrace of new ideas is part of our inheritance.

Africans have consistently learned from one another and from outsiders about how best to live. They are not any more reluctant or eager to change their ways of doing things than are the rest of us, even if media and some scholars have portrayed them that way. In fact, their history demonstrates a penchant for seeking out new ideas and new methods. Their long history allows us to see the power of cultural contact. Over centuries, some ideas and peoples are better suited, and probably more adaptable, than others and thus become more attractive and successful. (One way to look at it is that some memes were more successful than others.) One of the best illustrations of this in African history is the slow disappearance of most gathering and hunting peoples on the continent. For many centuries, they were not brutally forced out of their landscapes (until more recently in southern Africa) but absorbed into a more populous and economically diverse group of people who could make a living in a variety of ways and in a variety of landscapes. Similarly, modern Africans are eager to embrace new technology, such as cell phones, and new ideas and resources, such as those that come from foreign-educated Africans. Africans, like the rest of us, are the beneficiaries of cultural ideas and learning that have accumulated over millennia. Humans are culturally complex creatures due to our passion for ideas and the complex ways in which culture is created and recreated.

Suggestions for Further Reading and Viewing

John A. Distefano, "Hunters or Hunted? Towards a History of the Okiek of Kenya," *History in Africa* 17 (1990): 41–57. This article is an examination of previous disparaging and evolutionist views and ideas about the Okiek gatherer-hunters in Kenya. More recent linguistic and anthropological data suggest a culturally coherent and resilient identity that, while often bilingual, has maintained its gathering roots and close ties to both pastoral and agricultural peoples throughout the area.

Christopher Ehret, *The Civilizations of Africa: A History to 1800* (Charlottesville: University of Virginia Press, 2002). This book on African history is grounded in historical linguistics. Ehret traces the evolution of African societies in the four major continental language groups across four regions of the continent.

Jonnie Hughes, *On the Origin of Tepees: The Evolution of Ideas (and Ourselves)* (New York: Free Press, 2011). This is one of the most recent books published on memes. It is written in an engaging style and covers a lot of biological and evolutionary ground. A tour of the western United States is the backdrop for Hughes's intellectual inquiry into whether or not human life makes sense through the lens of memes. Seeing the world this way, or wearing these goggles, allows us to fully understand what makes humans different from every other living creature. Hughes has a very good bibliography of the ideas that led up to meme theory; he calls it a bibliography of the "goggle makers."

Kairn A. Klieman, *"The Pygmies Were Our Compass": Bantu and Batwa in the History of West Central Africa, Early Times to c. 1900 CE* (Portsmouth, N.H.: Heinemann, 2003). This book investigates Bantu and Batwa (gatherer-hunter) interactions in Central Africa using archaeology, historical linguistics, and oral traditions.

Rajend Mesthrie, "Language Shift, Cultural Change and Identity Retention: Indian South Africans in the 1960s and Beyond," *South African Historical Journal* 57, no. 1 (2007): 134–152. Mesthrie examines how over 150 years a variety of Indian languages disappeared but much culture remained intact.

James L. Newman, *The Peopling of Africa: A Geographic Interpretation* (New Haven, Conn.: Yale University Press, 1995). Newman has written an accessible overview of the major African language groups and the ways in which their speakers made a living and interacted with one another over millennia. The last half of the book looks at regional developments.

David Smith, "Africa Calling: Mobile Phone Usage Sees Record Rise after Huge Investment," *The Guardian,* October 22, 2009, http://www.theguardian.com/technology/2009/oct/22/africa-mobile-phones-usage-rise. This article is about the meteoric rise in cell phone sales in Africa in the first decade of the twenty-first century.

Tree of Iron, The, produced by Peter O'Neill and Frank Muhly Jr. (1988). This is an excellent video for two reasons. First, it demonstrates the deep interplay between culture and iron technology among the Haya in Tanzania. Second, it illustrates how ethnoarchaeologist Peter Schmidt works, using multiple sources (oral history, oral traditions, and archaeology) to piece together the history of ironworking in this area.

Jan Vansina, *Paths in the Rainforests: Toward a History of Political Tradition in Equatorial Africa* (Madison: University of Wisconsin Press, 1990). Vansina has a long section on historical linguistics and how historians use it to reconstruct history. Using historical linguistics, he then writes about several thousand years of Bantu speakers' sociopolitical history in Central Africa, an area with little written history prior to the publication of this book. It is an area that differs from neighboring societies in food production and types of political systems, decentralized (heterarchical) and large scale. A section titled "Tradition: Ancient and Common" might be of particular interest. It covers millennia of cultural continuity within these communities, examining housing, villages, farming, and foraging.

PART II

AFRICAN INSTITUTIONS IN THE MIDDLE TIME FRAME

IN THE WEST, and the United States in particular, we tend to think of culture as something good if it is mixed and if we celebrate it, so we have Black History Month, St. Patrick's Day, and a host of local cultural celebrations, as well as a strong movement within academia toward multiculturalism. Yet, such celebrations and curricular achievements are not enough to secure a deep appreciation for the tremendous varieties of the human experience. This part of the book seeks to broaden and deepen this understanding by examining some fundamentally different ways to organize societies than those that are the focus of most Western histories, such as matriliny, heterarchical social organization, and "wealth in people." Heterarchy is marked by overlapping arenas of authority as opposed to the more vertical and hierarchical model that has dominated our study of Western history. Chapter 5 discusses the various ways in which African societies have demonstrated, and still demonstrate, horizontal differentiation as opposed to vertical differentiation, or hierarchy. Such systems are widespread in African societies and offer a different way of looking at power and social connection. Chapter 6 considers matriliny as a system of social organization. For much of the African past, it was one of the primary ways in which Africans thought about their social connections and obligations because it made the most sense given their environments and challenges. Like all these other ideas, matriliny shaped behaviors and thought in significant ways. Chapter 7 discusses one of the primary ways that Africans have thought about their economies: through their connection to people. Some have called it "wealth in people," and others have called it the "gift economy." Regardless, it is a way to ensure security and well-being by making sure that individuals have solid, long-lasting connections of exchange, reciprocity, and debt. Starting in the late fifteenth century, Europeans entered this system valuing material objects as the path to security. As such, they sought gold, spices, and control of the Muslim trade that brought those goods to the international market. When they arrived in Africa, they found that Africans had slaves and were trading slaves, mostly within Muslim societies across the Sahara and Red Sea. Merging European material and mercantile interests with African interests in building strong societies of laborers and dependents resulted in a number of global changes, including the Atlantic slave trade that occurred from 1500 to the early 1800s.

5   Forms of Political Authority
Heterarchy

DEMOCRACY IS one of the most common forms of political systems in the world today, largely because it enables mass participation in political decisions. Yet, there is often some distance between the concept and its practice, as power tends to accumulate in the hands of few. One of the complaints about our current political system is that it does not adequately serve the interests of the majority of U.S. citizens, partly because wealth and political power are tightly connected. Sociologist Robert Putnam has clearly demonstrated our decreasing civic engagement. Both criticisms suggest a desire for a more active and accessible system of political and economic power. These concerns are not surprising given our hierarchical political system, where power and authority increase with status. It is this kind of vertical organization with concentrated power that has been at the heart of the study of history: economic and political authority as wielded by kings, states, churches, and landowners. Yet, as social and intellectual historians have amply demonstrated, there are often various sources of authority at any given time, acting with varying degrees of success, to check monolithic power. In the United States, for example, the religious right is a response to a perceived narrow political agenda and view. Similarly, groups of citizens have mobilized in recent years for various causes, including saving endangered species, prohibiting pollution, and maintaining trade unions. In each case, groups of people from cross sections of society come together for a particular purpose that is at odds, or in tension with, prevailing institutions.

Some societies are expressly organized around a variety of forms of authority. These societies can be called heterarchical rather than hierarchical. Heterarchy is a way of thinking about power and authority across and among social groups, institutions, and people. It implies diffuse, independent sources of power, rather than concentrated, vertical power. Many African societies for millennia had a variety of structures that included a chief or recognized wise elder who was respected for his or her wisdom, wealth, access to resources, link to the past, or some other culturally significant reason. But usually he (or she, more rarely) led in consultation with other older men and women to make decisions and judge cases. A chief often worked alongside others with competing realms of authority—religious, intellectual, or economic. Historian Walter Hawthorne made a useful distinction in this regard. Societies with heterarchy had unofficial leaders but not rulers. This chapter explores several African societies in the past, including a kingdom in East Africa that had multiple sources of authority and power. In West Africa, the focus is on an urban center with no significant status differentiation among its residents. Archaeologists Susan and Roderick McIntosh, whose work has illuminated history in West Africa, defined *heterarchy* as a complex political entity in which elements are "unranked vertically but may be highly stratified horizontally." In heterarchy, the goal is to understand the variety of ways that power and authority were manifest in a particular society, rather than focus on a small number of positions or people in whom most authority was vested.

While heterarchy has been widespread throughout the continent through different times and places, it has only been in the last 10 or 15 years or so that scholars of Africa have started paying attention to systems of multiple overlapping positions of power and authority. Political scientists, however, have been aware of such models for a much longer time. In fact, when Alexis de Tocqueville visited the United States in the eighteenth century, he noted that polycentric governance, or multiple overlapping arenas of political authority, was one of the strengths of early American society. Once aware of it, heterarchy is found in many places and times. Thus, like much in this book, a different lens on the evidence brings different ways of seeing and thinking about societal formation and values. Lifting up heterarchy will increase the chances that it will be found or created in contemporary organizations and institutions, as it has much to offer by way of thinking about renewing democracy and civic engagement.

Heterarchy reconnects us with the rest of the animal world. Kirkpatrick Sale, an independent scholar who writes about the interface between humans and their societies and the natural world on which they depend, notes that a human situation of diffuse authority is similar to the ecological situation of complementarity or mutuality, where members of a single species within an environmental niche act reciprocally and nonhierarchically to promote the communities' well-being. This situation, Sale argues, is the norm in the animal world, where distinction exists without rank. The aggression or coercion by some males in some species, such as baboons or wolves, he says, is often solitary rather than organized and institutionalized behavior. Quoting the founder of the social ecology movement, Murray Bookchin, in *The Ecology of Freedom,* Sale notes that what might appear to be hierarchical traits in animals are more like variations among individuals rather than organized stratifications that exist in most contemporary human societies. Sale maintains that most traditional societies also exhibit such complementary relationships where individuals possess specific skills and talents and a man or woman might gain status or admiration because of such skills, but other skilled individuals and customs can prevent such an individual from accumulating power. In both West and East Africa, large-scale complex societies have been built with attention to mustering the various skills and talents of a variety of citizens.

Geographical Focus

We examine two historical examples of heterarchy—one from West Africa in the first millennium CE and one from East Africa in the second millennium CE. One of the profound outcomes of colonialism and European influence was to significantly reduce complex webs of authority and power in many African societies in both western and eastern Africa. The major societies mentioned in this chapter can be found on map I.1.

Sources and Methodologies

As in much of the *longue durée* of African history, the study of heterarchy in the middle time frame relies on archaeology. Hierarchy is often visible in the archaeological record through rich burial artifacts, indicating a concentration of wealth in the hands of leaders. In heterarchy, little differentiation in burial practices suggests (but does not confirm) less concentration of wealth. Also, archaeology contributes to an understanding of local economic practices, such as agriculture, craftsmanship, and trade.

In the middle time frame, scholars can also use oral traditions, one of the primary sources historians use to write African history. Oral traditions are stories that are passed down within a community for generations, sometimes hundreds of years, about events of the distant past. Societies sometimes keep traditions alive for more than 500 years. Historian Neil Kodesh relies on well-known oral traditions to write his history of early Buganda. As you might expect, traditions often capture key moments in a society's past, either the ascension of a key figure to a position of power, such as Sunjata, the founder of the Mali Empire in the thirteenth century, or Kintu, the founder of the Buganda kingdom probably in the fourteenth century. Some oral traditions are origin stories that seek to account for people's existence in a certain geographic location. Others, as ethnoarchaeologist Peter Schmidt has shown with his study of ironworking in eastern Africa, remember sites of economic production, such as ironworking furnaces. Historian Jan Shetler worked with elders in western Tanzania to study their landscape and how old ideas about the landscape continued to shape contemporary societies, despite numerous changes. Kodesh, Schmidt and Shetler's work illustrates the power of place and memory. While reconstructing dates and chronology from oral traditions is often challenging, more consistent evidence is found between place and history through oral traditions. There is also a difference between the kinds of oral traditions that are preserved in a state society and those in a heterarchical society. In the former, a class or lineage of historians compile formal narratives that are conscientiously handed down from one generation to another. In decentralized societies, as Hawthorne found, no particular procedures or rituals with historic information are collected, so the narratives are handed down in a piecemeal fashion—during meals or while drinking or working.

Kodesh describes his approach to these traditions as an exercise in historical imagination. But this imagination is guided by other evidence from historical linguistics and comparative anthropology, as well as contemporary fieldwork that includes oral history and archival documents. Thus, by steeping one's historical imagination in a particular historical and cultural context, a historian can reconstruct some important elements of an African society's past. Both Kodesh and historian T. C. McCaskie (who works in Ghana) use oral traditions to reconstruct a more complex and fluid picture of precolonial African political changes.

Finally, when our examination turns to the nineteenth and twentieth centuries, then written documents and oral history become available for historical reconstruction. Colonial officials, for example, were interested in the histories of kingdoms and often tried to create kingship lists, usually derived from Africans' oral traditions. Colonial officials and the Africans who worked with them also compiled written cultural histories for the first time in many places. And these yield insight into African culture, politics, and the concerns of European authorities, among other things.

The Inner Niger Delta of West Africa

Archaeologists Roderick and Susan McIntosh were the first to use the term *heterarchy* for the society they were studying. The McIntoshes focused on an area south of the savanna states in West Africa known as the Inner Niger Delta (IND), particularly a site known as Jenne-jeno, where they made several significant discoveries. Jenne-jeno existed from about 300 BCE and reached its height in the latter part of the first millennium CE. The IND was a riverine zone with braided streams and complex environments that fostered different economic activities and thus local and long-distance trade (see map 5.1). Jenne-jeno was located at the southwestern extreme of the navigable and agriculturally productive inland delta. The IND was a natural transshipment point for trade in West Africa for centuries. Goods that came from the south by human or animal transport were taken further north either by boat or camel through the desert. In Jenne-jeno, copper and salt from the Sahara to the north were traded for dried fish, fish oil, and rice produced in the inland delta. Savanna products, such as iron, were traded there in exchange for salt, copper, rice, fish, and other staples.

Map 5.1 Jenne-jeno (located in modern-day Mali) on the Inner Niger Delta. From *The World Factbook 2013–14* (Washington, D.C.: Central Intelligence Agency, 2013), modified by Jessica Murphy, Xavier University.

The McIntoshes' fieldwork has provided a long-term perspective on settlement, social organization, and trade in this region. One of their conclusions is that urbanization and trade long predated the rise of the first centralized state in the area, Ghana, in the late first millennium CE. Centered on Jenne-jeno, they argue, was an earlier, African phase of urbanization. At its height in the ninth century, Jenne-jeno, with its accompanying 69 settlements, boasted a population of perhaps as many as 42,000 people. The city was the largest and most significant trading center in an intraregional economic network.

The Jenne-jeno site is comprised of multiple individual habitation mounds in close proximity, or clusters, as the McIntoshes refer to them, each exhibiting an economic specialization, though not everyone in a given settlement would have participated in the dominant activity. Archaeological work at Jenne-jeno suggests that authority was distributed among a variety of agencies that cut across society and bound together various ethnic groups, subsistence producers, artisans, and merchants. Roderick contends that most likely spatial segregation of the settlements coincided with craft specialization, or ethnicity, and was marked by various symbols such as dress, hairstyles, and scarification that preserved separate identities. While Jenne-jeno was a large settlement with residents engaged in a variety of activities, the cluster of settlements around Jenne-jeno was a network of specialized production.

Archaeology reveals that two sites near Jenne relied on rice and fonio (a type of grain) production in one case and millet production in another. In other areas, sites indicate that inhabitants specialized in such occupations as fishing (marked by fishing net weights), iron smelting, weaving (marked by spindle whorls), and trading (marked by imports and symbolic materials). Specialization would have enabled them to cope with environmental unpredictability. This can be looked at as a strategy for ecological resilience. When rains were unreliable and there were other uncertainties, economic diversity made sense. Rather than everyone in the area participating in the same generalized production for economic security, each group chose a particular economic activity and relied on the security of regional trade for other necessities.

This area also suggests relative economic equality. For these urban settlements, authority would have been based on networks of reciprocity rather than coercion. Communal memories of sacrifices made by one group for another during times of ecological stress or the privileges of "first arrivals" integrated disparate communities and encouraged cooperation. Even though some specializations, such as ironworkers, oral keepers of traditions (known as *griots*), and leather workers, would have accorded more authority than others due to their knowledge of the spirit world on which their work was based, their authority was checked by competition among various specialized crafts and by trade among competing factions. One member of society could belong to multiple groups as well. Social organizations such as kinship, age sets, secret societies, territorial and craft associations, and power associations also served as political associations representing various constituencies within the larger urban community. Age sets were groups of men (more rarely women) who had been born about the same time. They underwent an initiation ceremony together to teach them to be adults but also to bond them to one another as a group. Age sets cut across clan and lineage, linking people outside of kinship. Secret societies are another mechanism for initiating girls and boys into adulthood across kinship, common in places like Liberia and Sierra Leone. All these groups had competing interests and checked the tendency of charismatic individuals to monopolize or reinvent authority.

One feature of the archaeological layer associated with the ninth century CE is a particular ceramic ware with a coat of black and white paint applied after firing. If the ceramic vessel was used and washed, the paint would disappear; therefore, these ceramics must have been used for decoration and to mark status. In a hierarchical society, one would expect these items to be concentrated in certain areas and homes, but they are found throughout the Jenne-jeno mound. Another piece of evidence comes from the skeletal remains at Jenne-jeno. All the skeletons show evidence of good health, so there are no signs of unequal distribution of nutritious food or large differences in participation in hard labor.

One of the reasons heterarchy is common in early African history is that in most places in Africa during the middle time frame, land was widely available, but labor was not. In Europe at the same time, the situation was the reverse: access to land was concentrated and access to labor, in part as a result of concentrated ownership of land, was relatively easy. Thus, in Africa, if one wanted to escape from some form of authority (and experience the risks associated with cutting one's social ties), there was land available to start over. Susan McIntosh contends that the maintenance of multiple power relationships may tend to emerge among food-producing peoples where and when arable land is relatively abundant. This would have been the condition for some parts of sub-Saharan Africa until the present and was certainly the case for much of the continent in earlier times. It is even possible, she continues, that these various forms of social organization used to be much more widespread in the world.

As West Africa became more deeply integrated into long-distance trade associated with the Muslim world after the eighth century CE, several kingdoms formed across the West African savanna. Despite their apparent hierarchy, they also continue to demonstrate heterarchy. The first kingdom in the area, Ghana, was founded in the eleventh century CE and lasted for four centuries. It was followed by a much larger kingdom further to the east, the kingdom of Mali that lasted for several hundred years, incorporating a number of smaller, heretofore independent political entities into an empire. Mali's and Ghana's imperial strength rested to a large extent on taxation of the gold and salt trades across the Sahara. Salt came from the north, and gold came from the south. Both were highly desired commodities, salt as a dietary element and gold as ornamentation, a marker of wealth, and bouillon. During the middle time frame, much of the gold in circulation in Europe was minted from gold mined in West Africa.

The most famous oral tradition from West Africa, *Sunjata,* gives a glimpse into the founding of the kingdom of Mali, as well as many cultural and economic ideas from the middle to last half of the second millennium. In Mali, much like

Jenne-jeno, economic specialization came to be associated with particular families in the larger society, as described in *Sunjata*. For example, the oral tradition describes the role of blacksmiths, seers, and *griots* in Malinke society. Each king had a *griot* who accompanied him throughout his career, even prior to ascension to political power. The *griot* was a confidant; a historian, extolling the virtues of his king and the lineage of political power (often manipulated) to which his leadership was connected; and an aid. Seers were people with special ability to predict the future. They shared this trait with *griots,* blacksmiths, and hunters to some extent but did not possess their special skills.

All these specialists came to be associated with political power in the kingdom of Mali. Sunjata's rise to the kingship was deeply dependent on the cooperation of such specialists. For example, hunters and seers predicted Sunjata's birth and future destiny. Without their special knowledge and loyalty, he would have had little power. The oral tradition tells that Sunjata, son of a minor king and a spiritually powerful woman, did not walk for many years of his childhood. For this handicap, he was ridiculed and assumed to be no contender for his father's position upon his death, despite the seers' prediction. When Sunjata walked, it was only with the use of an iron bar that his father's blacksmith had crafted particularly for him. When Sunjata's *griot* disappeared, his ability to ascend to his father's position was temporarily, at least, eliminated. It is only upon his return that Sunjata was able to assume leadership. As Sunjata faces the final battle against his enemy, the Sosso empire, in the early 1300s, his *griot* exhorts him and his army to bravery and success by recalling the history of old Mali. He concludes, "I have told you what future generations will learn about your ancestors, . . . but what will we have to teach our sons about you?"

The oral tradition *Sunjata* also illuminates how oral traditions reflect accumulated ideas about a society and its history. After the fourteenth century, Islam came to be a source of both political and economic authority in West Africa, facilitating long-distance trade and connections between West Africa and the wider Muslim world to the east and north. Thus, the oral tradition describes some aspects of Sunjata's dress and behavior and the behaviors of those around him in terms now associated with Islam. So now the Malinke are heirs to a complex of political ideas, many of them more than a millennium old, some half a millennium old, and some much newer.

This evidence encourages us to think about political and economic relationships in a different way, outside of the Western norm of state development. Because mostly Westerners (and some Western-educated Africans) have been the authors of African history, it is important to be vigilant about the use of Western ideas and categories beyond our own time and culture. It is quite likely that Jenne-jeno never came to politically dominate the region as one might expect of its leading economic center. Susan McIntosh claims that their work "challenges deeply embedded evolutionary notions of complexity as differentiation by political hierarchization." Indeed, the concept of heterarchy describes the political relationships that have endured in the IND area over millennia.

Intensive archaeological research in the interior of West Africa has generated enough information to rewrite West African history in the first millennium CE, moving from a picture of state development driven by trade and Islam to one in which local trade among specialized producers and nonhierarchical regional urbanism are featured. Moreover, the archaeological evidence in the larger IND indicates that our earlier reliance on a few written sources for the history of the Sudan has misled us. Until recently, attention focused on developments in the early state of Ghana (at its height in the eleventh century CE) with a capital at Kumbi-Saleh, as recorded by Muslim scholars like the geographer al-Bakri. Yet, to the south, there were dense population clusters and evidence of societies linked to the trans-Saharan trade. African historian Jan Vansina contends that the vast IND was the demographic core and the economic dynamo of inner West Africa. Successor states, like Mali, retained elements of heterarchy as captured in the oral tradition *Sunjata*.

Buganda in East Africa

East Africa has a similar case of heterarchy within hierarchy. Buganda, where *kabakas,* or kings, reigned from the fourteenth century to the present day, was a heterarchical state. Buganda came to be the most powerful kingdom in East Africa in the eighteenth and nineteenth centuries and was one of many states formed in the second millennium CE on the rich agricultural land that surrounds Lake Victoria (see map I.1). The kingdom's institutions and population initially came from an earlier kingdom, Bunyoro. Many of these states, like Buganda, depended on banana growing for subsistence. Bananas are ten times more productive than grains like sorghum and millet. Thus, for the same amount of labor, bananas can support larger, denser populations. Villages were the basic settlement pattern and would have been found on hillsides, with dozens of families in each.

According to historian Holly Hanson, from the beginning the kingdom was assembled by connecting a host of varied relationships into the Buganda polity. Another historian, Neil Kodesh, examined Buganda history before the rise of the kingdom and in its early years and found a variety of social institutions (see table 5.1). Initially, people identified by kinship, sharing a spiritual leader who represented a spirit that could be called on to intercede in their affairs. Later clans came to be important. Thus, before the kingdom emerged, Baganda (the name of the people in the area) lived throughout the area, some under spiritual leaders turned clan leaders and some under simply leaders of people or chiefs. Baganda accepted multiple forms of authority, not just clan leadership, in the centuries before the fourteenth. Sometime between 1200 and 1700, a new kind of kingship

Table 5.1 Political authority in Buganda. Drawn from Neil Kodesh, *Beyond the Royal Gaze: Clanship and Healing in Buganda* (Charlottesville: University of Virginia Press, 2010); and Holly Hanson, *Landed Obligation: The Practice of Power in Buganda* (Portsmouth, N.H.: Heinemann, 2003).

Prior to c. twelfth century	Circa twelfth to seventeenth centuries	Circa seventeenth to nineteenth centuries
Leaders of people (NK and HH)		
Clan leaders as spiritual leaders (NK and HH)		Clans had specific royal responsibility (HH)
		Clan chiefs relied on followers through reciprocal obligation; this eroded with expansion of the kingdom (HH)
		Clans as collection of people with variety of skills and knowledge and connected by territorial spirits and their shrines (NK)
Territorial spirits (NK and HH)	Mediums for spirits provided for well-being of area (NK)	Territorial spirits became tied to *kabakas* (NK)
	Territorial spirits became delinked from specific areas with the rise of first king, Kintu (NK)	*Lubaale* deities were autonomous of the state (HH)
	Kabakas consolidated power from clan and healing institutions (NK)	*Kabakas'* rule both strengthened and challenged by wars of expansion and slave followers (HH)
		Queen Mother had a separate residence, officials, and decision-making power (HH)

with new royal rituals was established, but it had to adjust to and accommodate practices of power at the time.

Kodesh's work in Buganda illuminates some of those older practices of power. His work focuses on ways African communities sought to create arenas of collective action. Public healers, such as mediums and the spirits they embodied, provided for the well-being of the citizens over whom they presided. They were both political leaders and public healers. But even as power consolidated in the sixteenth and seventeenth centuries, the ideas that motivated their practice withstood increasing royal authority and influenced the state that developed. In the eighteenth and nineteenth centuries, even though public healing and political leadership became divided, healers still held significant authority.

For most African societies prior to colonization, there was a significant investment in the health of the land. If the land did not provide food in the form of crops or grass for livestock, people would go hungry. Most in industrialized countries think about the future and security in terms of individual efforts and support from close family. But this way of thinking is a product of our more recent history and reliance on scientific explanations for disasters and ill health. Also, access to great labor-saving technology has enabled most in the globalized North to escape a fair amount of discomfort and disease that their forebears had to endure and to accomplish tasks singly that before would have required multiple people. As a result of these developments and others, it is easy to assume that technology will continue to aid humanity as new problems occur. Most people throughout history, however, did not have such a view of the world. Their level of technology and low population numbers, among other things, meant that they felt far more vulnerable to natural occurrences. Thus, individual and collective actions to promote well-being were essential.

In addition, if people or animals were afflicted by disease, Africans and their societies would be weakened. People in the developed world can just visit a doctor to find out what is making them sick. For Africans, however, the illness might have an environmental or a physiological explanation, as well as an interpersonal explanation. People needed to be in a balanced relationship to one another if the entire society was to be healthy, as in the case of Buganda. Thus, there were a series of positions that controlled public affairs having to do with health, welfare, and prosperity subject to ritual control, such as spirit mediums, diviners, and oracles. In precolonial Malawi, for example, *Mbona* was a ritual healing association that people joined in time of illness, but it was also "a ritually directed eco-system." *Mbona* was able to protect fragile resources by restricting farming or grazing or by prohibiting such land-clearing practices as the burning of wild vegetation. Diviners in many places consulted the spirits before advising people on where to locate their villages. They chose areas that had a clean water source nearby and few insects. In the kingdom of Bunyoro in Uganda, senior mediums of the *Chwezi* spirits conveyed advice from the spirits to the king on how to maintain his fertility, achieve success in warfare, and increase the productivity of the land. In southern Nigeria, the *Aro* oracle gave people advice on health and fertility and was responsible for the maintenance of public order and the regulation of trade. In the Shambaa kingdom of Tanzania, healers and diviners were in charge of the maintenance of irrigation channels. Philip Curtin and his coauthors discuss these forms of ritual authority in their book *African History: From Earliest Times to Independence.*

Kodesh argues that clans grew out of earlier historical developments that included making territorial spirits portable by linking them to mediums rather than a specific area. Kintu, the founder of the Buganda kingdom and a medium himself, suppressed many local spirits as he came to exercise authority over a much larger area. Thus, his authority was linked to his relationship to a particular spirit that no longer presided over a small, local area. The oral tradition, for example, of Kintu's marriage to Nambi captures a part of this process. In this area, marriage is a common metaphor for entering into initiation as a medium for the territorial spirit. A medium would communicate with both the spirit and the living worlds and often dedicated his or her life to the work. Kodesh argues that it is likely that Nambi's community's well-being was jeopardized for some reason, so the resident healers and mediums no longer had the same authority over their people. In this situation, the community sought mediumship with Kintu, a powerful and portable territorial spirit. Through this process, Kintu gained authority, and Nambi's community gained protection and, presumably, prosperity. Kodesh uses an ancient oral tradition, anthropological and historical information from surrounding and similar societies, and more recent archival and written sources to unravel the meaning of the tradition for earlier Buganda history.

This change also accompanied the development of land-intensive banana cultivation. Unlike previous economic activities, banana land remained under continuous cultivation for decades. Thus, bananas made for a more sedentary population and provided more free time than the more arduous work of annual grain cultivation or pastoralism. They also increased emphasis on lineal inheritance, as there was significant wealth to be passed on in the form of banana groves. Increased royal authority relied on expanded notions of spiritual authority as well as greater food production.

Spiritual authority was one component of Baganda life, while clanship came to be another. As Buganda expanded in the eighteenth century, clanship became a means of connecting people who were not necessarily related or in face-to-face contact with one another through shrines of spiritual entities. As these new clans came into being, Baganda drew on a variety of bodies of knowledge to create communities that could thrive. Thus, clanship was formed to maximize a variety of knowledge and well-being rather than simply kinship. For example, the genealogy of the Otter clan describes a ritual priest, a talented doctor, a maker of mallets used in bark cloth production, a bark cloth artisan, and a famous diviner coming together. A clan formed on the basis of multiple skills would inevitably be stronger than one founded on a narrower set of skills. Through alliances with dispersed communities, the Otter clan combined necessary skills for a successful community. These alliances were sealed by the common practices of kinship, spirit possession, and public healing. Clan activities focused on a sacred site for the spirit and the nearby burial ground for the clan's founding ancestors. As later powerful royal figures rose to prominence, they sought to channel spiritual authority toward royal ends so that Baganda came to see their collective well-being as closely tied to the health and prosperity of the kingdom, rather than only a clan.

Hanson finds evidence for diffuse authority in memories of dense, overlapping webs of tribute in the past. She interprets these as markers of extreme competition for followers in the oldest parts of the kingdom. Evidence collected in the early twentieth century by British and Baganda investigators, histories recorded earlier in the nineteenth century, and testimony before a Commission of Inquiry of the British colony in 1920 all support the vulnerable nature of authority in Buganda. Dynastic tradition also remembers multiple *kabakas* whose authority was checked because they did not demonstrate requisite mutual obligation or love for their people. For example, in the early eighteenth century, Kabaka Kagulu was deposed for his unusual cruelty. Thus, the picture that emerges is not of an all-powerful king but of a king who was beholden to his followers by centuries of tribute and recognition of spiritual and clan authorities. Hanson describes the *kabaka's* relationship with his followers as one of reciprocal obligation.

The *kabaka's* authority was only as good as his follower's willingness to obey. The king and all other authority figures had to demonstrate their love for their followers. Hanson argues that rulers and followers created reciprocal obligation, and this became the glue that bound people to the Buganda kingdom. Reciprocal obligation also involved the giving of and asking for gifts. At one point in her book *Landed Obligation,* she notes, "The essential dynamic of power in Buganda was that chiefs needed followers and followers could leave their chiefs." Followers always had the option to dissolve the relationship by refusing to participate or leaving that particular piece of land.

The *kabaka's* authority was checked in other ways as well. The clans provided services to the king that helped to maintain the spiritual health of the king and the kingdom. The Mushroom clan were gatekeepers, the Buffalo clan carried the king and were responsible for a temple, and the Bird clan took care of spiritual medicines, including the one named for the territory itself. In addition, people provided the king with necessary items like canoes, beer, musical instruments and drummers, and servants. Pages at the court could leave the position if the *kabaka* ruled poorly.

Lubaale deities, or territorial spirits, were widespread in the Lake Victoria region from the sixteenth century on, and they checked the power of the *kabaka* as well. They were capable of influencing human affairs, had followers who actively worshipped them, and might intervene to help a petitioner. *Lubaale* had close connections to the state but were autonomous. The deities controlled lands dedicated to them, and those who lived there did not pay taxes or owe labor to the king. Control over the deity was passed from one clan elder to another, and the king had no say in this succession. The highest-ranking *lubaale* referred to the *kabaka* as his son-in-law. As sons-in-law, the *kabakas* offered gifts to the gods. The Queen Mother acted as an independent political figure in Buganda politics as well. With separate living quarters and the ability to depose the king, she acted as a rival authority figure with her own land and retinue of followers.

Hanson's description of heterarchical authority and its dissolution from the seventeenth century on demonstrates how wars of expansion and the captives derived from them dissolved the carefully crafted networks of obligation that had been the foundation of the kingdom. *Kabakas* with slaves did not need to satisfy their chiefs, and chiefs who controlled areas composed of nonfree laborers did not have to rely as much on the king. These events were followed by British rule in the late nineteenth century and, eventually, colonial division of land that greatly reduced the number of authority figures in Buganda society.

Prior to this, however, a person could follow many different authority figures, showing allegiance to one person during a time of crisis, for example, and to another at some other point in time. A person could show allegiance to a superior by recalling a particular obligation instead of a different one. Thus, power was not a zero-sum game where if one person gained more, another person got less. Instead, it was created and reenacted over time, and a person only had power if others agreed to it. Power was fluid, embodied in multiple positions of authority and skills, and had deep roots in ideas about spirits and relationships.

Modern Africa and Authority

With colonial rule and European notions of authority, forms and practices of power narrowed and flattened, to use Hanson's terms. She estimates that by the 1920s, thousands of positions of authority in Buganda had been eliminated by the British government. Nineteenth-century British and French and Western concepts of political authority generally have been far narrower than those of Europe and nonindustrialized societies like Africa. Moreover, the effects of conquests and demographic collapse that accompanied the establishment of colonial rule in many parts of Africa weakened various forms of authority.

Nineteenth-century Europeans, recent heirs to the rational, techno-scientific thought of the Enlightenment and Industrial Revolution, found it difficult to imagine how to negotiate with African ritual authorities. They were on familiar terrain when they negotiated with chiefs, but they could not imagine establishing a public order in which they shared authority with spirit mediums or oracles, even if these controlled practical knowledge. In many places Europeans came to think of diviners or mediums as enemies of colonial rule because of their foreign ideas and because they controlled the kind of survival knowledge that became implicated in wars of resistance in the late nineteenth and early twentieth centuries. In the case of Tanzania's Maji Maji rebellion, for example, Africans who felt their survival threatened by forced cotton cultivation, which was undermining subsistence farming, traveled in great numbers in 1904 to consult a spirit medium named Kinjikitile. They received war medicines from him and then rebelled. Also in Zimbabwe, leadership for the largest rebellion came from spirit mediums in the great Shona uprising of 1896–1897. Europeans in every colony attacked the ritual authority of African leaders. Both the British and the French enacted laws across Africa that made most forms of local healing illegal. They rarely enforced these laws when a healer treated a private patient. They were primarily meant to suppress large-scale ritual authority. In Tanzania after Maji Maji, many Germans attacked African healers.

For the remainder of Tanzania's colonial history, healers who organized public events were likely to be arrested. In Nigeria, a British military force dynamited the cave from which the *Aro* oracle spoke. In Uganda, the British made *Chwezi* mediumship illegal. Alongside government measures were missionary efforts. In the early colonial period, some Christian missionaries directly attacked the ritual authority of Africans—proving their own power by cutting down dangerous sacred forests and destroying shrines. At times they had ritual authorities arrested and detained, and they preached against what they saw as the falseness of African ritual knowledge.

Ritual leaders did not disappear entirely, but they were driven underground; their influence was felt more often than it was seen. As historian Stephen Ellis and religious studies professor Gerrie Ter Haar demonstrate in their book on religious thought and political practice, in Africa, it is still widely believed that all power has "its ultimate origin in the spirit world." This belief explains why things happen the way they do. As such, it is has been fairly resilient. These leaders learned to be secretive about their skills, so practical knowledge as expressed through ritual action, much of which had been performed publicly during the period before the conquest, was now concealed. When Germans started to attack healers in Tanzania, the healers did not stop practicing their art, but they stopped wearing the hair decoration that signified their profession, and they replaced their traditional medicine baskets with plain baskets. The healers were part of a more general phenomenon of African life under colonial control, where the things Europeans despised did not disappear but only became less visible.

But the long-term sustained colonial attack on ritual authority had profound effects. It left ritual leaders weaker than political ones, thus undermining the position of women, who were more likely to hold ritual rather than political authority. It also significantly narrowed the arena for effective social control. In the colonial economic order, Europeans occupied the top position. Other foreigners controlled many economic opportunities. Both East and West Africa still contain large immigrant populations—Indians and Lebanese, respectively—who were often given economic opportunities that Africans were excluded from, such as business ownership. Sometimes they, too, were excluded from economic opportunities that the Europeans had, such as landholding in Kenya. The result was serious limitations on opportunities available to Africans both politically and economically.

Africans' experience with colonialism has left many legacies, but one that is rarely mentioned in the literature is the restriction on multiple roles of authority and power. Without multiple forms of knowledge and skills, the political structure was much more rigid and less responsive. From this profound narrowing of opportunity, it is not too much of a leap to corrupt postcolonial African political systems. While there are many reasons for the current state of African politics, one must consider the role played by the collapse of heterarchy. As African governments became the singular avenue to power and wealth, it is not surprising that these positions were abused. The infamy of greedy leaders such as Mobutu Sese Seko (1965–1997) in the former Zaire (now Democratic Republic of Congo) who siphoned off much of the countries' mineral, agricultural wealth, and foreign aid for his own personal benefit for three decades is well known.

Corrupt African leadership is a staple of Western news. Yet, Western ideas of political leadership have played a role in its evolution. And the same leaders, such as Mobutu, have also demonstrated Africans' deep attachment to multiple forms of authority, particularly authority rooted in the spirit world. Ellis and Ter Haar argue that African politicians need to be adept at numerous political languages. As an example, they point out how Kenneth Kaunda, the first president of Zambia (1964–1991), used antiaircraft guns, spiritual protection, and communication gadgets to maintain power. Mobutu is often portrayed wearing a leopard-skin cap, and he faithfully attended Catholic Mass every Sunday. The leopard-skin cap resonates with a much earlier history of riverine settlement by Bantu-speaking peoples (of the Niger-Congo family) who now predominate in the Democratic Republic of Congo. The leopard, an elusive and dangerous animal, if killed by early settlers, would be transported upriver to the earliest remembered settlement where the recognized authority figure lived. The Catholic Church, of course, is a Western introduction and was closely associated with Belgian colonial power. While ordinary Congolese and Catholic officials wielded little independent authority in Mobutu's Congo, his attention to these symbols suggests their continuing salience in Congolese society.

One solution to such corruption is multiparty politics, as many African leaders, like Mobutu, stifled all political competition. But multiparty politics, while much more common in African countries since the 1990s, has not been a panacea for Africa's political ills. If former ideas of economic diversification, community well-being, and spiritual health had a place in modern African societies, African politics might be more transparent and responsive. Alexis de Tocqueville, coming from a much older society with a long history of kingship, admired the more fluid nature of American political authority, acknowledging that it was an important expression of democracy. Perhaps we and Africans have much more to learn about political authority from African history and its rich expressions of heterarchy.

The concepts of heterarchy, or dispersed rather than concentrated power, and their myriad historical expressions in African history for centuries offer us a different way of looking at both social and political organization. African anthropologist Wyatt MacGaffey argues that our modern view of the political is reduced to the use of material resources and secular power by "leaders, officials, pressure groups, and armed forces." Such a view is far narrower than our study of African history supports. The scale of our national political system is much larger than that of Buganda or Jenne-jeno and likely makes it harder for heterarchy to thrive at all levels, but reinvestment in heterarchy at some levels is surely possible.

Many critics of contemporary American society note that power is increasingly in the hands of a wealthy few who have ties to the political center, energy industries, financial services, and communications giants. Our current political system, although envied by many for its transparent elections and checks and balances, is very expensive and thus more attentive to the voices and interests of those with access to material wealth. The guardians of spiritual and social wealth, such as counselors, teachers, and ministers, have far less access to political power currently.

If concentration of wealth is a pattern in history, so, too, is the dispersion of power and investment in the well-being of communities, as Baganda concerns reflected. These histories indicate that a focus on the accumulation of power at the center is only one historical trend in the histories of many places and times. The other trend, heterarchy, is perhaps just as strong but far less widely studied. With such a perspective, reform of our system might include more than attention to campaign finance reform. What would happen if more were vested in spiritual and social communities? Or if schools became voices in the political process, voices that represented students, staff, and parents? If many earlier Africans are to be believed, these might be far more sustainable and democratic ways to organize communities of people.

Suggestions for Further Reading

Philip Curtin, Steven Feierman, Leonard Thompson, and Jan Vansina, *African History: From Earliest Times to Independence* (New York: Longman, 1995). One of the earliest books on African history, this was first published in 1978. It covers African history in three broad time periods: prior to 1500, between 1500 and the late 1800s, and from the colonial period to the present.

Stephen Ellis and Gerrie Ter Haar, *Worlds of Power: Religious Thought and Political Practice in Africa* (New York: Oxford University Press, 2004). The authors examine Africans' religious ideas—belief in the invisible, spirit world that has an influence on the visible, human world—as essential elements of power and authority. It is a rich study that opens up what are often rather narrow definitions of religion and politics both in Africa and in the rest of the world.

Holly Elisabeth Hanson, *Landed Obligation: The Practice of Power in Buganda* (Portsmouth, N.H.: Heinemann, 2003). Hanson is interested in the way in which reciprocal obligations shaped the Bugandan state. Like Kodesh's book, this book examines the ways in which the king's authority was bounded by others' authority and actions.

Walter Hawthorne, *Planting Rice and Harvesting Slaves: Transformations along the Guinea-Bissau Coast, 1400–1900* (Portsmouth, N.H.: Heinemann, 2003). Using oral traditions and historical documents, Hawthorne recreates the history of a decentralized society during the Atlantic slave trade era, noting the ways in which they adapted to significant economic and political changes.

Neil Kodesh, *Beyond the Royal Gaze: Clanship and Healing in Buganda* (Charlottesville: University of Virginia Press, 2010). Kodesh examines the role of public healing in community and political life in Buganda history. He situates his work within the growing literature on heterarchy and political power.

Wyatt MacGaffey, "Changing Representations in Central African History," *Journal of African History* 46, no. 2 (2005): 189–207. MacGaffey examines how scholars have narrowed or simplified African states and social structures to make them sound like Western narratives of history.

T. C. McCaskie, "Denkyira in the Making of Asante c. 1660–1720," *Journal of African History* 48, no. 1 (2007): 1–25. Using the history of Denkyira, McCaskie shows how oral traditions allow for a close examination of local history and culture, complicating previous ideas about state formation and ethnicity.

Roderick J. McIntosh, *Ancient Middle Niger: Urbanism and the Self-Organizing Landscape* (Cambridge: Cambridge University Press, 2005). Roderick McIntosh surveys the decades of work that he and his team have undertaken in the Inner Niger Delta, with particular attention to the cultural norms that governed settlement, such as urban clusters and ecological resilience.

Susan Keech McIntosh, "Pathways to Complexity: An African Perspective," in *Beyond Chiefdoms: Pathways to Complexity in Africa,* ed. Susan Keech McIntosh (Cambridge: Cambridge University Press, 1999), 1–30. This is one of many reports the McIntoshes made of their work in and around Jenne-jeno, in which they emphasize the evidence for heterarchy rather than hierarchy.

D. T. Niane, *Sundiata: An Epic of Old Mali,* trans. G. D. Pickett (Harlow, U.K.: Pearson Longman, 2006). This is the most widely published version of this oral tradition in Europe and the United States. It was collected in French in the 1960s from a *griot* and has been translated into English.

Kirkpatrick Sale, *Human Scale* (London: Coward, McCann and Geoghegan, 1980). Sale is an independent scholar and author. In this book, he examines the appropriate scale for a variety of institutions, including buildings, communities, and work environments.

6 Forms of Social Organization
Matriliny

THROUGHOUT HISTORY, individuals have had specific ideas about their families, marriage, and property. Societies typically define these relationships as a form of kinship. The most basic human relationships of kinship shape work roles, children's identities and caretaking, and political and economic institutions. How and why people in the past changed the way they thought about kinship is one aspect of African history. Matriliny is one specific way African people in the past and present have thought about their families, their work, and their economies.

Matriliny is deeply misunderstood by the general North American population. It is often mistaken for matriarchy or is seen as an ideal institution for female freedom or contrasted with some other, more familiar system, like patriliny, rather than being understood on its own terms. But it is true that the implications of matrilineal reckoning can be profound in terms of the way societies thought (and still think) about economic accumulation and distribution, obligations children had (and have) to their parents, spouses and other family members' relations to one another, and men's and women's political and economic rights in society. Patrilineal systems also have significant implications for those who live within them.

Africa is one of the best places in the world to explore the history of matriliny; many societies in the past practiced it. Despite its significance as a historical institution, it has been largely neglected as an element of historical study. As a result, scholars don't have a clear understanding of the significant role that matriliny has played in shaping human cultures in the past. The study of matriliny in Africa is also important because it can help us to investigate unquestioned cultural assumptions and societal constructions. In so doing, as inheritors of predominantly Western cultural ideas, readers can open themselves up to a wider variety of social, economic, and political possibilities than they might have previously considered. For example, matriliny forces us to question the normalcy of the nuclear family and to look at mother-daughter and sibling relationships as much as the husband-wife relationship. Finally, the study of matriliny and matricentric societies helps us to understand and value women's roles in society.

Many have questioned why matrilineal societies or societies that had more matrilineal aspects than patrilineal aspects developed in Africa. Increasingly, scholars are finding that matriliny has been as much the norm in early societies as patriliny, if not more so. In fact, in the late nineteenth century, as historian Christine Saidi notes in her study of women in East-Central Africa, most anthropologists agreed that early human societies were based on matrilineal descent groups and did not emphasize a nuclear family structure or patrilineal descent. This consensus was challenged by scholars and others in the early twentieth century who sought to promote capitalism and accumulation and believed that patriliny was essential to the promotion of such ideas.

Geographical Place

The geographic focus of this chapter is on a number of matrilineal societies that existed (and still do exist) within a "matrilineal belt" in Central Africa (see map I.1). All are descendants of the Niger-Congo language family and belong to Bantu-speaking societies. Some societies in this belt remain matrilineal or still practice elements related to matriliny; others used to be matrilineal but no longer exhibit any of the elements associated with it. Such societies include the Luapula, Fipa, Tonga, Sabi, and others of modern-day Zambia, Malawi, Tanzania, and the Democratic Republic of Congo. The Akan people of West Africa and the Baganda of East Africa are also discussed.

Sources and Methodologies

Like previous chapters, this one relies on historical linguistics to identify long-held ideas about kinship, as well as the field of cultural anthropology. The study of matriliny within the field of anthropology represents both the strengths and weaknesses of the discipline. Careful investigation of one aspect of a society and the ways in which it impacts other areas of society is one of the benefits of cultural anthropological study. Yet, it is a product of imperialism and has in the past been perceived as a study of the "other." For a long time, Africans, for example were seen as a people without history, simply possessing an unchanging culture and recounting myths instead of historical occurrences. For many in the late nineteenth and early twentieth centuries, the "other" was seen in hierarchical and racist terms. One result of this view was that African institutions and ideas were assumed to be aberrant and less effective than similar institutions from the anthropologists' home countries (usually in Europe or North America). Thus, for a long time, matriliny needed to be explained and studied, while patriliny was assumed to be normal.

Particularly regarding the latest phase of globalization since the 1980s, scholars have argued that any sense that cultures remain closed and their ideas limited to a particular geographic region does not hold up to empirical study. While anthropologists might never have made such claims, their intensive focus on a particular society with little concern for outside influences led to such readings and supported such popular assumptions. As anthropologist Emiko Ohnuki-Tierney wrote, every culture is a product of continuous interaction between the local and the external.

Of late, though, much work has been done by both anthropologists and historians to historicize anthropology, and vice versa. Though the fields remain distinct, history is concerned with significant events, people, and ideas that have shaped human societies based on the interpretation of evidence, while anthropology is interested in patterns and ideas within human communities or the relationships between human beings. Historians have also examined matriliny. Much historical work on matriliny describes it as a cultural attribute that may soon disappear—the assumption being that matriliny cannot coexist with Christianity or other strong outside influences. Yet, both anthropologists and historians have much to learn from each other. Both approaches are used in this chapter to explain the institution of matriliny and put it into context, acknowledging the perpetual forces that act on an institution to change it, while it maintains salience and meaning for those who practice it.

Explicating Matriliny

Descent is one way of remembering and emphasizing membership in one or, sometimes, both parents' families. Bilateral or bilineal societies recognize descent from a relative several generations back on both sides of the family, while matrilineal or patrilineal families recognize descent from just one side of the family. Matrilineal societies place emphasis on one's membership in the mother's family. Patrilineal societies, like the contemporary United States, place emphasis on membership in the father's family, most noticeably marked by children usually taking the father's last name at birth. In the past, many African societies traced descent through women, or matrilineally (some still do today). This means, practically, that an individual lives, works, and shares resources with those related to her mother more often than with those related to her father. But this was hardly ever used as a rigid system; instead, people imbued it with significance by their actions and ideas. Thus, ideas and practices were always being negotiated, reaffirmed, and altered. They lasted a long time in many places because they were particularly helpful in ensuring successful reproduction of society in difficult circumstances.

One of the most fruitful ways of looking at matriliny is as a set of ideas, ideals, or strategies regarding social relationships that are available to members as they seek to survive and thrive. Just because people have biological relatives does not mean they must interact with these relatives in set ways. People typically shape and reconstruct their ideas about relationship based on changes in their environment, economy, and society. For example, you have probably heard your grandparents grumble about the lack of respect children have for their elders in our society today. Such a change is a result of our culture and methods of child rearing that have fundamentally changed over the last 50 years. And just because people in a society hold ideals does not mean they live by them. Thus, the ideals people in a matrilineal society hold might be quite different from their actual practices, as most of us can recognize in our own societies. For example, Americans hold up marriage as a lifetime commitment, yet over 50 percent of marriages end in divorce.

Nonetheless, many societies have long-term ideas and beliefs or core ideas that have withstood many changes. As Rhonda Gonzales has noted about the early history of eastern Tanzanian societies, how they understood their world was broad and pliable, but people used a set of core ideas to make sense of their worlds and come to decisions about their lives. People are able to live together more peacefully and easily by observing common values and norms that govern behavior. Matriliny does not define a group of people as much as it describes patterns of behavior that are both malleable and somewhat resistant to change.

Some commonly held practices typify many of the more recent matrilineal societies. These include matrilineal descent (one is primarily the child of the mother and her family), matrilineal succession and inheritance (one inherits status and possessions from the mother's family), and uxorilocal or matrilocal residence (married couples and young families reside at the wife's family's compound rather than with the husband's family). Again, it is important to remember that not all matrilineal societies would be matrilocal, for example. In many African societies, past and present, a man or woman could choose whether to reside with his or her mother's or father's family, but in many societies it made more economic sense to live with the mother's family; thus, a trend of matrilocality emerged. Note that each of these terms beginning with *matri-* indicates a woman's role in the particular institution associated with the rest of the term: *-lineal* for descent and *-local* for residence.

Generally, a matrilineal society affords women far greater security, economic control, self-confidence, and freedom, but matriliny does not mean a reversal of the roles of men and women. Matriliny never meant exclusion of men and their roles from society. Though matrilineal societies usually traced descent (and thus bequeathed wealth) through the women's family, often it was technically from mother's brother to sister's son and therefore from man to man rather than through female relatives. For example, a man's wealth would pass to his sisters' sons rather than his own. But some societies passed wealth directly from mother to daughter. The father's role in reproduction was also usually recognized and given status. Authority is more diffuse in a matrilineal society, with the mother, maternal uncle, and father all having roles. Another way of looking at matrilineal societies is through the idea of heterarchy, or diffuse authority, rather than authority concentrated in one person or a small number of people. In contrast, authority in most nuclear families is located in the father figure.

Mothers and Reproduction

Such diffuse authority likely comes from the desire to maximize the successful raising of children in very difficult circumstances. In more familiar societies, the expectation is that as one matures, one's primary allegiance is to one's spouse and shared offspring and that one's relationship to siblings is of secondary importance. In matrilineal societies, one's relationship to siblings usually remains more important. As historian Christine Saidi shows, for many East-Central African societies, the sororal group, composed of adult sisters and their mothers, has existed for at least 2,000 years. This group would oversee girls' initiation, the length of bride service for grooms, and when a girl would be allowed to own her own household after marriage. One can readily understand why people would emphasize sibling relationships. Most human communities have recognized the stronger ties of kinship versus the looser ones of marriage. Thus, the brother-sister or sister-sister relationship tends to be strong and permanent, despite marriage. As anthropologist Chris Knight has argued, there are some straightforward reasons why early human kinship was matrilineal. If a woman relies on her brothers for long-term support, then she can turn to them for personal support and support for her children in case of conflict with her sexual partner. Thus, strong bonds between brothers and sisters, and mothers and daughters ensured women's energy could be directed toward their children. In many more recent gatherer-hunter societies, the groom lived with the bride in her camp and worked for her family, ensuring that mother-daughter and sister-sister bonds remained secure. As anthropologists have noted, the attention and energy that parents and other caregivers devote to human offspring is far greater than in any of our primate relatives.

With an emphasis on sibling relationships, marriage tends to be loose, not necessarily monogamous, or long lasting. Often there is a preference for cross-cousin marriage (a cross-cousin is the child of one's parent's sibling of the alternate sex, so a mother's brother's child or a father's sister's child) in order to preserve relationships of common descent. Over time, two lineages would intermarry, reinforcing their own lineages and retaining more of their wealth in the process, rather than distributing it to a series of different lineages. This practice, however, challenges another desirable aspect of marriage: creating more extensive networks. Marriage outside the lineage creates broader social networks and, thus, more people to rely on in difficult times.

A related societal construct is matrifocal societies. A matrifocal society is one in which the family unit is centered on the mother as the biological and social reproducer of society. Certainly, one of the characteristics of many African (and African-American) families is respect for the work and role of mothers. Scholars have drawn attention to broad patterns of gender equality and complementarity throughout the continent, even in areas that today do not practice aspects of matriliny. Many African societies are matrifocal, with a cluster of ideas emphasizing the centrality of motherhood, even if they are classified as patrilineal. And some societies—particularly in difficult times—might emphasize matrifocal units if the authority and responsibility of men as husbands and brothers of women are eroded by economic insecurity or social upheaval.

Anthropological and historical studies suggest as well the importance of the role of the grandmother in various African societies. For example, anthropologist Marja-Liisa Swantz found that in some Tanzanian societies, when a woman's first female child reached puberty, her maternal grandmother would celebrate the event because it guaranteed lineage continuity. Considerable ethnographic evidence exists regarding the importance of grandparents to their grandchildren in terms of nurturance, education, and intimacy. Among other things, grandmothers are stores of significant cultural knowledge and power. Thus, as one scholar speculates, there is much more to understand about the role of grandmothers in African communities.

Clearly, families and societies have many ways to recognize the crucial role that mothers play in recreating society. Matrilineal societies (and many patrilineal societies as well) emphasize the womb as a metaphor for family, noting the importance of woman's reproductive role in society. Anthropologist Karla Poewe has studied the Luapula of Zambia, for whom the social unit of greatest inclusiveness is the womb, or *ifumu*. *Ifumu* stands for the Luapulan world, where everyone has access to natural resources. Thus, their world is seen as a fertile space with sufficient resources for successful human reproduction. Among the Fipa, in southwestern Tanzania, the "key" ethnic myth identifies strange women as the founders of the royal Twa dynasty between the sixteenth and eighteenth centuries. The leader's name is related to the Fipa word for "womb," likely emphasizing his role in creating a new society. In both these examples, one can see how language reinforces the view that women's role in society is paramount. Matriliny and its study also help to illuminate facets of society that might otherwise be neglected, such as pottery making, female sexuality, and the role of sisters and mothers. To the extent that researchers have neglected women's roles in societies, they have also neglected matriliny as a social institution. This is another area in African history that requires much more research.

One other manifestation of the importance of women in African societies that is worth touching on is the role of queen mother, a position that was common in kingdoms throughout East Africa and among the Asante in West Africa for hundreds of years prior to colonialism. For example, historian Holly Hanson reports that, beginning in the sixteenth century CE in East Africa, the queen mother had as important a position as the king in a number of Great Lakes kingdoms. The queen mother of Buganda was the king maker in a number of ways. A candidate for the kingship relied on his maternal relatives, under the leadership of the queen mother, to support him against other contenders. The historical linguistic evidence suggests that the positions of both queen mother and king were created at the same time in many of these societies. In Buganda, for example, the significance of this role continued late into the nineteenth century and was seen as parallel to that of the king in many ways. For example, the queen mother had her own set of ministers who lived on land under her control and who returned to her a portion of the taxes they collected. Her lands were exempt from the king's plundering, and her chiefs did not have to obey the king. Her residence was across a river from the king's residence, marking her independent control of land and people. In addition, in Buganda, two other royal women had substantial power: the queen mother's sister and the queen's sister, who was chosen from among the half-sisters of the king by the same father. Clearly, women in these societies were important socially, politically, and economically.

Matriliny in Ancient Africa

If matriliny was, indeed, the standard form of social organization in Africa and elsewhere for much of human history, it must have satisfied some general needs of early societies. Such societies were generally smaller in population and valued people rather than access to land. As Jan Shetler has noted, Africans developed "land-rich cultural traditions." With land being a widely available commodity and people being scarce, they valued fertility, mobility, and control over labor as sources of wealth. In such societies, setting porous kinship boundaries and the ability to attract diverse members were successful strategies. The more networks one had, the more likely one and one's society were able to withstand economic and environmental challenges. The heterarchical nature of matrilineal societies was especially adapted for incorporating strangers and for expansion on a land-rich continent both as human species evolved and as *Homo sapiens* developed agriculture.

About 10,000 years ago, according to historian Christopher Ehret, two of the four original African civilizations, the Middle Nile (which became the Nilo-Saharan) and Niger-Congo, were matrilineal—that is, they reckoned descent and familial belonging through the mother's line. These two societies were located in western Africa and across northern Africa in the Saharo-Sahelian belt, respectively (see map 6.1). As agricultural Bantu-speaking Africans (descendants of the Niger-Congo) moved from their homeland in Cameroon to other areas of

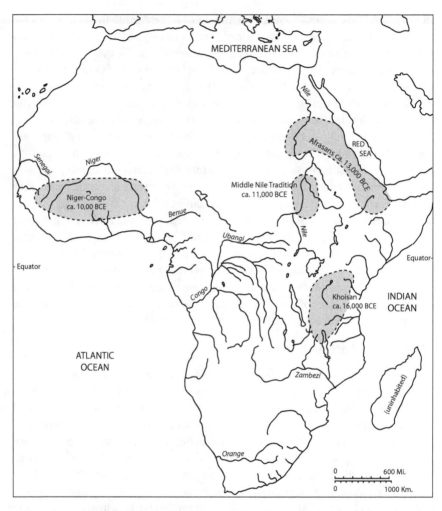

Map 6.1 Proposed early lands of four major linguistic groups in Africa: Afrasan, Middle Nile, Khoisan, and Niger-Congo (the one covered in this chapter). From Christopher Ehret, *The Civilizations of Africa: A History to 1800* (Charlottesville: University of Virginia Press, 2002), 37. Courtesy of University of Virginia Press.

the continent starting about 5,000 years ago, matriliny spread. Thus, for thousands of years, matrilineal societies occupied a broad (though not continuous) swath of the continent, from West to East Africa and covering parts of Central Africa as well. Across this area, there remains today a scattering of matrilineal peoples, as well as many societies that retain aspects of matriliny; thus, a section of this area is often called the "matrilineal belt" of Africa and includes portions of

Tanzania, Malawi, Zambia, and eastern Congo (see map I.1). These societies were responsible for settling much of sub-Saharan Africa. They did not create entirely new societies, however, but built on old traditions and incorporated the customs of their new neighbors. Frontiers, in particular, required broad networks for as much security as possible, as families sought to find and learn about new economic resources (such as food and medicine), while ensuring their survival.

From about 5000 BCE on, Bantu speakers lived in matriclans, a kinship group larger than a lineage that recognized a common, distant ancestor but could support the more geographically dispersed settlements of frontier people who were moving into Central, eastern, and southern Africa. One concept that has a long history in the Niger-Congo language family is the word for "matrilineage." As Bantu speakers spread to Central Africa between 3500 and 1000 BCE, they maintained their matrilineal reckoning and, by 2500 BCE or so, had terms for both "matrilineage"—*-cuka*—and "matriclan" (a number of lineages that recognize a common ancestor)—*-ganda*. Scholars such as historian Kairn Klieman know this from the reconstruction of proto-languages. The term *-cuka* also refers in many languages to a termite mound and, metaphorically, a hearth. Klieman believes this is because this type of termite mound is often used as a cooking support for pots. Another explanation is that termite hills were considered receptacles for the ancestral spirits of the land's original owners—the Batwa—an association that exists from southern Central African Republic to Zambia. And the founders' ancestral spirits would be responsible for the contemporary fertility of the community. Either way, the connection between society and its successful reproduction is clear in the use of the term *-cuka*.

In Bantu-speaking societies starting about 4,000 years ago, the two most important events in a girl's life were puberty and the birth of her first child. At puberty, a girl was initiated into the status of a *mwali,* or young woman. The term comes from the verb "to grow." The initiation was marked by public ceremonies that framed a period of seclusion. During this time, rituals concentrated on ensuring the girl's fertility and thus her contribution to the matrilineage. The girl received instruction on culture and her roles as a woman, mother, and wife. This instruction is in keeping with the priorities of a matrilineal or matrifocal society. In contrast, foreign researchers have emphasized the significance of the sexual aspects of female initiation. Such a focus, historian Rhonda Gonzales argues, would be more appropriate in a patrilineal society, where a partner's sexual satisfaction and stable marriages would be important. In matrilineal societies, marriages were easily dissolved, and a woman's role and purpose were defined within the matrilineage, not within her marriage; thus, the initiation would focus on ensuring the continuation of the matrilineage.

The second rite occurred after the birth of her first child and marked a Bantu-speaking woman's transition to full adulthood. Whereas in the patrilineal contemporary United States, the chief rite of passage is marriage, when a woman becomes the wife of a man, the two significant rites for girls in much of Central Africa for hundreds of years revolved around their biological capacity to bear children. Western culture believes that a woman's importance is not based on her reproductive capability, but many psychologists feel this abandonment of biological imperatives comes at great emotional and social cost. An American woman's place and role in society are not as narrow now, but neither are they as secure.

Evidence exists that many Bantu-speaking societies in Central Africa recognized both the female and male lines by the first millennium BCE. Thus, speakers in this region had a broad spectrum of lineal ideas from which to draw. Since the early centuries of the Common Era there has been a trend toward increasing patrilineal organization, though there are significant exceptions. More intensive cattle keeping, likely due to contact with Khoekhoe (from the Khoisan language family) pastoralists, is one probable reason for this shift among many southern African Bantu-speaking societies. Recently, two anthropologists studied the link between the loss of matriliny and cattle keeping, including among many Kusi (or southern) Bantu societies (who were descendants of the Mashiriki Bantu). In their study of 68 Bantu-speaking populations, acquiring cattle led formerly matrilineal cultures to change to patrilineal or mixed descent. They argue that livestock tended to be accumulated by men and passed on to sons in the form of bride wealth and inheritance. Thus, cattle were a male-based investment. As a counterpoint, in predominantly agricultural economies, residence will tend to be matrilocal, as the greatest economic investment is in land and the risk of paternity shifts the balance toward women as stewards and inheritors of land. Access to land for one's daughter is more secure than for one's son because he might have an unfaithful wife and thus be charged with raising offspring who are not his own. In this case, it is more secure for grandparents and parents to bequeath land to their daughters rather than their sons. There are, however, important exceptions. According to historian Jan Vansina, when the Kwandu of Zambia turned from pastor-foraging to cattle keeping and farming after they lost their sheep in an epidemic, they adopted corporate matrilineages to cope with the economic and social changes that came along with the switch.

In contrast, from 300 to 1450 CE in Congo, Angola, Zambia, and Malawi, matrilineal reckoning and the importance of female roles solidified in many places. Jan Vansina has written about the early history of Angola and western Congo and notes that between 700 and 1000 CE, the adoption of cereal agriculture and agropastoralism brought the necessity for new social institutions to help larger numbers of people relate to one another. Also, cattle keeping required residents to disperse at various times of the year, so the new institutions needed to help bridge these occasional geographical divides between relatives. Here, cattle keeping was practiced in conjunction with farming in matrilineal societies, in contrast to the above discussion. Matrilineages and matriclans served these purposes well. Matriclans recognized common descent from an ancestress, a common name, a praise name, and food avoidance. And they would have enabled cattle owners to send their herds to their mother's relatives in different locations, thus reducing the risk of a single herd being decimated by disease. In this region, Africans practiced virilocal residence (a newly married couple lives with the husband's family), often more closely associated with patriliny.

Sabi-speakers, who lived during the last millennium BCE in eastern Congo, practiced matriliny. Historian Christine Saidi has studied these cultures in some depth and notes that they were centered on women. They created an ideology that is marked by gender equality, matrilineal inheritance and control of children, matrilineal principles of decentralized political power, an emphasis on community, and the distribution of goods instead of individual accumulation. At the same time, these societies partially or entirely abandoned the practice of male initiation. They considered matriliny a more useful and convenient method of social organization than the more bilateral one they had been using previously. Female initiation was an important social rite, and male initiation increasingly became less important and eventually disappeared completely in many societies. Sabi-speaking women demanded bride service from their daughter's husband and thus commanded both their daughter's and their son-in-law's labor.

Sabi speakers also had a prefix for female officeholders, indicating that leadership was open to both genders. Twentieth-century ethnographies did not reveal that as late as the 1960s, women were chiefs and leaders of many East-Central African societies. In some societies, women were instrumental in picking a new chief. In fact, Bantu languages do not distinguish between male and female. Thus, based on language alone, it is not possible to tell whether an office or position was gender-specific.

They also adopted a new term for God—*Leza*—from the verb "to nourish." This, too, likely marks the shift toward emphasizing women's roles in society, as nurturing was widely assumed to be primarily the job of women. The descendants of some of these peoples remain matrilineal until today, such as the Bemba of Zambia, the Chewa of Malawi, and the Makonde of Tanzania. Finally, Saidi argues that the rituals associated with ironworking, such as the workers themselves maintaining abstinence from sexual intercourse during the smelt, are likely borrowed from a much earlier, female-dominated technological invention: pottery making. She contends that men took elements from an already existing suite of female rituals to build a male-dominated ritual authority.

What these more focused studies of some Bantu-speaking societies demonstrate is the salience, even if not the continuous presence, of ideas closely associated with matrilineal societies. These values include highly dispersed kin networks, ensuring distribution or resources and connections, and the ability to readily absorb newcomers and their ideas. These values were held in many places and times as peoples occupied more and more of the African continent over the last 5,000 years or more. Thus, how and why societies emphasized one form of lineal organization over another are highly variable and must be carefully studied. Unfortunately, such careful study has not always been carried out.

Previous Ideas about Lineal Shifts

Previous studies of matrilineal societies, particularly those that sought to answer how and why societies shifted from one form of lineal reckoning to another, have been based on erroneous, but understandable, assumptions. Theories about lineal shifts reflect as much about the researchers' assumptions as they do about the subject under study. Most scholars' work in this area has until recently been based on beliefs about matriliny.

One belief was that her spouse would become a woman's most important relationship as an adult. One aspect of kinship in many places worldwide is the fact that siblings occupy similar positions in the social structure. Thus, a daughter might refer to her mother's sister as her mother, to her father's brother as her father, and so on. This sibling equivalency may be surprising to those who assume individual identities and strategies within the family, but it provides bonds of sisterhood and brotherhood that facilitate networks of interdependence rather than solitary achievement. If sibling relations are key, then marital ones cannot be; thus, the nuclear family is just one possible mechanism for securing a successful future.

Many feel that matriliny itself needs to be explained—something that is certainly not the case for Africa. Others believe there is an inherent contradiction or "puzzle" within matrilineal societies for the father who feels bound to his children but owes his ultimate allegiance to his matrikin. Of course, women would feel a similar contradiction within patrilineal societies. Thus, matriliny only looks puzzling to those engaged in a different system.

Early on, many proposed that changes associated with the market economy or cattle keeping enabled men to acquire earnings and a livelihood independent of the family and, in turn, led to an increasing preference for bequeathing his money and property to his children rather than his matrikin. Karla Poewe notes that in twentieth-century Zambia, both the government and the church worked to create and support (rather ineffectively) "stable nuclear families" that promoted the father's role in the family. Similarly, different religions traditions, such as Christianity, Hinduism, or Islam, brought attitudes about appropriate family life from Europe, North America, and Asia that emphasized a nuclear family and close relationships between husband and wife, while other adult relationships, such as brother and sister, were accorded less importance.

Historians today are discovering that scholars often missed signs of matriliny in societies that were transitioning from one system to another or that had both matrilineal and patrilineal features. Anthropologists, for example, tended to privilege the elementary family as the core kinship unit, obscuring the importance of siblings in matrilineal society and thus sometimes underrepresenting matrilineal features. Since the first half and the middle of the twentieth century, when these arguments were at their height, there has been an attempt to interrogate some of these claims, and scholars have found that matriliny, or at least some aspects of it, continues in light of participation in the modern economy and Western or Eastern monotheistic religions. For example, historian Liazzat Bonate demonstrates that in northern Mozambique, contrary to Islam's ideological preference for patriliny, virilocal marriage, and spatial segregation of genders, Islam and matriliny coexist. Thus, the region stands as an example of the resiliency of matriliny.

The Tonga are a group of cattle-keeping people in the matrilineal belt of southeastern Africa. Thus, they are an exception (along with some Central African societies studied by Vansina) to the trend mentioned earlier. The Tonga practiced matrilineality until the middle of the nineteenth century. According to historian Margot Lovett, this included matrilocality, so a newly married man resided with his wife, and later their children, in her parents' compound. There he worked for his in-laws in male-specific tasks such as clearing bush for new fields, building and repairing houses, and, if the household was situated near a lake, providing fish for its members. This work was known as bride service.

In the late nineteenth century, husbands were granted the right to appeal for the chance to live near their own kin. Then, by the turn of the twentieth century, there is evidence that the Tonga had started to practice bride wealth (from the husband's family to the wife's) rather than bride service. Yet, Tonga maintained matrilocal residence after marriage and matrilineal descent. Three events caused the Tonga to switch from bride service to bride wealth: the arrival of the patrilineal Ngoni about 1850; the establishment of the Free Church of Scotland's Livingstonia Mission in 1878 at Bandawe station; and the inauguration of male labor migration a few years later. As a result of these factors, Lovett believes, by the mid-1950s, the Tonga lived virilocally, and a man bequeathed at least some of his property to his sons. In addition, the social role of the father and patrilateral kinship ties became more important. Over time, individually and collectively, Tonga decisions changed their kinship norms. Yet, matrilineal factors were still important, as matrilineal descent was still privileged, and adult sons and widows evidenced a distinct preference for residing matrilocality. Thus, the Tonga, a cattle-keeping people, retain matrilineal features to the present day.

Thus, assumptions about the inevitable collapse of matrilineal societies seem unfounded. Matrilineal characteristics can be very resilient in the face of

dramatic religious, social, and economic change, and matrilineal societies function just as well as patrilineal societies. These societies represent tremendous
depth of historical experience as present-day inheritors of kinship ideas that are
as old as some African societies. All of this suggests that further study of early
African societies without these preconceived notions could reveal even greater
matrilineal influence.

More Recent Matrilineal Societies

The African continent today is home to more matrilineal societies than any other.
Moreover, matriliny has recently emerged in some societies, such as the Uduk in
Sudan and the Kwandu in Zambia. African peoples are not automatically shed-
ding the practice when confronted with societal changes, such as those brought
about by greater access to the wage economy, higher education, or urbanized
living.

One of the best-studied African matrilineal societies in Africa is the Akan
(including the Asante) in what is now Ghana. According to anthropologist R. S.
Rattray, who studied the Akan in the early twentieth century, the Akan believed
that children inherited their soul from their father and their flesh and blood from
their mother; thus, the children were considered members of the mother's family.
They also believed that, if at all possible, birth should take place in the mother's
natal home. As a result, maternal siblings were more important than the spouse
in many spheres of life. In fact, the husband and wife did not always co-reside;
often the husband visited the wife's home in the evening. Somewhat less than half
of the Asante lived in matrilineal households with female heads, and only one-
third of married women lived with their husbands. Despite the other characteristics that follow a matrilineal pattern, Asante believed that ideally their children
should grow up in their father's house. But there could be a fair amount of variation in terms of household makeup; households could be under male or female
heads. A female-headed household would likely be composed of the head and
her children, her sister and her children, and maybe their grandchildren. On the
other hand, a male-headed household might include his wife and children as well
as his sister and her children. Individual autonomy and negotiated mutual aid are
the key features in Asante relations. Instead of pooling income, labor, or assets
for central decision making, these were held individually. The Asante also have
an important role for women in politics. Some accounts recall women chiefs long
ago, perhaps prior to the rise of the Asante kingdom in the seventeenth century.
In addition, women have maintained the role of queen mother, who, according
to the Asante Constitution, was "next to the king" and who, in fact, was often the
king's sister.

For the Luapula of Zambia, the notion of illegitimacy is irrelevant, because the mother of the child is always known and the most important parental

connection. Thus, the determination of paternity is not nearly as significant as it is for us, in our patrilineal society. Also, the primary function of the man is to help replenish his wife's lineage rather than his own. Marriages tend to be fluid, and a man or woman can have many partners throughout their lives. Economically, women have guaranteed access to land, their offspring, and remittances from their adult children. Politically, women and men participate equally in meetings and are able to defend their rights. The Luapula have shifted toward patriliny in the last decades of the twentieth century, thanks in part to increased participation in Protestant Christianity. These studies demonstrate that matriliny and the ideas that can be associated with it are practices with as many variations as there are societies. Moreover, these ideas do not represent a package or institution so much as a variety of responses to achieve successful management of families and resources.

Our study of matriliny raises a number of questions about some historical and anthropological assumptions. For example, it reminds us that emphasis on mother-daughter or sister-brother relationships is perhaps just as natural as an emphasis on father-son or husband-wife relationships. In addition, the fact that a number of African societies still practice matriliny and many are matrifocal suggests that our idea that social change and progress are linear is incorrect. Similarly, a focus on matriliny demonstrates that all societies will not react to profound economic and social changes in similar ways. Matrilineal ways of thinking about family give us much to reflect on in terms of our own societies and their structures and ideals. Finally, as the previous material suggests, matriliny is not a historical remnant but a living institution with great depth and meaning for many African peoples. It is a constellation of ideas that has contemporary relevance, even though for a long time it served the relatively scattered populations during long, drawn-out processes of settlement. Africans have created many such social structures that are worthy of our attention and understanding.

Suggestions for Further Reading

Christine Choi Ahmed, "Before Eve Was Eve: 2200 Years of Gendered History in East-Central Africa" (Ph.D. diss., University of California, Los Angeles, 1996). This is a study of early central African societies from the perspective of gender. Ahmed uses linguistic and archaeological evidence to explore the ways in which women shaped these societies.

Critique of Anthropology 17, no. 2 (1997), special issue. This journal contains a variety of studies of matriliny and the ways in which previous explorations of it were hindered by researchers' assumptions about the normalcy of patriliny.

Rhonda M. Gonzales, *Societies, Religion and History: Central East Tanzanians and the World They Created, c. 200 BCE to 1800 CE,* http://www.gutenberg-e.org/gonzales

/index.html. This is one of the most recent works using historical linguistics to reconstruct the cultures of ancient Africans. Gonzales focuses on the Ruvu societies along the central Tanzanian coast and interior, particularly noting the roles of women and religion.

Clare Janaki Holden and Ruth Mace, "Spread of Cattle Led to the Loss of Matrilineal Descent in Africa: A Coevolutionary Analysis," *Proceedings of the Royal Society of London Biological Sciences* 270, no. 1532 (2003): 2425–2433. These two anthropologists studied 68 Bantu-speaking societies in sub-Saharan Africa, testing the hypothesis that when matrilineal societies acquire cattle, they become patrilineal. Their results supported the hypothesis. They used a language tree and secondary ethnographic data with statistical analysis.

Ladislav Holy, *Strategies and Norms in a Changing Matrilineal Society: Descent, Succession and Inheritance among the Toka of Zambia* (Cambridge: Cambridge University Press, 1986). Holy examines the changes that have occurred in kinship as a result of Toka switching from hoe agriculture to ox-drawn plowing.

Emiko Ohnuki-Tierney, "Historicization of the Culture Concept," *History and Anthropology* 12, no. 3 (2001): 213–254. A Japanese anthropologist discusses criticisms of anthropology as being without history and argues that culture has always been changing and influenced by a combination of local and external ideas.

Karla Poewe, *Matrilineal Ideology: Male–Female Dynamics in Luapula, Zambia* (London: Academic, 1981). This is a relatively accessible treatment of the myriad ways in which the Luapula practiced (through the 1970s at least) matriliny.

R. S. Rattray, *Ashanti* (Oxford: Clarendon, 1923). This is one of the earliest and most frequently used accounts of early-twentieth-century Ashanti culture. It suffers, as do many accounts from this era, from a sense of timelessness but nonetheless captures many aspects of the matrilineal society.

Christine Saidi, *Women's Authority and Society in Early East-Central Africa* (Rochester, N.Y.: University of Rochester Press, 2010). Covering more than 2,000 years of African social history, Saidi incorporates evidence from historical linguistics, archaeology, comparative ethnography, oral traditions, and art history to demonstrate the authority and power of women in precolonial Africa. She examines technology, social relations, and sexuality.

Marja-Liisa Swantz, *Ritual and Symbol in Transitional Zaramo Society with Special Reference to Women,* 2nd ed. (Uppsala: Scandinavian Institute of African Studies, 1986). Anthropologist Marja-Liisa Swantz discusses the role of grandmothers in Zaramo society, as mentioned in this chapter, among a wide variety of cultural features.

Jan Vansina, *How Societies Are Born* (Charlottesville: University of Virginia Press, 2005). Using archaeology and historical linguistics, historian Jan Vansina reconstructs the creation of large-scale central African societies from c. 900 BCE to 1600 CE.

Trudeke Vuyk, *Children of One Womb* (Leiden: Centrum voor Niet-Westerse Studies, Rijksuniversit, 1991). In this contemporary anthropological look at matrilineal societies across Central Africa, Vuyk challenges a number of ideas, particularly the preoccupation with the conjugal or nuclear family as the basis for understanding social relations and work roles. Instead, a broader look at social relations within matrilineal societies illuminates larger cultural ideas.

7 Forms of Economic Thought

Wealth in People and the Entrustment Economy

As HISTORIAN John Iliffe wrote, among the Africans' chief contributions to world history is their ability to survive and thrive in a very challenging landscape. As in all preindustrial societies, Africans had to use their bodies to work for a living and to ensure the health of the next generation. Until the twentieth century, Africa's history was primarily shaped by a combination of its vast landscape and sparse population. Therefore, the resource Africans lacked was people, not land, as it was for Europeans. One product of this situation is an African value system that is largely derived from the importance of human relationships for survival and success and particularly the availability of people for labor, reproduction, and security. Such "rights in people" have been at the heart of African economic and social history, as historian Jane Guyer has noted.

The related term "wealth-in-people" captures the value of relationships (and their collective knowledge and skills) in African accumulation and wealth reckoning. The term was first used in the 1970s to express the ways in which elders controlled the labor of others, such as children, in their societies. The term is now used much more broadly to note characteristics that are common throughout Africa, such as interpersonal dependency and network building that require investing in relationships at the expense of accumulating material personal wealth. The network of people, particularly dependents, upon whom one could rely for production and reproduction brought security in numbers and energy, as well as a variety of ideas, skills, and talents that would make for stronger families and societies.

This outlook about what is important and valued is much different from the Western focus on wealth—a "wealth-in-things." In the West, particularly in the last few hundred years, the accumulation of money and material things was the primary goal in life, and relationships were of secondary importance. Like so much else, however, this was not a cut-and-dried distinction in either place. Africans pursued the accumulation of things, such as livestock, but they were often secondary or tightly linked to ensuring a wide network of people.

This valuing of people is one way to consider the era of history that drew the African continent into much closer relationships with the Americas and Europe: the Atlantic slave trade that occurred from 1500 to 1800. During this time, approximately 12 million Africans were forcibly transported across the Atlantic to serve burgeoning mining and agricultural industries in the New World. Most of what American students first learn about Africa is as the source of slaves. This book focuses on African societies and the ways in which they responded to and helped to perpetuate slave trades within a broader social and economic context both within and outside the continent. An emphasis on relationship, kinship, and people can be seen in more recent African economic history as well. It is one of the reasons why Western development, aid, and ideas about economics do not always succeed or fit well with African priorities.

Geographical Focus

The Atlantic slave trade was concentrated on the West and Central African coast, stretching from modern-day countries of the Gambia and Senegal to Angola in southern Africa. By the end of the slave trade, in some places, like Angola, the catchment area for slaves went inland for almost a thousand miles. All kinds of societies were impacted by the slave trade—large-scale and small-scale, centralized and not, some that eagerly participated and others that did not or that traded other goods but not slaves. The last part of the chapter focuses on contemporary African economies and relies on a study from western Kenya near Lake Victoria.

Sources and Methodologies

Much of our reconstruction of the African slave trade comes from European traders' documents. A rich database on the slave trade is maintained at Harvard University (www.slavevoyages.org/), particularly statistically. European traders were mostly interested in the numbers associated with their business: the number of slaves captured in Africa, the price paid for them, the number lost at sea, the price they brought in the New World, and the costs associated with trading, such as food, water, and fuel for the voyage. But they also needed to maintain relationships with African leaders and traders and to understand the nature and quantity of goods that Africans wished to trade for their slaves.

Prior to the creation of the database, information about the slave trade was in various archives across the Atlantic world, so scholars who wanted to research the impact of the slave trade in Africa focused on the data that were available, and that mostly was in the form of numbers. During the 1970s and 1980s, debate raged about how many Africans were captured during the Atlantic slave trade; numbers ranged from 8 million to an admitted estimate of 100 million. The most accepted number was between 10 and 20 million, the latter taking into account deaths before slaves were put on the ships and during the Middle Passage. The implications of the numbers are, of course, significant in terms of the disruption caused to African societies from which they came. Smaller numbers were used to downplay the significance of the trade both in terms of European culpability and African consequences. But verifying the impact on Africa is difficult because we don't know exactly where slaves were captured and the size of the populations from which they were taken. This is not to say that the figures and implications of them are guesswork, but they are not as accurate or complete as would be desirable.

European documents usually contain little information about the names of African slaves or the slaves' specific points of origin, listing just the embarkation point. As a result, little is known about the interior slave trade, the ethnic origins of many slaves, and the ways that individuals and families responded to the insecurity and opportunity afforded by the trade. We know more about the slave trade from autobiographies of slaves who were captured and then freed, such as Olaudah Equiano. The slave trade database also contains biographical vignettes from enslaved Africans. All of these sources humanize a dehumanizing topic: the trade in human beings. You can see three such stories (about Dobo, Ayuba, and Catherine) at http://www.slavevoyages.org/tast/assessment/essays-intro-01.faces.

The numbers are also significant in terms of European culpability. For a long time, the slave trade was painted as an evil act perpetrated by Europeans against unwitting Africans. More focus on Africans involved suggests that for African leaders and traders there was often a benefit in terms of wealth and status, and participating was a conscious choice. For the victims, of course, the story is different, and very few, if any, would have chosen to become slaves. European involvement is not as difficult to parse. The slave trade was highly lucrative and, at the time, one that was not seen as morally repugnant as it is today.

An increasing number of scholarly accounts that use oral traditions, oral history, and anthropology explain some of the cultural and historical dynamics at work in African societies during the slave trade. Tracking African ideas about the economy during the slave trade and in more recent times requires oral history and anthropology and sensitivity to the ways in which different cultures construct holistic systems of meaning. Such ideas are not usually included in European sources or data. Anthropological and historical accounts of slave-trading societies, such as those by Charles Piot of the Kabre, help to explain why some Africans participated in the slave trade. They also illuminate how societies maintained an emphasis on personal relationships during an era that is often associated with dehumanizing those relationships.

African Economies in the Past—Wealth in People

African ethnography, from West and Central Africa, including areas involved in the slave trades, indicate that wealth could be both animate and inanimate and that personalized objects could be interchanged with human beings. In southern

Cameroon, wealth came in the form of wives, indigenous currencies, and livestock. And in Kongo, certain medicines (*minkisi*) were functionally interchangeable with human beings. Among the Igbo, wealth had two categories: wealth that multiplied or self-replicated, such as animals, crops, and people, and wealth that one "caught" or acquired. For many Africans, a wide variety of animate and inanimate objects were valued for their capacity to ensure health and security. But generally, most inanimate or non-self-replicating wealth served to strengthen relationships between people.

Africans clearly saw the economy as composed of objects and living things, and relationships among people, animals, and objects were closely monitored and regulated. What distinguishes preindustrial economies from capitalist or market economies of our modern era is that economics, trade relations, and exchange are embedded in social relations. Development studies expert Gilbert Rist argues:

> In most societies other than modern society, the circulation of goods is organized according to relations of kinship or hierarchy, and this confers on things a special role in which they are subordinate to social ties. Certain goods (e.g., those set aside for a dowry) can be exchanged only between certain persons (the eldest of the family) and only in precise circumstances (restricted exchange); in other cases, the social bond is expressed through the exchange of identical goods; or the "big men," in order to maintain their prestige, have an obligation to redistribute goods obtained through the fruits of their labour, and so on.

A market economy, on the other hand, deals in autonomous objects and people, without ties between these categories or within them.

French anthropologist Marcel Mauss thought of the preindustrial economy in the form of gifts, tracing the meaning of human life through the obligations of gift-giving and gift-receiving. Much like Rist's description, there was an art to the practice so that gift-giving was required for certain ritual activities, and formal relationships were established based on gift-giving. Moreover, how, when, and with what a gift was repaid were important judgments that communicated much about the relationship.

The term for gift-giving in much of Mali is *dama*, and it maintains social connections; celebrates the essence of humanity and sharing; and promotes community well-being so that members are protected from poverty and encouraged not to accumulate too much wealth. One study indicated that each person in the capital of Mali was obligated to give an average of one and a half gifts per day.

Another example of these formal relationships has been described by anthropologist Polly Wiessner, who discussed the practice among gatherer-hunters in the Kalahari Desert in Botswana. *Xaro* was a partnership between two people marked by the exchange of goods. An individual would have multiple *xaro* relationships. In his book *Heart of Dryness*, James Workman quotes Wiessner as saying, "*Xaro* was one of the most powerful bonds within the social fabric, because a partnership would last for life." *Xaro* people would be friends eager to return gifts and to continue the relationship.

Political scientist Goran Hyden and others have written about a moral economy or economy of affection to describe agricultural (or preindustrial) societies and their economic values. Hyden recognizes that the economy of affection is a universal phenomenon but argues that it is more significant in Africa than elsewhere. It is an economy that emphasizes developing and nurturing personal relationships. Africans' economic behavior is driven by a logic that is not represented in the academy or in international financial institutions, he argues. It has also been scrutinized for its contributions to postcolonial African political corruption. Within a moral economy, one's ties to relationships and friends are often more important than wider obligations. Within a small-scale community without much institutional framework, the systems run well. But when grafted onto a national government, the moral economy poses some profound challenges, such as a tendency toward nepotism and political corruption. Like any cultural idea or institution, the moral economy has both good and bad sides, and whether one is more prominent than the other depends on the context.

Historian Tadasu Tsuruta has argued that Tanzania's moral economy has been shaped by both existing communal values and a response to external forces, including a capitalist economy that "has expanded rapidly since the early nineteenth century." Tanzanians met this global economic expansion with their own economic relations and concepts. One of these is *utani*, often defined as a joking relationship. *Utani* is characterized by joking with one's peer, but such jesting marks a deeper relationship involving the exchange of money or goods between the joking partners. If one has an *utani* relationship with another, it is a way of elevating that relationship and the economic expectations associated with it.

These relationships also had a leveling mechanism, a means of ensuring greater equality within society. A variety of leveling mechanisms are found in African societies. Tsuruta asserts that *utani* ties were either based on equal relationships or developed to promote equality and harmony. *Watani* (those engaged in the joking relationship) could take each other's property without permission and without blame. They also played an important role at funerals, particularly if one died away from his homeland, providing meals and support for the bereaved. Thus, *utani* was an economic support system in a society that had no formal institutions (such as a nation-state might have) to provide such support.

Although originally confined within ethnic groups, *utani* relationships spread between ethnic groups as Tanzania became incorporated into a wider global economy in the nineteenth century and as people moved greater distances and needed aid and support in unknown lands. By the mid-twentieth century, *utani* was not as widely practiced due in part to a wider acceptance of individual property rights. These rights, introduced by Europeans, meant that access to one another's property in difficult times was inappropriate, if not taboo. African ideas about the economy, such as *utani*, do change, as this example shows, but socially embedded economic ideas and transactions tend to be resilient and long-lasting, such as those described by the joking relationship. Although Africans have always participated in economic relations and ideas in a wide variety of ways, they still place a lot of emphasis on building interpersonal relationships.

The Atlantic Slave Trade Era

While Africans in many parts of the continent valued personal relationships more than material things, access to people and the resources they commanded was still respected. African societies consisted of members along a continuum of dependency and lack of freedom. Dependents were the source of a male or female elder's wealth and security. Think about an extended family in terms of relative freedom. Generally speaking, in most precolonial African societies without much hierarchy, grandparents had the most freedom due to their age and potential wisdom. The following generation—the parental generation—had some freedom but not the same level as their parents' generation because they were still expected to labor and provide for those related to them. Also, their resources and time could be commandeered by the older generation. The last generation—children—had even less freedom. Children would be expected to do as they were told and would have little control over their time and have few resources to call their own. Possibly equal to, or even lower than, children in the family would be nonbiological members of the family who had to be provided for: debt pawns or slaves. Debt pawns were children from one family who were given to another family for a period of time during hardship. The family receiving the pawn would provide the natal family with food or livestock or some other resource in exchange for the labor of the child for months or years. Slaves, of course, would have no relation to the family, and their labor and possibly sexuality would be under the family's control.

Thus, in ways that seem strange to Americans in the twenty-first century, most Africans' lives until very recently were constrained by expectations of older generations. The concept of freedom, while important for Africans, was not the salient means by which they measured the value of their lives. Significant lack of freedom sometimes brought security in the form of housing and food, as in the case of a debt pawn whose natal family might be facing hunger or danger. Taking in children or others is another aspect of a "wealth-in-people" economy in that it emphasizes taking care of people who might not have the resources to rely on themselves. Also, through marriage or other close relationships, dependents became a part of kinship networks, mitigating the original servile circumstances.

In addition to personal dependency, after the first millennium CE in northern Africa, Africans were engaged in slave trading with the Muslim world. Slaves were used internally by Muslim states in the military and government, particularly. But many were taken out of the continent to southern Europe and the Middle East. When Europeans first landed on the West African coast in the late fifteenth century, they found Africans trading and using slaves and, initially, simply tapped into this system. They were there seeking spices and gold that had come to them overland for centuries. Now, with navigation skills, seaworthy boats, and financial backing, European explorers were able to travel to Africa.

The Portuguese initially helped to transport slaves from Benin kingdom to Elmina along the modern-day Ghanaian coastline, where Africans bought them. There, slaves carried goods inland and brought gold to the coast. Eventually, the Portuguese began using slaves on sugar plantations on Atlantic islands, like Sao Tome, and eventually across the Atlantic in Brazil and elsewhere. Dutch, British, and French traders later joined the Portuguese trading for slaves and other goods like spices and gold along the African coast.

Thanks to the Trans-Atlantic Slave Trade Database, scholars have solid estimates of the number of slaves who were forced to leave their homes to work in another land—approximately 12.5 million between 1500 and the mid-1800s. The peak decade in terms of the trade was the 1780s. During those years, approximately 870,000 slaves were shipped across the Atlantic. Then, beginning in 1808, countries started to outlaw the trade. It took several decades before the trade across the Atlantic ended completely. Ironically, slavery within Africa increased, as societies that had become used to securing large numbers of slaves now sought to engage slaves in their own economies, as well as to provide labor for a growing raw material trade with Europe. Though three European countries dominated the trade, they did so at different times. The Portuguese were the most active in the fifteen and sixteenth centuries. The Dutch played an important role in the seventeenth century, and by the eighteenth century, the English dominated the trade.

Slaves were taken from seven broad regions in West Africa running from east to west: Senegambia, Sierra Leone, Windward Coast, Gold Coast, Bight of Benin, Bight of Biafra, and West Central Africa. Numbers exported from these regions varied significantly both across the region and across time. At the height of the trade in the eighteenth century, the Bight of Benin contributed 23.2 percent of the slaves exported. But between 1676 and 1730, almost half of the slaves taken from the continent came from this region. Central Africa contributed over 40 percent of the slaves overall, particularly after the 1700s.

About 50 percent of the African slaves were taken to the Caribbean islands, more than 33 percent were sent to Brazil, and just 6 percent went to the United

States. Once there, their experience in slavery was as chattel, or property, rather than on a continuum of dependency that might eventually allow for full adult status in the community, including marriage. Who was taken across the Atlantic reveals much about African societies and economics. Generally, in the Atlantic slave trade, more men were sold than women and children. Women, in particular, were often kept in African societies, perhaps initially as slaves, but they would eventually become members of the society, probably after they had married and borne children. Their ability to reproduce was of critical concern to Africans. Men could be sold without a similar loss of reproductive potential. If more women had been sold, it is likely that the demographic toll of the trade would have been even greater than it was.

Some slaves were already circulating in trade networks when Europeans arrived, but the numbers available increased over time. Slaves were obtained primarily through kidnapping, selling of convicted criminals, raiding, and interstate warfare. The last was likely the most significant and could be a result of state expansion, such as was the case with the Kingdom of Kongo in Central Africa in the fifteenth century or Oyo in the Bight of Benin in West Africa in the eighteenth century. Scholars disagree on Africans' motivation to participate in the trade. One question is whether African leaders responded to the market in slaves by purposefully engaging in warfare to obtain slaves or if they had primarily political reasons and were happy to channel their prisoners into the slave trade after conquest. It seems likely that much of the warfare was a result of political ambitions rather than naked interest in accumulating trade for slaves. A number of societies—like Benin, for example—chose to limit their participation in the slave trade during some periods out of fear of the consequences, but they readily traded other goods with Europeans. The consequences included loss of security for their own people, thus jeopardizing the welfare of society. Benin's example demonstrates that African leaders sought sovereignty and control first and foremost and took advantage of aspects of the Atlantic trade when it served their purposes.

Another question is whether the slave trade brought about political fragmentation or political augmentation. Historian Paul Lovejoy argues that the only way that increasing numbers of slaves could reach the African coast was through political fragmentation, while historian John Thornton argues that states like the Kingdom of Kongo, at least for a period of time, were strengthened by their alliances with Europeans and their access to guns, cloth, and other luxury goods. While some states did develop as a result of the slave trade or dynamics associated with the slave trade, there were a significant number of nonhierarchical societies that continued to exist alongside the larger, stronger ones. Researchers have found evidence (supporting the subject of this chapter) that it was through mechanisms for securing personal relationships that these societies weathered the challenges posed by slave trading, warfare, and raiding. Small-scale and large-scale societies continued to play a role in African history throughout the Atlantic era.

Another ongoing debate about the Atlantic slave trade is what Africans got in return for the slaves and what kind of long-term economic consequences the trade had on African societies. One argument proffered by historian Walter Rodney, among others, is that Africans bought worthless goods in exchange for able-bodied men, thus setting African societies and their development back. Other scholars have argued that the reality was far more nuanced. It is true that African leaders traded people for cloth and metal goods that were used to enhance status in the case of the former and to perpetuate insecurity and access to slaves in the case of the latter. Recall that material goods were used to strengthen social relationships, so Rodney's argument weakens because it is based on a Western notion of wealth and security. Africans also wanted a much broader range of goods, including beads and other decorative items, alcohol, gunpowder, salt, and pepper. In fact, Africans often set the terms of trade, demanding, for example, certain types of cloth with preferences that shifted regularly. As a result, European traders brought a wide variety of cloth and other goods the next time they came to Africa because they did not know what would be popular or in fashion. Africans were not wasting their resources but obtaining goods that enhanced their abilities to attract followers and build relations.

Case studies of the slave trade and its impact exemplify African economic thought, as well as some of the consequences of a trade in people within cultures that value relationships more than transactions. Smaller, decentralized societies help to illuminate the ways in which hundreds of small-scale societies struggled internally and across communities to shape their own histories, though not under conditions they had much control over. The Kabre live in northern Togo and found themselves between two major slave-trading states during the Atlantic slave trade: the Asante to the southwest and the Dahomey to the southeast. The Asante kingdom was founded around 1680 by Osei Tutu, the *Asantehene*. He initiated a series of reforms that created a sense of national identity among differentiated chiefdoms, including an Asante-wide legislative body and a "stool of office" for each chief that bestowed authority and tied the chief to the king's "golden stool." Early in the Atlantic slave trade, Asante provided gold and imported slaves to work in the gold mines. But after 1660, due to Asante military activity and connections with Muslim trading networks to the north, Asante society became a slave-trading society and, increasingly, a slaveholding society.

Dahomey was founded about the same time as Asante and developed a number of representative institutions to tie lineages and professional groups to the king, or *oba*. By the early 1700s, the availability of firearms from the European trade allowed Dahomean rulers to exert authoritarian rule. And in 1720, the *oba* defeated two states near the Atlantic Ocean and gained access directly to European traders. Dahomey eventually situated itself as a middleman in the trade, collecting revenue from the slave trade as slaves came from the north on their way to the coast.

When faced with large slaveholding and trading states as neighbors, a small-scale society, like the Kabre, could either ally with one such state and risk raids by the other or pursue sovereignty and be prepared to sell or offer slaves when necessary. The Kabre responded to the raids and other economic activities that accompanied the European slave trade by retreating to the mountains in northern Togo and offering some of their own citizens, often children, for sale at slave markets. This reduced the likelihood of raiding and the need for the Kabre to form alliances or tribute relationships with the more centralized states. This gave them some control over the slaving dynamic, which could be violent and unpredictable.

Anthropologist Charles Piot researched why the Kabre were willing to sell their own people during the slave trade. The explanation lies within a broader cultural framework of relationships and exchange that were central to Kabre culture. If a visitor entered a Kabre household and found a child eating something, a parent would tell the child to offer the food to the guest. Before speaking or walking, Kabre children were taught to generously share their food with others. As the Kabre matured, they exchanged labor, grain, and animals for beer, land, help with the transport of harvest, and so on. The Kabre distributed their material wealth to establish wide-ranging alliances that served as a source of security and stability, sometimes for decades. Lifelong relationships of exchange had a special name and were carefully built over years.

Moreover, an unused field or animal could be claimed by someone who could demonstrate a need for it; small portions of harvests were claimed by ancestor spirits; and those who had more resources often took land or animals from others so they would not always be expected to give away their resources. The emphasis was on dependency as the glue of society, even if one's material circumstances did not require it. Also, because much of a person's land and animals might belong to the needy instead of those with whom he wanted to build a lifelong relationship, the Kabre made sure at least some of their land and animals were always in the hands of those with lifelong commitments to exchange.

The Kabre also acknowledged that one's bodily labor was an investment. If an individual had put labor into something (such as food), then he or she had the rights to it. In this context, the Kabre could also pawn a child to another family in exchange for food or livestock during difficult times. The expectation was that once the family could pay back the food or livestock, the child would be returned to the natal family.

The Kabre maintained some matrilineal features, including that a mother's brother was responsible for her children until they were initiated. When a child reached adolescence, the father's responsibilities increased. Kabre children had a mother, a father, and an uncle invested in their welfare. This idea of multiple ownership extended to material things as well, so, for example, land could be worked by one individual but owned by someone else. Access to wealth in people and things was readily contested and malleable. The slave trade offered Kabre uncles the opportunity to establish control of children who, eventually, were more under the authority of their natal father than their mother's family. When an uncle sold the child, the father would never be able to make a claim on the child. Also, the cowrie shells paid for the child would be divided among the child's family members, further reinforcing those relationships. Rather than focusing on the rupture caused by the sale, the Kabre could emphasize the way other relationships were strengthened. Another advantage of selling a child into slavery was that it could be more beneficial than pawning because no repayment could be claimed by the host family in the future. In this way, the Kabre used institutions, full of ambiguity and opportunity, to respond to the slave trade in a way that preserved their autonomy and overall well-being.

Historian Sandra Greene has chronicled changes in social relations among the Anlo-Ewe of the eastern Gold Coast and western Slave Coast during the slave-trade era. To the west of Anlo territory, Akwamu, a polity just south of Asante, was in conflict with Accra over direct access to the coastal trade for much of the seventeenth century. An influx of refugees from Akwamu in the late seventeenth century led to a scarcity of arable land in Anlo. Only one-fifth of Anlo land was arable, and much of it at any time had to be left fallow to regenerate plant material that could be tilled back into the soil to increase its fertility. In response, the Anlo developed a clan system (beyond the already existing lineage system) to distinguish older residents from the newer ones. In this way, land belonged to clans, and young women were encouraged to marry one of their father's sister's sons to keep the family land within the clan even after marriage. If a woman married a man of a different clan, her land could be forfeited to the clan because her children technically belonged to their father and his clan.

Anlo only became involved in the slave trade in the early eighteenth century when continued conflict to the west along the Gold Coast sent traders looking for other outlets. Then they did so as middlemen, trading salt, fish, and European goods for slaves and ivory from the north. Anlo established new trade routes to the north during the eighteenth century, expanding their access to northern products. Like many other societies, Anlo kept female slaves and exported mostly male slaves because females provided Anlo with much-needed labor as well as the ability to produce children. Female slaves worked to smoke, dry, and salt fish, and many became second and third wives. In this way, men increased the size of their families and productivity and then displayed their increased wealth with beads and cloth and other trade items from overseas. Involvement in the slave trade increased inequality in Anlo. Free wives also benefited from having a slave co-wife because the second wife would contribute labor and children to the family, reducing the expectations on the first wife and allowing her more freedom to visit and maintain relations with her own kin. The Anlo did not seek out participation in the slave trade, and they did not become victims of it, but instead amplified their economic efforts, both in terms of fish production and trading, in response to European interest. Anlo society changed as a result, but it had changed prior to their participation in trade as they incorporated strangers and would change again with colonialism.

A final example from the Guinea coast in what is today Guinea-Bissau illustrates another form of response to European Atlantic trade. Historian Walter Hawthorne worked among the Balanta for more than a year, collecting oral traditions and less-formalized historical memories in the form of stories, songs, and memories encoded in names and places. Reading European historical documents as well, he pieced together a detailed history of a small-scale society inland from the coast over five centuries.

Much like the Kabre, the Balanta used extant social divisions—the relative lack of freedom among children and younger men and women—to respond to the violence and challenges of the slave trade. The Balanta and others in the region moved from upland regions that were difficult to defend and settled in more isolated, marshy, and riverine coastal areas—areas that became the location for rice production. They fortified these settlements to protect themselves from raids and organized young men into age grades. These age grades protected the villages from raids, became raiding parties themselves (likely a reformulation of cattle raiding that young males had previously engaged in), and became the chief rice producers as well, all in response to the authority of older males in society. In turn, though, elder males had to grant some privileges, such as the future right to sit on elders' councils, to keep younger men working within their own society and not running off for better opportunities, or at least more freedom, elsewhere.

Balanta village age grades conducted slave raids on neighboring villages and merchant vessels on rivers. Few in number, they generally preyed on unsuspecting women and children who were easier to transport over long distances. Children could also be integrated into Balanta age grades. As in other places, criminals were also sold as slaves. Such a focus also made sense in terms of economic changes within Balanta society. The Balanta prized European iron and used it to forge hoes and other agricultural tools that made it possible to grow a new crop suited to their wetter location: paddy rice, which slowly replaced the previous staple crop, yams. Men became the chief rice growers, so the Balanta prized male slaves more than females. They also used iron to produce weapons for defense and raiding. The Kabre, Anlo, and Balanta weathered the tumult of the Atlantic era with some of their institutions and values unchanged and many of them altered in response to European trade and other societies' and individuals' participation in it. These societies remained intact in large part because they valued people and the labor they provided and maintained conditions that ensured successful agricultural production as well as biological reproduction. Though no one knew it at the time, other challenges lay ahead, challenges that would further alter African economic ideas and institutions.

At the end of the formal Atlantic slave trade in the nineteenth century, slave trades within the continent flourished, and the use of slavery expanded in many parts of West Africa. For the most part, African societies did not undergo the same kinds of economic and social transformations that Europe did during the 1700s and early 1800s that led to abolition of the Atlantic slave trade in the first decade of the nineteenth century and then the abolition of slavery in Europe and eventually in European colonies. A good number of African societies depended on export trade in slaves for at least part of their income. Recall that the 1780s was the peak decade in terms of the number of slaves shipped across the Atlantic. The slave trade was a thriving business for both Europe and Africa, and its abolition would take time to get used to. Societies inland still engaged in slave raiding and trading, and coastal societies still received and traded slaves as well.

Thus, ironically, although slave trading was slowly dying outside of Africa, it was still embedded in African economies. Historian Paul Lovejoy chronicled this transition, noting that European trade in slaves continued on the east coast of Africa well into the nineteenth century, as French and Arab demand for slaves increased export numbers there significantly. Approximately 1.5 million slaves were brought to the Swahili coast in East Africa, bound for French islands off the coast (Madagascar, Comoros, and Seychelles), as well as Arabia, Persia, and India. Many stayed on the coast or on islands, such as Zanzibar, growing grain or cloves or other spices for both domestic consumption and export trade.

Another irony of the European transition away from slavery is that traders continued to rely on African commerce for their industries and economies. The European-African trade of the first half of the nineteenth century became known as "legitimate" trade to differentiate it from the illegal slave trading that continued despite laws to the contrary. This legitimate traffic included goods that had long been exported from Africa, such as ivory and gold, but also newer commodities like palm oil, peanuts, and cloves. What Europeans ignored, however, was that most of these goods were either produced by slaves or transported by slaves, so legitimate trade was bound up in African economies that had become increasingly dependent on slavery during the course of the overseas slave trade.

Another dynamic of nineteenth-century African history was the increasing prominence of Islam in the savanna region of West Africa. Through a series of religious revolutions, several Muslim states were formed between the 1700s and the mid-1800s. Many of these states were large and commanded a sizeable population. Many also relied heavily on slaves to grow food for the leaders and the military. Slaves also served in the military and filled harems. Estimates are that between one-third and one-half of the populations of these Muslim states, such as the Sokoto Caliphate in what is now northern Nigeria, were composed of slaves.

Asante, north of the Gold Coast, provides a vivid example of the impact of abolition of the Atlantic slave trade on African leaders. Historian Adu Boahen quotes Asantehene Osei Bonsu's conversation with British consul Joseph Dupuis in Kumasi in 1820:

> "Now," said the king, after a pause, "I have another palaver, and you must help me to talk it [sic]. A long time ago the great king liked plenty of trade, more than now; then many ships came, and they brought ivory, gold, and slaves; but now he will not let the ships come as before, and the people buy gold and ivory only. This is what I have in my head, so now tell me truly, like a friend, why does the king do so?"
>
> "His majesty's question," I replied, "was connected with a great palaver, which my instructions did not authorise me to discuss. I had nothing to say regarding the slave trade."
>
> Taking up one of my observations, he remarked, "The white men who go to council with your master, and pray to the great God for him, do not understand my country, or they would not say the slave trade was bad. But if they think it bad now, why did they think it good before[?] Is not your law an old law, the same as the Crammo (Moslem) law? Do you not both serve the same God, only you have different fashions and customs? Crammos are strong people in festische, and they say the law is good, because the great God made the book; so they buy slaves, and teach them good things, which they knew not before. . . . If the king would like to restore this trade, it would be good for the white men and for me too."

The Asantehene is incredulous about the abrupt change in European interest in slave trading and acknowledges that he benefits from it. Slaves continued to flow into Asante through war and tribute from the north. Asante responded to abolition in the early nineteenth century by making more use of slaves within their own societies, in the army, as political advisers and, increasingly, as workers on kola nut plantations, in gold mines, and as transporters of goods. Most slaves were owned by lineages, and Asante leaders feared high concentrations of slaves anywhere in the kingdom, so they sought to disperse them throughout society. Matrilineal inheritance helped to redistribute slaves among dispersed kin. The Asante government also pursued policies to encourage even the Asante of moderate means to afford slaves so they would have a stake in the perpetuation of the slaveholding system. Some descendants of slaves assimilated into Asante society but were often more vulnerable than freeborn descendants.

Hundreds of years after European demand for African slaves had begun, slavery had become an important institution in much of western, Central and eastern Africa. It was only with colonization, mission Christianity, and a series of laws that formal slavery in most societies came to an end. But what remains in most places is an investment in people as a form of security and well-being.

Wealth in People in Modern Times

Parker Shipton's work in Kenya, described in a trilogy of books, has demonstrated how Africans' investment in personal relationships has withstood slave trading, colonialism, and neocolonial ideas and institutions. Shipton writes about the Luo people of western Kenya. They live along Lake Victoria and make their living in a variety of ways, including farming and small-business enterprises. In elucidating Luo ways of thinking about the economy, Shipton uses the term "entrustment" to capture the way Luo think about economic exchange and the relationships enmeshed with it. In Shipton's words, from his first book:

> Entrustment implies an obligation, but not necessarily an obligation to repay like with like, as a loan might imply. Whether an entrustment or transfer is re-turnable in kind or in radically different form—be it economic, political, symbolic, or some mixture of these—is a matter of cultural context and strategy.

Entrustment includes an obligation to the dead and unborn as much as the living, so Luo transactions are mindful of generations past, present, and future. Thus, a loan of animals may last many years or longer than a generation. Entrustment also considers that exchangeable commodities have different categories, as Rist highlighted earlier. Thus, hens and roosters are not interchangeable, and one homestead's rooster is not readily exchangeable for another's rooster, embedded as it is in a particular family. Luo are also reluctant to convert animal wealth "downward" into inanimate or easily divisible forms of wealth. And they prefer to sell surplus maize shortly after the harvest when the price is lower than it will be later. Luo who sell are then able to invest in something tangible and notice-able when their neighbors and relatives have food and money available. Waiting and selling only when others are hungry risks social alienation or accusations of witchcraft, another leveling mechanism.

For Luo, land is not seen as a commodity interchangeable with others or sub-ject to the same kinds of risk as other things. Because land belongs to the lineage, contains burial sites, and is still tied to economic survival, it is too precious "to be gambled away" with a mortgage. Land is intimately linked to social identities and histories, and losing it would fundamentally alter not only the borrower's situa-tion but the situation of many of his kin. These ideas clash with those of colonial officials of the past and international financiers and national government officials of the present who assume that land titling and the mortgaging that follows from it will raise agricultural productivity. The logic is that if farmers can take out loans against their land, they will invest more heavily in it. These politicians and bankers remain unaware of the role that land played and continues to play in Luo life. Shipton concludes in his second book that the freehold-mortgage process has come to seem natural in Europe and the United States, where wage work is readily available, but in dry-land agrarian farming, where rain, transport, prices, and markets are all unreliable and wage work is scarce, a mortgage is "a threat to African agrarian life."

Entrustment also recognizes that the relationship is long lasting and marked by debt. "In Africa or elsewhere, a life in which all debts were settled would be a frozen life of atomized individuals—no life at all," says Shipton. In other words, entrustments create bonds between Luo and others that bring meaning to their world. Thus, financial independence would mean social isolation. Without this debt and credit, life would not be as rich—socially or economically. This is very similar to the way the Kabre thought about relationships as well.

Yet, Shipton notes that Luo operate not only in an economy of entrustment but also in a market economy, and it is not clear to him that they are moving from the former to the latter as much as modernization thinking has assumed. Unfortunately, neglecting the existence of the former has led to poorly executed foreign projects and schemes in eastern Africa, such as land mortgaging. Another foreign assumption has been that Luo don't repay loans at high rates because they are inexperienced with credit. In reality, Luo are very familiar with credit, as seen above. Most Luo have debts to pay, as well as credit or obligations to collect. These webs of indebtedness stretch from rural to urban areas and are of a higher priority than those due to a bank or other institution; less familiar, distant lenders usually rank as least important. Shipton writes in *The Nature of Entrustment:*

> In Luo eyes, the claims of distant creditors, like cooperatives, state banks, or international aid agencies pale in comparison with the perpetual, living and breathing debts between in-laws; and this is among the reasons, for better or worse, why institutional financial loans tend to be repaid as scantly as they are.

Luo loans are also interest-free and not expected to be paid back if a harvest fails. This is certainly not the case with Western-style loans.

These differences suggest that both colonial officials and development professionals run great risks in making assumptions about Luo understanding of debt and credit. Shipton clearly describes an economy embedded in the modern world but holding fast to economic transactions embedded in the social fabric that developed out of an agricultural and a subsistence lifestyle. Despite the strong presence of the global market economy, much of Luo economic decision making lies outside of processes and ideas that dominate in the study of economics.

Not so long ago in many places in North America and Europe, people thought of economics as embedded in society, just as the African societies described here. One of the consequences of modern society has been a fascination with rationality and reason as employed in scientific inquiry. As chapter 8 illustrates, the field of economics has been deeply influenced by this way of thinking so that economists and policy makers now assume that economic behavior can be analyzed much like the laws of science without attention to social relations. Africa's participation in the slave trade is a reminder that any kind of economics concept can serve some in society more than others.

But it also is a reminder that for much of human history, there has been a need to build relations with people and things to achieve security. One of the ways this occurred was by recruiting members within the family who were servile or dependent long before the Atlantic slave trade. Dependency was a fact of life and a situation that brought one into closer relation with others and ensured immediate welfare but also longer-term security. Given this increased interest in slaves engendered by European traders in the sixteenth century, Africans responded by trading those in their society who were more dependent or recently incorporated, through warfare, pawning, or as perpetrators of criminal activity.

But even within those categories, they often made choices based on relationships. Traders and leaders in most societies were more willing to sell men than women because they did not want to jeopardize their families' and societies' ability to reproduce. They also used institutions and relative degrees of freedom within their societies to address increased demand for slaves, turning debt pawns into slaves or their sister's children into slaves. For those traded, the result was often heartbreaking and also could be deadly, but for the wider African society from which they came, it was a means by which they could navigate a changing trading environment. It was also a means for ensuring continued success of their societies.

Suggestions for Further Reading

Beverly Bell, "Mali's Gift Economy," *YES! Magazine*, http://www.yesmagazine.org/new-economy/malis-gift-economy. This article describes the *dama* economy of gifting in Mali. It is primarily women who are involved in it, and members of the 2007 World Social Forum, an alternative to the World Trade Organization and other organizations that promote globalization, sought to learn about this view of the economy as another way of thinking about exchange.

Sandra E. Greene, *Gender, Ethnicity and Social Change on the Upper Slave Coast: A History of the Anlo-Ewe* (Portsmouth, N.H.: Heinemann, 1996). This is a study of the Anlo-Ewe of southeastern Ghana between the seventeenth and nineteenth centuries as the community absorbed traders, refugees, and conquerors.

Walter Hawthorne, *Planting Rice and Harvesting Slaves: Transformations along the Guinea-Bissau Coast, 1400–1900* (Portsmouth, N.H.: Heinemann, 2003). Hawthorne's study of small-scale societies during the Atlantic era on the Guinea-Bissau coast emphasizes the ways in which Africans responded to larger economic trends within specific geographical and cultural contexts. His work is a valuable contribution to our understanding of the era, as he demonstrates that decentralized societies responded to the slave trade in a variety of ways—some of them much different from larger-scale societies.

Goran Hyden, "Why Africa Finds It Hard to Develop," *Nord-Sud Aktuell* 18, no. 4 (2004): 692–704. Political scientist Hyden seeks to get to the root of Africa's recent development challenges, arguing that understanding culture and behavior is particularly important, especially the economy of affection that is prevalent in many societies but particularly salient in Africa. It is important because it shapes behaviors in ways that differ from the logic of social science models.

Charles Piot, "Of Slaves and the Gift: Kabre Dale of Kin during the Era of the Slave Trade," *Journal of African History* 37, no. 1 (1996): 31–49. Piot conducted fieldwork among the Kabre in Togo in the 1980s. His article continues a conversation started by Jane Guyer and Samuel Eno Belinga initiated with the article "Wealth in People as Wealth in Knowledge," published in 1995. Piot demonstrates how what seems incomprehensible to a modern Western sensibility, the selling of other Kabre, fits within indigenous economic ideas, including the circulation of gifts in order to build relationships.

Parker Shipton, *Mortgaging the Ancestors: Ideologies of Attachment in Africa* (New Haven, Conn.: Yale University Press, 2009). This is the second in Shipton's trilogy on Luo and their economic systems. All three books are sensitively done and help to illuminate the ways in which Luo to this day view economics and how that changes the decisions they make and the way they behave.

Parker Shipton, *The Nature of Entrustment: Intimacy, Exchange and the Sacred in Africa* (New Haven, Conn.: Yale University Press, 2007). This is the first in Shipton's trilogy.

PART III

RECENT HISTORY AND POLITICS

AFRICA HAS BEEN a significant player in the increasingly globalized world of the late nineteenth and twentieth centuries. In this period, Africans became part of nation-states as well as national economies. At the same time, their national economies were tied to a much broader global economy. Unfortunately, for Africans, though, the nation-state, market economies, retributive justice, and other ideas that were introduced with colonialism have become hegemonic in the global community in that they have been assumed to be the best possible way to construct societal systems. In most cases, Africans have combined previous ideas and institutions with these newer ones. Yet, Western media attention is often focused on narrow avenues of African participation in such global systems, often as impoverished victims or as senseless perpetrators of violence.

Even seemingly more benign terms that are often used to mark the most recent phase of global interconnection since the 1980s, such as *globalization,* tend to favor Western or Northern views and experiences. Globalization is a term with much greater resonance in the industrialized North than in the rest of the world. From the perspective of African history, it can only be seen as an extension of the relationships and ideologies of the colonial era (from the late nineteenth to the mid-twentieth centuries). Thus, since the 1800s, Africa has been largely defined by its relationship to other places in the world. As a result, the predominant narratives are of economic and political colonization and the resultant poverty and underdevelopment. These narratives largely come from outside the continent and define what the continent and its people are lacking rather than what they possess.

More than this, though, the outcome of colonialism has been a profound division in global society between those countries that were colonizers and those that were colonized. While some of the division is real in terms of unequal access to educational and economic opportunities, much of the division is perpetuated by global stereotypes. In contrast, this section highlights some of the ways in which Africans contribute to both mainstream and alternative economic, political, and social developments. Chapters 8, 9, and 10 seek to elucidate two things:

how Africa has remained the intellectual and practical "other" over the course of the twentieth and early twenty-first centuries and why such a view reflects only a small part of the African experience in the last 150 years.

Chapter 8 covers the history and experiences of Africans under colonialism and in the early postcolonial period through the lens of development. It argues that while development was couched as a mechanism for bringing the benefits of Western industrialization and state making to African countries, it was (and is) practiced as a result of historically shaped relationships of power and dominance that have resulted in a lack of significant development or improvement. Chapter 9 looks at Africans' contributions to economic thought, justice, and peacemaking, including historical examples from South Africa, Liberia, and Tanzania. Finally, chapter 10 examines the recent experience of Somaliland, a country free of piracy and with a robust government. Somalilanders have created an independent state, free of the more chaotic southern Somali society. The international community has yet to recognize their independence. Since 1991, Somalilanders have returned to some of their local political and economic institutions to rebuild their country after war. This country offers us a glimpse of some of the kinds of institutions that might help guide previously colonized countries and their colonizers toward a smaller-scale future where political and economic development meets the needs of people first rather than the elite.

8 African Views on Colonialism and Development Assistance

With Heidi Frontani

THE GROSS DOMESTIC PRODUCT (GDP), a measure of a country's goods and services, in Tanzania is again growing rapidly. Between 2000 and 2008, growth was 7 percent per year, and between 2009 and 2011, it was 6 percent per year. At the same time, Tanzania is ranked as one of the poorest countries in the world in terms of per capita income, according to the *CIA World Factbook*. The first statement indicates that "things" are going well in Tanzania; the second that they are not. How can both be true at the same time? Both are measures of purported progress or development as determined by a Western-dominated economic and intellectual system. Both statistics mark the ways ideas and institutions that have developed out of a deeply contingent Western historical process have come to determine African countries' trajectories and to be largely accepted by African leaders, if not Africans themselves.

One way to resolve the seeming contradiction between these economic facts is to ask: How are the fruits of economic growth distributed? Anthropologist Arturo Escobar notes that economists took some time to realize that the "Brazilian miracle" of growth rates of more than 10 percent per year masked increasingly unequal distribution of income and left low-income groups worse off than before. In 2006, physician and researcher Hans Rosling, using visualization software to animate statistical data, showed, among other things, how country-level statistics can hide wealth disparities in a country with a robust economy. In early-twenty-first-century China, people in the most well-to-do province had wealth and a life expectancy on par with that of the United States, but those in China's least-well-to-do province experienced wealth and a life expectancy on par with Ghana. Likewise, Tanzania's GDP numbers above are country-level statistics that mask great inequality among its citizens.

The way in which the United Nations, the International Monetary Fund, and a variety of non-governmental organizations (NGOs) measure the status of countries is with economic statistics and, frequently, a narrow range of them, like the GDP. These statistics and the ideas they represent are drawn from Western history and particularly from the discipline of economics, not Africa's past or present. These kinds of statistical approaches and the assumptions behind them have defined the West's relationship with Africa. They also contribute to notions of the West needing to "develop" other world regions because they belong to a substandard category of progress and humanity. What if statistics and the ideas they represent, such as development, not only fail to capture certain aspects of positive change in African societies but are part of the problem because they represent the world in a narrow way?

Geographical Place

In the colonial and postcolonial era, continental trends are more prominent than in earlier eras as external forces, such as a European interest in overseas territories, acted in similar ways across broad swaths of the continent. Many of the policies and ideas behind development during the colonial period were experienced throughout the continent with only minor variations, depending on whether colonial officials focused on resource extraction, labor migration, or the cultivation of cash crops and whether they made English or French the language of government and schools. Yet, specific examples are helpful, so this chapter focuses on Tanzania in East Africa. There, the first president of the country, Julius Nyerere, embraced a particular form of economic development that gained worldwide attention for its boldness and vision.

Similarly, since independence in the 1960s, most African leaders have sought to close the GDP, educational, and health gaps between their countries and the former colonizing powers. Initially, most countries, including Tanzania, chose to follow a socialist path to development, but by the early twenty-first century, most were following a more capitalist approach. The variations in success at this agenda have more to do with politicians' actions than a country's geographical location or resource base or the characteristics of the societies living there. One significant geographical factor that does limit economic development is the size of most African nations. With small populations there are limits to the size of the labor force and to consumption. Julius Nyerere recognized this and created a regional institution to pool resources and populations: the East African Community.

Sources and Methodologies

In this chapter, the discipline of economics generally and the ways in which the debate about economic growth and development have been framed more specifically are essential to understanding Africans' experiences over the last hundred years or so. Nation-states require a means to measure economic functions, such as the production of goods. Most nations have measured such production with the gross domestic product. While the number is useful for measuring some kinds of economic activity and comparing it from one country to another or from one year to the next within one country, the statistic masks economic activities that have been a critical part of African history for millennia, such as subsistence food production and the keeping of livestock for personal use and wealth.

Similarly, per capita income, usually calculated by taking the GDP and dividing it by the country's population, is measured based on official reporting to the state. Someone who takes care of a neighbor's children or who sells crafts out of his home or who grows all of her own food does not have her income measured by the state. In these ways, the statistics, such as those for Tanzania above, tell a particular story about how well Tanzania is fitting the mold of industrialized production and economic growth as determined by the experiences of Europeans.

More than statistics, though, economics as a discipline over the past 200 years has increasingly become separated from social reality. Development studies professor Gilbert Rist argues that since the nineteenth century, economics has become more of a science with an emphasis on laws rather than a humanities discipline with an emphasis on the complexities of human interactions, particularly recognition that people engage in economic acts for emotional reasons, such as love and pride, as much as rational ones. One of the ways in which economic prominence in our discourse is clear is the wide use of the term *economic development* as the primary focus of our relationship with southern countries as well as a key measure of success.

Just as there are biases and gaps in information derived from archaeological or cultural anthropological study, there are also challenges involved in viewing more recent African history through the lens of Western-derived economic development. Before looking at the foundations of colonialism and development, it is important to examine the history of the idea of development. This is intellectual history, tracing the roots of an idea, much like historical linguists try to trace the roots of an idea in African societies. The difference is that there are written documents going back thousands of years for the idea of development.

Development—The Idea

While development as a project to apply to a society only became operational in the 1940s, it has a longer intellectual history that includes colonialism, which helps explain why activities in the century before the 1940s differed only in degree and name from the "development era" that followed. Gilbert Rist writes about the long history of the idea of development. He argues that it is a Western invention and one that for the last 50 years has maintained momentum by drawing in other societies. Rooted in seventeenth-century Enlightenment thinking, development, founded on the ideas of progress, linear history, and growth, became the dominant way of thinking about human societies. Previously, nature had been used as a guide for human possibilities, recognizing that, like any living organism, human societies grew for a while but eventually contracted and died. With the new way of thinking came three important points: history is the same as progress; all nations travel the same road; and all societies do not advance at the same speed as Western society. Thus, colonization became possible as a means by which to aid more "backward" societies along the road to what the West had already achieved.

Belief in development has become so widespread that southern leaders have embraced it. Yet, 50 years after beginning to develop the South in earnest, not much has changed. In business, research, or politics, continual failure would lead to the end of the career or project, but in development, each failure leads to another attempt. Rist calls development a "religion" for this reason, and his definition of development is far different from those of international organizations or Western governments. He states:

> "Development" consists of a set of practices, sometimes appearing to conflict with one another, which require—for the reproduction of society—the general transformation and destruction of the natural environment and of social relations. Its aim is to increase the production of commodities (goods and services) geared, by way of exchange, to effective demand.

Virtually all major, planned colonial activities in Africa are captured by Rist's statement, as are many postcolonial development initiatives undertaken by the World Bank and others operating at a large scale.

More common definitions of development include other positive and more measurable outcomes than Rist's and often center on decreasing poverty by raising income. The United Nations produces annual country reports for its Human Development Index that include income, school enrollment/literacy, and life expectancy and lists countries according to a Gini coefficient. Named for the Italian statistician Corrado Gini, this is a measure of dispersion that can be used to chart variances in residential segregation, traffic flow, and other factors.

The Gini, as with virtually all statistical measures, can be used to make rather different kinds of statements about a society, all of which are true. Sweden is often held up as a model country not only in terms of the high percentage of development assistance given to the global community and its people's overall measure of happiness, but also for the relative equality among its citizens. Yet, Sweden has a low Gini coefficient when based on income and a much higher Gini coefficient when based on wealth/assets because the earnings measured in a given year make everyone appear more equal than when inheritance, opportunities for advancement, and other factors that span a lifetime are considered.

Economist and Nobel Laureate Amartya Sen argues that development is a measure of a people's ability to make choices about their own futures. He, like

Rist, favors a definition of development with an emphasis on quality of life and challenges Western assumptions about the superiority of material plenty, comfort, economic growth, industrialization, and urbanization.

Colonial Development Initiatives

Although development was not the language of the early colonial period (the late nineteenth century) in Africa, the colonizers had the same goals but under different names: civilizing, introducing Christianity, and encouraging commerce (or a market economy). These three goals are referred to as the three Cs of colonialism. As with most development work to the present day, the civilizing mission reflected Europeans' belief that they had much to offer Africans in terms of improved social systems, land use, and wage labor and thus should be in charge of Africans' betterment. What they did not make explicit was the primary drive behind colonialism, which was to gain access to tropical areas rich in mineral wealth, such as gold, copper, and aluminum, and where desirable tropical commodities could be grown, such as sisal for making rope; rubber for waterproof clothes and eventually tires and many other goods; coffee, tea, sugar, and cocoa for warm morning beverages; and peanut and palm oils for soaps, candies, and lubrication.

Although there were certainly exceptions, Europeans believed African religions were based on superstition; health care systems used witchcraft; and land use was unplanned, disorderly, or irrational. In addition, similarities between European and African systems were downplayed. For example, some African religions were monotheistic, like Christianity, and herbal medicines were used in Europe as in Africa.

Major early efforts by European colonizers forced Africans to tame what were viewed as wild, disorderly landscapes by introducing neat, straight lines via city streets, fenced-in homesteads, and regional roads and railroad tracks. Houses, schools, clinics, and churches were built with straight walls, not the rounded architectural traditions found on much of the continent. Loss of life among Africans forced to labor on European-inspired projects was viewed as a necessary evil on the path to a more civilized life.

Once civilization and Christianity had taken hold to some extent, a major focus of the colonial enterprise became commerce. Colonizers sought to obtain valuable resources from Africa at relatively low cost, often under the guise of developing the region through the introduction of cash crops and mining particularly. Their economic goals included encouraging European settlement that in turn led to ranching and national parks. To facilitate the export of plant, animal, and mineral products, Europeans built infrastructure improvements.

All of these economic changes brought significant cultural consequences to African societies. Subsistence farming on small, scattered plots with multiple crops using the labor of family members and neighbors gave way in some places to cultivating single, large, monocropped plots. Colonizers inadvertently increased gender inequalities by teaching men how to grow cash crops, like coffee and tea, and granting titles to land almost exclusively to males. Women became the primary subsistence producers in many societies, while men sought employment in the wage economy either through agriculture or education. Monocropping reduced soil resiliency, increased the need for additional capital inputs via pesticides and herbicides, and contributed to the loss of indigenous technical knowledge related to traditional farming practices.

When farmers protested the multitude of changes thrust upon them, colonizers generally attributed their complaints to ignorance of the benefits of the new farming methods, laziness, or an unwillingness to change. What the colonizers failed to note was that farmers were rightly concerned about time invested in cash crops at the expense of food crops and that "inept" farmers whose crops failed to grow might be rebels employing "weapons of the weak" (anthropologist James Scott's term)—methods of protesting available to those who hold less power—by boiling seeds before planting them in an effort to be rid of the colonizers and the new crop.

Advances in herding were akin to those undertaken in farming. Colonial leaders effectively created ranching schemes for pastoralists so they could transition from moving about in search of water and pasturelands to settling down near a newly created well and raising fewer fatter, more marketable cattle. As with farmers, changes in lifestyle were challenged but attributed to negative personal attributes such as cultural conservatism and fear of modernization. In reality, some pastoralists fled ranches to make it harder for the tax collector to find them or to keep larger herds with multiple cattle breeds that did not require the veterinary investments associated with the dense congregations of genetically similar cattle found on ranches. In addition, large herds contributed to soil compaction around wells and required considerable capital investments in terms of feed and shelters.

Development initiatives associated with wild animals generally took the form of enclosing areas as hunting preserves and, by the early to mid-twentieth century, enclosing them as conservation areas and national parks for which entry fees could be charged. Those who had relied on subsistence hunting found themselves in need of a new livelihood and uncompensated for lost access to hunting grounds. Many continued to hunt as poachers, risking fines and imprisonment, to be able to feed their families. Hunting animals for sport, but only by the colonizers themselves, was initially allowed under the logic that a gunshot wound to the head made for a rapid and relatively painless death, unlike local people's snares, pitfalls, and poisons. When local people hunted in areas designated for conservation, colonizers attributed their actions to a disregard for animal life and ignorance of the need to protect certain species.

Colonizers also sought to modernize mining practices, moving operations from smaller-scale and largely surface activities to larger-scale production down to considerable depths. For development of the mining industry, dams were constructed for hydroelectric power. While dams did provide the intended energy, they also altered the ecology of the rivers on which they were built and contributed to dramatic rises in the incidence of certain diseases, such as schistosomiasis, which is associated with slow-moving or still water. Mining changed labor dynamics also. Men were the primary mine laborers and often traveled for days to reach a mining camp. They stayed there, usually under contract, for months at a time, returning home with their wages or with clothes and other Western goods bought with their wages; some returned home with venereal disease or Christianity. Women and children remained behind to run the farm and take care of the livestock.

Africans' reluctance to participate in new colonial economic activities drove officials to implement taxes in order to force Africans into the cash economy. Initially taxes could be paid in kind with a measure of grain or a small animal, but by the early twentieth century, most colonies required a tax per family or per male adult that had to be earned through wages or the sale of crops or livestock.

Europeans and their policies also inadvertently introduced and spread diseases and other conditions, including syphilis, influenza, chiggers, rinderpest, and trypanosomiasis (sleeping sickness). Clinics and hospitals created by the colonizers to modernize the existing health care systems often could do little to offset the tremendous loss of life and poor health brought on by their other activities. Rinderpest killed 50 to 90 percent of cattle across much of the continent in the late nineteenth century and led to starvation among pastoralist groups for whom cattle represented wealth as well as a source of nourishment. Starvation was also accelerated by the colonizers' imposition of high, flat taxes that did not take into account the quality of harvests, the amount of rainfall, and other factors considered by local leaders when setting tax rates in earlier times. Geographer Michael Watts documented how within a few years of the arrival of colonial rule, drought became equated with starvation among the Hausa of West Africa. Prior to colonial rule, starvation was a rarity; it only befell populations after several consecutive years of drought depleted their grain reserves. Colonialism brought wholesale changes to African subsistence economies, as Europeans sought to extract economic wealth from the colonies for their own development.

Africa since 1940—The Development Era

After 1940, Europeans began to more directly develop their colonies. In the late 1930s and the 1940s, Africans made increasing demands for more political and economic opportunities, particularly in urban areas. These demands, as well as the devastating impact of World War II, led to a Europe more willing to engage and invest in their colonies. The interwar period marked the beginning of a far more proactive approach. Thus, historian Frederick Cooper has dubbed the years 1940 to 1973 the "development era." European countries used development to hold on to their colonies. In particular, the British Development Act of the 1940s was a response to challenges to imperial power. Even the United States adopted a similar outlook, partly to ensure a role in former colonies. In 1949, Harry Truman, in his inaugural address, announced his concept of a "fair deal" for the entire world. An essential component of this concept was his appeal to the United States and the world to solve the problems of the "underdeveloped areas" of the globe. His words sound very much like those of today's celebrated economist Jeffrey Sachs. He noted that humanity had the capacity to relieve suffering through "more vigorous application of modern scientific and technical knowledge." Projects in the 1950s and 1960s followed the thinking that African countries must imitate the industrial trajectory of Europe, promoting a large role for national planning and for industrial development in many countries. After independence, socialist planning and a desire for industrial development continued.

In a recent study of the most dramatic failure of the ambitions of British late colonialism, the East African Groundnut Scheme of the late 1940s, African economist Matteo Rizzo underscores the impacts of the Groundnut Scheme on Tanzania's Southern Province:

> It funded a dramatic rise in the number of people in wage employment, the improvement of roads, and the building of better health and educational facilities, but it also stimulated rampant inflation of both goods and wages, and social unrest, of which the spread of alcoholism, prostitution, and theft were the most obvious symptoms.

The Scheme's intended outcome was groundnut (peanut) production on a massive scale to provide British corporations such as Unilever with vegetable oil for their products, including soap such as Lux and Lifebuoy and margarine like Blue Band. Alan Wood noted in *The Groundnut Affair* that clearing the land for planting went forward even though the equipment available, tractors and heavy chains, was hardly up to the task, and the soil in the areas with better fertility and more favorable climatic conditions was too compact. Other areas had many trees that needed to be cleared and were home to vicious bees that hospitalized tractor operators. Furthermore, Southern Province was relatively far from any existing ports and railway lines, raising the question of how groundnuts would be transported if successfully grown.

Tanzania was viewed as the recipient of considerable British "aid" and investment, although virtually all of the approximately £49 million spent on the Groundnut Scheme was lost. When Britain withdrew from its African colonies as a condition of independence, it frequently held the new states responsible for repayment for "development projects" and investments. Other colonizers similarly placed conditions on independence: Rwanda could only gain freedom from Belgian rule if it agreed to set aside 10 percent of the country for protected areas for wildlife.

The Groundnut Scheme is an example of some of the potential consequences of outsiders imposing large-scale economic projects. James Scott has critiqued this type of "high-modernist, planned social order" because it excludes local knowledge and experience. In Tanzania, the locals were aware of some of the challenges of the area and thus had not exploited them, making it possible for the British to envision a scheme at all. That it failed was more surprising to the British than to Tanzanians.

After independence in the 1960s, newly emerged African states legally had charge of their natural resources for the first time in more than half a century and assumed that controlling development themselves was their key to political legitimacy. Most Africans and their leaders at the time sought (and still seek) to emulate some variant of classic modernization strategies. They built schools and clinics and increased access to roads, railroads, and major cities. There were, however, some variances. In Tanzania, for example, the colonial discourse about development that saw subsistence-producing peasants as part of the problem shifted under African rule to viewing peasants as part of the solution.

Julius Nyerere, the first president of Tanzania, stated in his inaugural address and later addresses that the country was at war against ignorance, disease, and poverty and was going to fight them with economic and social development that would raise the standard of living. He called on every Tanzanian citizen to join the war effort through what he believed were traditional African ideas of self-help and familyhood (*ujamaa*). He also believed that development was based on using human capital, particularly people's labor and intelligence. These new efforts gave the state great control over development processes. As a result, what development constituted widened, while the number of actors associated with control over that development radically narrowed. Just like under colonialism, these projects tended to be top-down, lacked feedback from local people, and lacked accountability when projects ran amok socially, financially, and/or environmentally.

Despite an auspicious beginning in many newly independent African countries, a combination of factors led to significant indebtedness in the 1980s and 1990s. Many, like Julius Nyerere, sought to improve their people's welfare. Unlike Nyerere, though, many believed that industrialization and big projects, like hydroelectric dams, were part of the solution. Many of these projects, such as the Akosombo Dam that created Lake Volta, the largest reservoir in surface area in the world, in Ghana, did not achieve projected output and saddled the country with a debt to repay that was out of proportion to the benefit of the project. Other large projects included factories to make soap, matches, clothes, and other items that African countries had been importing during the colonial period. Most of these companies were owned by the state and operated inefficiently, resulting in loss of capital.

Internal policy and planning choices in Tanzania merged with some external factors to create a difficult economic environment by the early 1980s. In the mid- and late 1970s, two oil shocks, periods during which the price of oil increases steeply and suddenly, occurred. For African countries trying to develop, the rising cost of a key economic input was detrimental. It was even more disruptive, however, because their main revenue generators—minerals and cash crops like coffee, sisal, and tea—were no longer earning as much on the world market as they had in the late 1950s and early 1960s. Also, African farmers had little control over these fluctuating prices because they were usually set by cartels based elsewhere. Thus, the combination of increasingly expensive imports and decreasing payments for exports put African leaders in a bind. If they wished to continue to build industries, roads, schools, clinics, and so on, then they needed to take out loans.

As African leaders failed to deliver on development promises in the 1970s and 1980s due to a number of external economic factors, such as increasing oil prices and decreasing prices for African exports, the world's financiers saw an opportunity for investment and aid. The International Monetary Fund (IMF) and the World Bank had been lending development money to Latin American countries for several decades, and they were eager to provide loans for African countries as well. Ample resources were available for loan because oil-exporting countries were generating tremendous revenue and were looking for places to invest their petrodollars. The IMF and World Bank promoted loans based on the idea that the money would build industries and lead to economic growth that would enable African countries to repay their loans.

By the early 1980s, a new framework for development was in place that focused on liberal market philosophy and the role of the individual and NGOs rather than the state. This phase was marked by the dominance of economic ideas coming from the United States and exemplified by Ronald Reagan's presidency. This view, dubbed the Washington Consensus, advocated a relatively narrow focus on economic growth based on a balanced budget, exchange rate correction, liberalization of trade and financial flows, privatization, and domestic market regulation. Governments that were willing to undertake these reforms got loans for large-scale development projects, such as road building and agricultural assistance. The result of such reforms for Africans was often higher prices for imports, loss of government jobs, and a rise in health care and education costs, among other things.

In contrast, most African states in the first decades of independence, eager to own their own political and economic processes after decades of colonial rule, had opted for state-led growth (much like the former Soviet Union used between 1930 and late 1980). In the neoliberal view, a productive state needed to open its markets to the rest of the world, thus producing competitive and efficient industries and attracting foreign investment. In the state-led model, African nations would control their industrial and infrastructure development from inside, ensuring access to resources and income for their own citizens. A second priority was that with neoliberalism, African countries were asked to privatize their industries, utilities, health care, and education instead of having them under government control or providing government support for them. One of the aspirations of many early African leaders, like Julius Nyerere, was to ensure widespread access to health care and education. IMF and World Bank policies that subjected Africans to fees for these services restricted access substantially. The third outside expectation was that African countries would reduce the size of government by eliminating jobs and reducing spending. Unemployment led to an increase in the informal economy, such as selling goods on the street or starting an egg-laying business in a peri-urban backyard. Altogether, the expectations that were tied to loans to African governments in the 1980s and 1990s were known as structural adjustment programs (SAPs). African governments thought of them as strings attached to their loans.

While elements of the SAPs had proved successful in other countries at other times, what the promotion of these policies failed to take into account was the fact that most of the industrialized nations backing the loans had not followed such an economic recipe during their formative years. According to economist Ha-Joon Chang, all successful developed countries used infant industry protection, among other measures, during their catching-up periods. In other words, they did not open their industries and markets to those of more developed countries, as African nations have been expected to do. Since the 1980s, the result of opening markets in many African countries has been devastating to local industry. For example, due to importing used clothing from the United States, Zambia went from running several dozen textile factories in 1991 to only eight by 2002. Reducing government expenditures on health care and education meant that access to both is more class-based than it was before in many countries.

While it is arguable how successful SAPs and their accompanying loans have been for African countries, there is little doubt that as a result of these policies, coupled with a significant increase in population and sometimes corrupt leadership, most African countries were not any better off at the beginning of the twenty-first century than they were in 1960 (see map 8.1). One significant reason for this is that African countries never succeeded in generating enough revenue to pay back the loans, in part because they were made to dictators or other corrupt leaders who wasted the money. As many countries transitioned to democratic leadership in the 1980s and 1990s, debt continued to amass from loans as

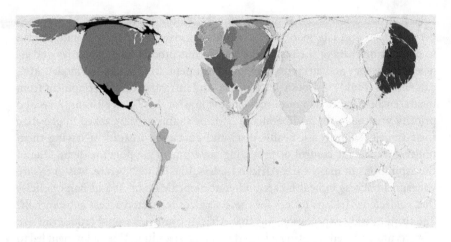

Map 8.1 Proportion of worldwide growth in wealth that occurred there between 1975 and 2002. Courtesy of Sasi Group (University of Sheffield) and Mark Newman (University of Michigan). worldmapper.org, map 171.

leaders sought to catch up to Western standards. By 2005, total debt for Africa continued to rise, despite ever-increasing payments, while aid was falling. Developing world countries were paying $13 on debt repayment for every $1 received in grants. From 1975 to 2005, the poorest 60 countries, dozens of them in Africa, paid $550 billion in principal and interest on $540 billion in loans, but they still had a $523 billion debt burden.

A third phase of postcolonial development began in the late 1990s with increased attention to poverty as it was realized again that aid was benefiting an upper stratum of society rather than the lower strata. The current era is hailed as more participatory and with a focus on sustainable growth, poverty reduction, human development, environmental protection, gender equity, and human rights protection, among other things. It involves significant multilateral aid (from the World Bank and IMF), bilateral aid (from one country to another, such as the United States Agency for International Development giving to the Tanzanian government), and aid from international non-governmental organizations (NGOs), such as World Vision and Care. One sign of this most recent direction is the Heavily Indebted Poor Countries' Initiative (HIPC) of the World Bank that has given well-performing countries debt relief. Yet, Tanzania and other countries contracted large new loans at the same time that old debts were being forgiven. It is not clear that HIPC is a new approach so much as an attempt to make unsustainable debt burdens sustainable and thus more likely to be paid back. This, of course, would benefit the donor countries. As of December 2011, 33 of the world's 39 HIPCs were in sub-Saharan Africa. Thus, their debt ties to the lending countries remain as strong as ever.

Some also argue that this most recent era is marked by the collapse of heretofore accepted distinctions between external and internal actors. Thus, what began in the second half of the twentieth century as a distinct form of external intervention—foreign aid—has come around to merging with African states' political and economic goals in an unprecedented way. The result is a state that receives a large amount of funds from international donors and answers to their priorities as much as, if not more than, their own citizens. Thus, as governance specialist Geir Sundet argues, development has become the African state's most important legitimizing tool. And as political scientist Graham Harrison claims, it makes the most sense now to think of donors as part of the state. African gatekeeper states are as concerned with exports as they are with the flow of aid. "Gatekeeper state" is historian Frederick Cooper's term. Such states focus their attention outside their boundaries for the revenue flow that is essential to their existence. The consequence, however, is that leaders of such states have little incentive to pay attention to the needs and voices of their own citizens. A gatekeeper state is a legacy of colonial rule.

As the above suggests, foreign development aid has played a massive role in many agriculturally based countries over the last 50 years as they have attempted to "catch up" with more industrialized countries. In 1990, aid constituted 30 percent of Tanzania's entire GDP. In 1992, *Family Mirror,* a private newspaper in Dar es Salaam, reported that two-thirds of the national budget was comprised of foreign aid. According to another Tanzanian newspaper, in 2007–2008, foreign aid accounted for 42 percent of the national budget. In the Rukwa region of western Tanzania, 80 percent of the development budget came from NORAD, the Norwegian Development Agency during the 1970s, 1980s, and 1990s.

Such significant foreign support of a nation's budget meant at least two things. First, monies were targeted at specific projects or interventions, such as road construction and repair, health, or clean water projects that could easily be tracked. Second, foreign development projects helped to expand an African state's power because they could intervene in projects that they otherwise would not have the funds or personnel to engage in, such as those studied by historian James Ferguson in Lesotho.

Development Now

Decades after colonialism has ended, African leaders, foreign governments, and Western development experts are still trying to develop Africa. Jeffrey Sachs is one of the best-known economists of our time. He has called on his current generation to bring an end to worldwide poverty. His book *The End of Poverty* outlines how to make it happen, and his Millennium Development Villages are his plans in action. He argues that with very little money, people in the United States could do a tremendous amount to improve the lives of those in poverty, including promoting more productive agriculture and digging wells for clean drinking water. It sounds promising and doable. The problem is that his call to action and similar ones have antecedents that remind us that such an approach is not new. (A good example is Greg Mortenson's Central Asian Institute, which was building schools in Afghanistan and Pakistan until a *60 Minutes* report on the organization revealed that it had spent more money in the United States than overseas and that many of the schools were not in operation.) Recall Truman's plea in 1949 and the three Cs of colonialism. In fact, calls to develop Africa stand in a long line of attempts to improve the lives of those in the South by those in the North.

Truman's call played on a common feeling among those in the United States and other developed countries: that they are materially, at least, better off than those elsewhere and that material well-being is the primary goal of human societies. Further, it is assumed that the latter would benefit from our help. The implication is that development is easy and anyone can effectively help improve others' lives by writing a check or contributing time or labor.

But development is not easy. It does not have simple fixes, unfortunately suggesting otherwise would discourage people from giving; development is a huge industry, one that, sadly, encourages us to think ahistorically. Between 1960 and 2000, approximately $1.7 trillion was spent on development aid, with very little to show for these efforts. Despite such knowledge, there remains a strong impulse to give aid. An April 2012 report in the *Washington Post* on the provision of clean cook stoves to families in developing countries illustrates this reluctance to give up even when evidence points to the lack of efficacy of a project. Traditional cook stoves are made of mud, and they use charcoal, wood, or dung for fuel. They are usually located inside a building with poor ventilation. The fire from the stoves releases particulate matter that causes pneumonia, lung cancer, and heart disease. Because women and girls do most of the cooking, they are most affected. In addition, the cook stoves' use of wood and charcoal contribute to deforestation.

Since 2010, the United States pledged $105 million to provide clean cook stoves to 100 million households. Former secretary of state Hilary Clinton and actress Julia Roberts are two well-known people who have spoken out about the problem, promoting clean cook stoves that don't require as much fuel and that have chimneys to vent the particulate matter out of the house.

But as the newspaper reported, a three-year study of clean cook stove use in India that involved 2,600 households in 44 villages found little long-term impact. By the end of the study, most families were barely using the stove at all, and those who were still using them were not using them correctly. The result was no significant difference in the air quality of the home or the health of the family members. From the perspective of a historian, perhaps what is most troubling about the article is its conclusion that simply more information would make a clean cook stove development program a success. While that is no doubt possible, a serious examination of what made the program a failure would be more helpful than a relatively innocent optimistic attitude. For the entire article, see http://articles.washingtonpost.com/2012-04-16/national/35451170_1_indoor-air -air-quality-lung-cancer.

Like the clean cook stove project, as anthropologist Arturo Escobar noted more than a decade ago, much of what Westerners have sought to do under the rubric of development has been narrowly conceived and ultimately detrimental to the interests of the intended beneficiaries. Our statistics, our plans, and our notions of success (and failure—i.e., poverty) are all a product of our particular historical trajectory, sometimes intertwined with our guilt over our awareness of materially having much more than most. Development expert William Easterly attributes development project failures partly to the egos of those in charge. He suggests that many development economists, Jeffrey Sachs included, as well as the World Bank, United Nations, USAID, and most others engaged in development work, continue to operate as "planners" as opposed to "searchers" and impose their development initiatives based on what they think should work elsewhere with relatively little consideration for how local conditions and cultures might make such plans less relevant. Easterly is a proponent of incentives rather than "conditionalities" (conditions put on loans, or "do as we say, or you will not get the loan") and notes that without accountability, grand goals simply get pushed from one decade to another without having been reached. For example, in 1977, the UN set 1990 as the year to have universal access to water/sanitation; now the goal is 2015. Also in 1990, the UN set 2000 as the year to achieve universal primary school enrollment, and now the goal is 2015 as well.

Almost 150 years since the beginning of colonization and 70 years since Truman's speech, Africans' relationship with the rest of the world has been determined to a larger extent than anyone could ever have imagined by such ideas. Both Africans and Westerners have much faith in development, in part because all are living in an economic era, one in which the most salient measures of success are in terms of economic production and growth, and labor employment. For example, the possible reactions to the two seemingly contradictory economic indicators at the beginning of the chapter both have inherent within them a sense that African poverty is a problem that needs to be solved. Such a reaction leads to an unwarranted sense of power and responsibility for complex problems, far away, that are unlikely to be "solved" more successfully than before.

As Escobar argues, development as an agenda (or underdevelopment as a reality that must be modified) has defined the Third World since the close of World War II. And development economics has been the ideology supporting efforts to change that "reality." Development economics is a culturally and historically constructed solution to an equally culturally and historically constructed problem (poverty). African ideas regarding their needs and cultural values are rarely considered.

There are many cases in which Western assistance has not had the outcome anticipated due to limited understanding of and experience with local cultural conditions and decision making in households faced with chronic material poverty. In *The White Man's Burden,* development economist William Easterly describes how the gift of millions of mosquito nets to Zambia by one large aid agency had no impact on malaria rates because recipients used the nets for wedding veils, fishing, and other unanticipated uses. He contrasts the failure in Zambia with that of an aid agency, Population Services International (PSI), in which members are held accountable for outcomes. In Malawi, PSI staff followed a locally devised distribution plan in which local nurses received a minor financial incentive to explain the nets' importance to pregnant women and new mothers and sell them at a fraction of their true cost. PSI-distributed mosquito nets in Malawi cut malaria rates dramatically.

Providing effective development assistance is difficult and has rarely occurred because outsiders do not hold the answers to African development. Aid donors and African governments have failed to listen to the real concerns and ideas of ordinary people. And such ordinary people have made extraordinary contributions to the world economy.

African Contributions to Development

Despite the widely held view that the West must help Africa, Africans, both on and off the continent, are helping to develop and otherwise improve the lives of their fellow Africans. African countries' development assistance is substantial relative to the continent's resources and demonstrates an innate capacity for development that is often ignored. By highlighting such activities, outsiders' perceptions of Africa as a charity will become more in line with reality. Moreover, Africans contribute to the welfare and development of wealthier nation in ways that are rarely acknowledged.

Whereas many in wealthier countries view themselves as generous for donating their time or funds to those in need, their level of giving is often much less than they imagine. In *The End of Poverty,* Sachs notes that when asked what percentage of the U.S. federal budget Americans think goes to foreign aid, their median estimate is 25 percent, and when asked how much of the budget *should* go to foreign aid, the median response is 10 percent; yet, less than 1 percent of the federal budget is spent that way. Not only do Americans tend to overestimate what the United States does for others, but they are unaware of the substantial self-help initiatives undertaken in Africa or that much of the development work undertaken on their behalf has not been effective.

Africa's Development Assistance to Wealthier Countries

One significant way that several African countries assist those with much higher GDPs and other measures of wealth is via the provision of medical professionals, including doctors, nurses, midwives, and pharmacists. According to the World Health Organization (WHO), there is a global deficiency of approximately 4.3 million health workers and 3 million health professionals. In many countries, these issues are caused by a combination of local factors, including poor planning of human resources, deficient or unsafe working conditions with heavy workloads, long hours, work locations with little infrastructure, inadequate pay, and little professional independence. Thus, although African countries often train a sufficient number of health professionals to meet the needs of their people, many face a severe shortfall of medical professionals because once they have obtained their degrees, they leave the continent to take jobs in wealthier countries. This represents a very large investment in education and training provided by African states that does not benefit their own citizens but those of wealthier countries. The outmigration of health professionals from poorer countries to wealthier ones is a global phenomenon that weakens already strained and inadequate health care systems. But Africa, with only around 1.3 percent of the global health workforce and approximately 25 percent of the disease burden and the largest number of HIPCs, can least afford to lose its physicians, nurses, midwives, and pharmacists, as the recent Ebola outbreaks testify. Although there has been some improvement in the number of health professionals in Africa since the 1980s, in the early twenty-first century, Africa still has only 1 health worker of any kind for every 1,000 people. This is well below the recommended 2.5 per 1,000 needed to meet the United Nations' Millennium Development Goals (MDGs) that seek to end poverty, improve maternal and child health, combat HIV/AIDS, and more by 2015 (http://www.un.org/millenniumgoals). Furthermore, 37 of 47 sub-Saharan countries do not meet the minimum recommended WHO standard of 20 doctors per 100,000 people.

In sub-Saharan Africa, Ghana and South Africa have some of the highest rates of emigration by highly educated individuals, including health professionals. According to a 2005 World Bank study, 47 percent of college-educated Ghanaians live abroad, and 54 percent of physicians who trained in Ghana between 1999 and 2004 left to work elsewhere such that in 2004, Ghana had only 0.15 physicians per 1,000 people and 0.92 nurses per 1,000 people. In 2004, South Africa had 0.77 physicians per 1,000 people and 4.08 nurses per 1,000 people, but the outmigration of nurses relative to other health professionals was especially high. South Africa reported more than 4,000 doctor vacancies and over 32,000 nurse vacancies. Outmigration of health professions reduces the likelihood of Ghana, South Africa, and other African countries meeting three MDGs directly related to health: reducing child mortality; improving maternal health; and combating

HIV/AIDS, TB, malaria, and other diseases. At the beginning of the twenty-first century, of the approximately 5,330 physicians from sub-Saharan Africa practicing in the United States, 86 percent come from Ghana, South Africa, or Nigeria. The statistics are similar for Europe. For health professionals in particular, unless migration is temporary, the financial capital accrued back home via remittances (funds earned and sent back home by Africans living outside of their home country) by health professionals does not balance the detrimental effects of losing a much-needed health workforce. Until very recently, there was a large private health care sector in the United Kingdom that actively poached health professionals, often providing assistance with visas, relocation expenses, and housing. Complaints from African governments have helped to slow this practice.

In addition to supporting health care systems in wealthier countries, Africans also support the well-being of non-Africans in surprising ways through civic service opportunities such as the Peace Corps and other agencies. While the stated objective of the Peace Corps may be the support of African development, the reality is often different. Testimonials, memoirs, blogs, and other reports from returned Peace Corps volunteers who served in Africa suggest that U.S. volunteers almost unanimously agree that in their two or three years of service, they received more from Africa and Africans than they gave. The following case study is from Ghana, but it reflects broader trends.

In 1961, Ghana was the first African country—indeed, the first anywhere in the world—to receive Peace Corps volunteers (PCVs). For the first three decades, 50 to 80 percent of PCVs in Ghana, as throughout West Africa, worked in education, yet PCVs generally helped to very temporarily address teacher shortages without improving the overall education system via teacher training. Many finished their assignments questioning whether their service had improved the socioeconomic standing of the country in which they served because their suggestions for improvement of the Peace Corps program generally were not implemented if they did not fit with the U.S. government's image of the program.

In more recent decades, PCVs have been engaged in a wider variety of assignments, including assisting refugee populations, halting deforestation, and assisting with the establishment of small businesses. But more recent PCVs, like those before them, do not believe that they make substantial contributions to their African host country in their official areas of assistance. Instead, PCVs report personal benefits from their PCV experience in Africa: romantic attachments (70 percent of PCVs marry another PCV); career choice and advancement; and personal fulfillment through self-development, maturity, and friendships.

Whereas African states invest many years training doctors and other health professionals who frequently wind up providing health care services to the world's wealthiest for decades, PCVs only receive three months of training and generally return to the United States after two years of service. Others who provide assistance to Africans via mission trips, study-abroad programs with a service component, and other volunteer opportunities generally spend no more than a few weeks on the continent and lack even the three months of country-specific training of PCVs. As such, there is a major disconnect between the informal, but effective, long-term development assistance provided by African medical professionals to wealthier countries and what is typically provided by well-meaning but generally untrained or undertrained individuals from the United States and other wealthier countries through more formal programs to African communities. In these examples, instead of Westerners effectively helping Africans, Africans are helping Westerners.

Africans' Self-Help and Service Initiatives

Kenya's Harambee and Green Belt Movements

In 1963, Jomo Kenyatta, the first president of independent Kenya, used the Swahili term *harambee,* which loosely translates to "let's all pull together," to encourage all communities, especially poor rural ones with no elementary or secondary schools, to work together to hold fund-raisers to build schools and rewarded those that did so with government-paid teachers. Twenty-five years later, there were more than 600 *harambee* schools, and three-quarters of all Kenyan secondary school students obtained their formal education at them. Beyond transforming Kenya's educational system, local communities have applied the *harambee* concept to complete health facilities, water projects, cattle dips, churches, soil erosion, and afforestation projects.

In the mid-1970s, Wangari Maathai began a reforestation project in her home region, seeking employment for her neighbors through planting trees in central Kenya. Her work eventually became known as the Green Belt Movement, through which rural Kenyan women plant trees to combat deforestation, slow soil erosion, and restore their primary fuel source for cooking. Since the movement was established, over 40 million trees have been planted, and more than 30,000 women have been empowered via training in food processing, bee keeping, ecotourism, and other income-generating trades. In 2004, Maathai became the first African woman to receive the Nobel Prize. Maathai died in 2011, but her legacy lives on through the books she wrote, the lives she touched, the Green Belt Movement she created (http://www.greenbeltmovement.org), and the Wangari Maathai Institute for Peace & Environmental Studies at the University of Nairobi named in her honor.

African Entrepreneurs and Intellectuals

Africa is the birthplace of many entrepreneurs and creative thinkers like Maathai, but not many beyond Nelson Mandela and Archbishop Desmond Tutu of South

Africa and former UN Secretary General Kofi Annan of Ghana have their work widely advertised. Sudanese-born mobile telephone tycoon and philanthropist Dr. Mohamed "Mo" Ibrahim is one of the few to have his work somewhat regularly appear in the popular press—namely, his prize for good governance and excellent leadership in Africa that has been granted via his foundation (http://www.moibrahimfoundation.org/en) since 2007. Other telecommunications pioneers include the D.R. Congo's Miko Rwayitare and Zimbabwe's Strive Masiyiwa. Many African leaders receive little recognition for their impressive work.

African Volunteers and Service Providers

Western media portrayals of African states frequently highlight political instability, civil unrest, famine, and the generation of refugees. Such stories highlight outsider efforts to assist Africans via the United Nations High Commission for Refugees (UNHCR), the United Nations Children's Fund (UNICEF), Oxfam, and related agencies, but they rarely showcase what Africans are doing to assist others during times of crisis. Yet, African assistance to other Africans and the global community has been large scale and, in terms of development assistance, at times more effective than that of official relief agencies.

During World War II, more than 1.35 million Africans from what became 30 independent countries served in the armed forces. Approximately 166,500 Africans fighting in Asia helped defeat the Japanese. Some Africans enlisted, many were conscripted, and most were treated poorly. Ethiopia suffered 95,000 civilian and 5,000 military deaths; South Africa had around 11,900 military dead, but for most of Africa, the number who lost their lives in the fight against fascism is not known.

As African countries gained independence, many were not content to have their freedom while others remained colonized. Ghana sent troops to what would become the Democratic Republic of Congo and Zimbabwe to assist in liberation struggles there. While still colonized, liberation troops in Rhodesia (now Zimbabwe) assisted independence efforts in neighboring Mozambique. By the 1960s, dozens of newly independent Africa countries became members of the Organization of African Unity (OAU), which helped to end colonial and minority rule on the continent by giving weapons, training, and military bases to liberation groups in Rhodesia and the African National Congress and Pan-African Congress in apartheid South Africa. In the late 1970s, Tanzanian troops helped to oust Uganda's dictator, Idi Amin.

As power struggles took place in still relatively newly independent states, Africans continued to assist other Africans in need. In the 1990s, over 100,000 Togolese and more than 100,000 Liberians sought refuge in Ghana. Togolese who crossed into neighboring Ghana, like the Liberians coming from farther away, were offered assistance at UN-established camps. Within months, the British

Broadcasting Corporation (BBC) noted that the predominantly ethnic Ewe Togolese refugees had largely "disappeared" into Ghana's Volta region, having been absorbed into local Ewe people's homes. Refugees frequented local clinics and paid for health services there rather than use the free services offered in UN refugee camps. Liberians arrived from a nonneighboring West African country; they did not share ethnicity with Ghanaians and wound up relying on UNHCR camps that quickly grew unwelcoming in terms of sanitation, security, and other amenities. In 1990s Ghana, local people provided refugees with more effective assistance than the world's primary organization devoted to the same. Such assistance rarely makes the popular presses of industrialized countries, but it occurs regularly.

During the 1994 Rwandan genocide, many Western countries pulled out their UN peacekeepers, but those from Ghana and other African countries continued to serve. During the crisis in Darfur, Sudan, many made their way to shelter in the Democratic Republic of Congo. There are many success stories in Africa, but the success is rarely considered newsworthy beyond specialized news programs, such as CNN's *Inside Africa* or the reports of development agencies.

Africans also provide considerable service in times of peace and stability. In recent decades, many African countries have required a National Service commitment of one or more years, especially from those who have received educational support from the government. Men and women perform their National Service in health, education, and other areas. Since the establishment of Ghana's National Service Scheme in 1973, more than 50,000 individuals have assisted with nation building via service to schools, the health sector, and the government. In Botswana, from 1980 to 1999, around 5,500 individuals were called on to perform a year of National Service annually in remote schools and health clinics. Akin to Teach for America, the secondary goals of National Service include providing employment to recent graduates, enhancing the personal development of participants, and exposing participants to other languages and cultures in their country.

Remittances

In addition to these self-help and development initiatives on individual, community, institutional, and country levels, remittances—funds earned and sent back home by Africans living outside of their home country—rank among several African countries' top foreign exchange earners. The informal channels on which many rely to transfer money home (such as cash carried by a friend rather than a bank transfer) make precise accounting of remittances impossible. Approximately 25 million adult Africans live abroad whose annual financial contributions to their families and communities collectively amount to around $40 billion. For Africa as a whole, remittances represent 50 percent more than net Official Development Assistance (ODA) from all sources, including individual governments and multilateral agencies and for most countries also exceed foreign direct investment from businesses and other nongovernmental sources. World Bank studies suggest that remittances represent 5 to 25 percent of GDP in the top recipient countries. Lesotho obtains about 25 percent of its GDP from remittances; Togo, Cape Verde, Senegal, Guinea-Bissau, and the Gambia get about 8 to 10 percent; and Liberia, Sudan, Nigeria, and Kenya get about 5 to 6 percent. Although Nigeria is only around tenth in percentage of GDP from remittances, the country leads in dollar amount received: around $10 billion annually. Remittances are not currently viewed as part of official aid to Africa, although development specialist Roger Riddell notes there have been discussions to include remittances when calculating ODA.

Africa's Development Assistance: Perceptions and Reality

Africans' self-help initiatives do not fit with outsiders' images propagated in the media of needy, starving people awaiting handouts in a conflict-ridden region. Believing that Africans need us makes us feel better and reinforces our overestimation of the value of our assistance. Africans generally do not desire charity, but they appreciate gifts and reciprocal relationships. In Zimbabwe, the majority Shona population distinguishes among a "free gift" (*handwa*), a "generous gift" (*gomborero*), and a "gift given to predispose the receiver in the giver's favor" (*tsinzo*). Thus, used clothing from Westerners might be *handwa* or even *tsinzo*, but not *gomborero*. In Ghana, a true gift is one that "hurts" because it is difficult, financially or emotionally, to give away. Similar sentiments exist in other African countries, such that remittances sent by family members who are struggling financially may be valued more than somewhat larger sums of money, material goods, or even time and labor given by outsiders who are viewed as sacrificing relatively little. Much ODA falls into what the Shona called *tsinzo*—a gift given in the hopes of getting something in return—because donor governments generally expect positive or improved international relations from recipients of their aid.

A major disconnect between the image of African development assistance and reality stems from aid organizations doing very little in the way of self-assessment or keeping themselves accountable for assistance given; thus, aid failures can be blamed on Africans, not donors. Although much donor lingo has shifted to "partnerships" as opposed to charity or aid, the reality remains that they are uneven partnerships. The donor gets to set the rules and frequently decides what development projects to pursue and in what areas. Even today, Africans have very little say in whether they are recipients of development aid and, if so, for what projects.

Africans' assistance to wealthier countries and other Africans is not only underreported but for several reasons is more likely to be effective than that from outsiders. Africans assisting other Africans are more likely to understand the cultural context.

Recognizing that African cultures and economies offer us as much as we might offer them is an important first step in ensuring that Westerners do not continue to repeat the mistakes of the past. Wealth in Africa is as much relational as material. Western development has not recognized this reality. It has been based on a narrow version of economic development that focuses on material poverty.

Standard measures of wealth, including GDP, suggest that the West has much to offer Africa, but alternative measures of well-being, several in the field of "happiness economics" that have been developed since the late twentieth century, offer a more nuanced picture. In 2006, the New Economics Foundation released its first Happy Planet Index (HPI), an alternative means of measuring fulfillment by country based on experienced well-being, life expectancy, and ecological footprint. In the 2006 HPI study, 31 African countries ranked higher than the United States. Although the United States' lower ranking was due in large part to its substantial ecological footprint, the high scores from so many African countries suggest a greater ability to appreciate what one has, including strong social relations built in part by investing in social capital, rather than suffering the "affluenza" of the world's wealthiest—the anxious condition of having much material wealth but always wanting more.

Giving is a way of feeling good, and the United States has a substantial history of philanthropy but almost none in assessment of the actual outcomes of the same. For the most part, Americans have exemplified the "headless heart"— those who give out of compassion but without first meaningfully learning about Africans' self-help initiatives and whether our aid will undermine or support those efforts.

It should be clear by now that ordinary Africans' experiences with development do not reflect their own experiences or desires so much as those that have resulted from their engagement with the West and its institutions and ideas over the past 150 years or so. For all the advancements that colonialism might have brought to different colonies, they are minuscule compared to what the major colonial powers shared in terms of their approach to development in Africa— namely, to "civilize" or "Europeanize" Africans. Sadly, many postindependence African leaders followed in the colonizers' development footsteps, placing a premium on catching up with the West. These ideas are often most easily expressed through statistics that often show that Africans have failed to develop by traditional measures, such as income and industrialization. Such representations of Africa and Africans result in development projects for the continent and its people. But these projects reveal much more about the preoccupations and prejudices of the colonizers and do-gooders than Africans themselves.

As this chapter demonstrates, and as subsequent chapters will illustrate, many forms of economic transaction have been sidelined by a focus on official development assistance, the market, and rationality within economics. What outsiders might call "generosity," people in other societies might see as a different kind of economic relationship. Illuminating these behaviors in societies outside of the West will render such values and activities more visible in our own societies.

Foreign economic development needs to be pushed aside to make way for local development based on ideas and programs that stem from African values. Few Westerners would welcome foreign ideas for how to direct our country's future. African approaches are not necessarily superior, but they emphasize the value and contributions of local knowledge and practices, including African ideas about economics, and they build on the strengths of African societies, including their own efforts to develop themselves and to contribute to the global economy, which are the subjects of chapters 9 and 10.

Suggestions for Further Reading

Deborah Brautigam, *The Dragon's Gift: The Real Story of China in Africa* (Oxford: Oxford University Press, 2011). This book examines China's decades of involvement with African countries, comparing China's policies and actions with regard to development assistance with what has been publicized in the Western media.

Robert Chambers, *Rural Development: Putting the Last First* (Harlow, U.K.: Longman, 1983; repr., Harlow, U.K.: Prentice Hall, 1995). Chambers contends that rural poverty is often unseen or misperceived by outsiders, including researchers, scientists, fieldworkers, and administrators. He describes how development is undermined when we fail to appreciate the richness and validity of rural people's knowledge.

Ha-Joon Chang, *Kicking Away the Ladder: Development Strategy in Historical Perspective* (London: Anthem, 2002). Chang returns to economic history to demonstrate that the policies and institutions currently recommended to developing countries are not the same as those used by developed nations as they were industrializing and modernizing.

Frederick Cooper, *Africa since 1940: The Past of the Present* (Cambridge: Cambridge University Press, 2002). Cooper seeks to revise the chronology of recent Africa history, suggesting that there is great continuity between the late colonial and early postcolonial periods, from 1940 to the 1970s. It is a convincing analysis and helps to illuminate the choices that early African leaders made.

William Easterly, *The White Man's Burden: Why the West's Efforts to Aid the Rest Have Done So Much Ill and So Little Good* (New York: Penguin, 2006). Easterly argues that most development aid has failed as a result of top-down planning (much like Scott below). One reason is that aid planners are not accountable to the population their projects are designed to help but instead to their own organization or donors back home.

Stephen Ellis, *Season of Rains: Africa in the World* (Chicago: University of Chicago Press, 2012). With a foreword by Desmond Tutu, *Season of Rains* notes the need to rethink Africa's place in time to understand it beyond the typical media images and in all its complexity.

Arturo Escobar, *Encountering Development: The Making and Unmaking of the Third World* (Princeton, N.J.: Princeton University Press, 1995). In some ways, this is an earlier version of Rist's book, but the focus here is on the Third World and the ways in which it has been shaped and defined by the idea of development.

Graham Harrison, "Post-Conditionality Politics and Administrative Reform: Reflections on the Cases of Uganda and Tanzania," *Development and Change* 32, no. 4 (2001): 657–679. Harrison traces the ways that states with extreme external dependence lose sovereignty as donors' and creditors' roles in budget allocations and political decisions become integrated into the state.

Moky Makura, *Africa's Greatest Entrepreneurs* (London: Penguin, 2009). Mo Ibrahim and more than a dozen others are profiled.

Steven Radelet, *Emerging Africa: How 17 Countries Are Leading the Way* (Washington, D.C.: Center for Global Development, 2010). With an introduction by Ellen Johnson Sirleaf, *Emerging Africa* describes the often overlooked positive changes in democracy, technology, and economic management that have taken place on much of the continent since the mid-1990s.

Gilbert Rist, *The History of Development: From Western Origins to Global Faith*, trans. Patrick Camiller, 3rd ed. (London: Zed Books, 2009). This powerful book argues that a Western idea has spread across the globe and become a religion for political and economic leaders everywhere.

Matteo Rizzo, "What Was Left of the Groundnut Scheme? Development Disaster and Labour Market in Southern Tanganyika, 1946–1952," *Journal of Agrarian Change* 6, no. 2 (2006): 205–238. The East African Groundnut Scheme is the most dramatic and most cited British development failure. Rizzo examines the role of the labor supply in the failure of the project, as well as the impact of the need for scheme labor on the subsistence economy.

Jeffrey Sachs, *The End of Poverty: Economic Possibilities for Our Time* (New York: Penguin, 2005). Sachs believes that with more financial commitment from the United States and other countries, some of the fundamental development challenges that African and other countries face can be eliminated. Sachs is also behind the Millennium Development Goals of the United Nations and Millennium Development Villages.

James Scott, *Seeing Like a State: How Certain Schemes to Improve the Human Condition Have Failed* (New Haven, Conn.: Yale University Press, 1988). Scott analyzes a variety of failed large-scale authoritarian plans. His conclusion is that local, practical knowledge is essential to successful political, economic, or social change. For this reason he is skeptical about the potential success of any large-scale development planning.

Michael Watts, *Silent Violence: Food, Famine, and Peasantry in Northern Nigeria* (Berkeley: University of California Press, 1983). Watts examines the food crisis of the African Sahel during the 1970s, arguing that famines are socially produced, not natural occurrences.

9 African Contributions

Economics, Politics, and Society

With Heidi Frontani

As GLOBALIZING FORCES encourage homogenization and integration into limited and powerful institutions, societies are losing myriad ways of thinking about economics, politics, and society. This chapter highlights the ways Africans have constructed and thought about their societies, particularly in response to oppressive colonization and accompanying economic ideas. Africans have made substantial contributions to the ways human societies have sought to solve economic and political problems. Many solutions build on their own cultural ideas and practices but result in institutions and responses that are emulated elsewhere and recognized internationally. When the focus is only on why Africa needs our help, these kinds of ideas and institutions do not receive as much attention as they deserve.

This chapter examines three kinds of responses to challenging problems. The first is a series of political and judicial organizations aimed at changing the racist policies of South Africa in the twentieth century. The second contribution is the powerful role that women have played in African politics in many places, with particular focus on the role of Liberian women in ending the civil war in Liberia. The final contribution is the development of a huge informal economy as a response to a weak formal economy that does not have the capacity to absorb the numbers of people who desire gainful employment. These responses illuminate Africans as actors in their own history, diagnosing problems and working to fix them by using a variety of tactics. Their solutions might not always look like solutions North Americans would employ, but this wider range of possibilities suggests that problems can be solved in a variety of ways. Their solutions also suggest that culture can play a role, although not an exclusive one, in the kinds of solutions that are considered and in their effectiveness. Thus, it is not always the case that outsiders can help mobilize opposition or organizations that will be as effective as those that grow organically.

Geographical Place

This chapter highlights three places: South Africa, Liberia, and Tanzania. The first two are sometimes difficult to include in a broad coverage of the African continent because their histories were somewhat different from the more generalized African experience. South Africa remained under white minority rule until 1994, decades after most of the rest of the continent had achieved African majority rule. South Africa was a settler colony like Southern Rhodesia, Kenya, and Algeria. Although it experienced a fair amount of violence in the transition to African rule, it never fell into full-scale rebellion or revolution like Southern Rhodesia and Algeria, due in part to the charismatic and courageous leadership of Nelson Mandela and others.

Liberia was never colonized by a European power. Like Sierra Leone, its neighbor, it became the focus of African resettlement in the nineteenth century. As freed slaves increased in number in the United States, Britain, Canada, and the Caribbean, whites living in those societies feared having to live near a large free black population, and they encouraged blacks to return to Africa. Thousands did and settled in the coastal areas of both Liberia and Sierra Leone. The result of such repatriation efforts in both places was, similar to colonialism, a cultural imposition in the sense that Americo-Liberians, as they came to be called, were usually Christian and considered themselves superior to the native Liberians because of their religion, experiences, and education. Americo-Liberians controlled the Liberian government; bestowed favors on American corporations, such as Firestone Tire and Rubber Company; and received sporadic aid from the U.S. government from 1820 to 1980. Following the collapse of Americo-Liberian rule, a civil war ensued, enabled by illicit trade in diamonds. The transition to a more democratic regime in the late 1990s was hard-fought and involved children and women.

Sources and Methodologies

Several of the events discussed in this chapter occurred recently, and many websites are available for more information on African solutions to these issues. Links to documents, organizations, and film trailers provide a multimedia approach to the content, as well as the ability to investigate related ideas. But it also brings the challenge of sifting through information to find what is most useful. Like any source, the Internet is only as valuable as the rigor of the author. The motivations of those posting information must be considered in the same light as the motivations of colonial anthropologists or Muslim travelers. The background and affiliation of website authors are important factors in determining the reliability of the content. Citations and attributions are just as important online as in other forms of scholarly work. One way to assess the validity of website content is to see if it cites other authors or scholars. This is a sign that the author is cognizant of a wider network of ideas to which theirs contribute. Similarly, using Internet sources alongside other sources makes for a stronger and likely more accurate representation of the past.

Ethnicity in Africa

The first two examples covered in this chapter illuminate efforts that bridge African ethnic divides. Ethnic identities have become an integral part of the narrative of African history, both inside and outside the continent. But like much else, these identities have histories of their own, revealing more flexibility and nuance than is often assumed from an outside glance.

Before formal colonialism, cultural identities (largely tied to linguistic differences) were important, as previous chapters reveal. Baganda identity from some time after the twelfth century was associated with a language, an enlargement of political scale, and geographical location that in turn was tied to a variety of spirits. Sabi speakers emphasized matrilineal relationships during the Middle Time Frame and recognized a common deity. There also were important distinctions in terms of subsistence strategies so that Bantu-speaking farmers and Batwa gatherer-hunters in Central Africa 4,000 years ago or more interacted across recognized cultural divides. Such divisions began with the development of agriculture and the practice of pastoralism and choices different peoples in different regions of the continent made. Africans, then, have always had identities that differentiated them from others on the basis of language, subsistence, political organization, spiritual practice, or a combination of one or more of these factors. Yet, people outside the society and after the fact have named some of these distinctions (such as Sabi speakers) and applied labels, neglecting other distinctions. Cultural and linguistic identity was one of several ways Africans could choose to relate to others in times past. Clan membership, identification with spirits, and marriage could provide different ties. Previous chapters also make it clear that such identities were fluid and malleable, depending on the circumstances, so the Ariaal are a recent ethnic identity forged out of several pastoral societies with longer histories.

Christian missionaries and colonial officials in the mid- to late nineteenth century played a prominent role in solidifying ethnic identities. Missionaries came from a variety of societies, and each society tended to work with one or a few related ethnicities at a time. One of the first tasks for both Protestant and Catholic missionaries was to translate some of the Bible, hymns, or the catechism into the local language. Doing so often meant choosing one language or ethnicity to represent multiple groups, as translation into every language in the area would have been onerous. African translators were essential in carrying out this work, and they, too, helped to shape ethnic identities by their affiliations, choices, and knowledge. In this way, some ethnicities gained more prominence and stature than others. Similarly, metropolitan countries sought to minimize investment in their colonies for the first decades. One way to do so was by establishing a system of indirect rule, whereby Europeans occupied the highest levels of authority and Africans the lowest levels. But cohesive administrative units had to be established, and they often were created around perceived ethnic boundaries. One example of an ethnicity that was created by colonial officials is that of the Gusii in western Kenya, as described by historian Timothy Parsons. In the nineteenth century, those whose descendants would become Gusii identified as members of clans not an ethnic community. Gusii was what other Africans with different cultural practices called them. Colonial officials picked allies to help administer Gusii people and thus created chiefs and an ethnicity where neither had existed before. Such labels became a source of identity and belonging in a rapidly changing society, as historian Bruce Berman has argued.

Typically, Africans served as Native Authorities for a particular ethnicity, tasked with relaying directives and initiatives from the capital, representing the interests and needs of their people, and collecting taxes and sometimes recruiting labor on behalf of the colonial state. Native Authority tasks were often at odds with those they represented, as Africans rarely wanted to pay taxes or to follow directives from hundreds of miles away that were not tailored to their particular situation. Thus, the Native Authority, while trying to maintain the respect of his people and represent their views, had to engage in tasks that were odious to those same people. Not only was the position of Native Authority challenging, but finding the appropriate person to serve required colonial officials to favor one leader over another, and sometimes one subgroup over another, thus solidifying some identities, while weakening others.

In settler colonies, where Europeans hoped to establish a home and viable economic enterprises, land was taken from Africans who administered it by lineage or family. To compensate for land loss and ensure administrative ease, in Kenya, Southern Rhodesia (now Zimbabwe), and South Africa, Africans were relegated to reserves that had ethnic associations. As historian Timothy Parsons argues regarding Kenya, the British introduced tribes to Kenya by linking law, civil society, and geography with communal identities, but they could not define the ways Kenyans responded to such identities. As African populations grew in colonial Kenya, some tribal reserves could no longer contain their ethnic populations, so the government agreed to ethnic interpenetration to relieve pressure on some communities. Interpenetration permitted those from one ethnic group to live in the tribal reserve of another ethnic group as long as they did not provoke the original community and adopted their culture and ways. In other words, the colonial government recognized the flexibility of cultural identity that they had originally wanted to believe was rigid and immutable! Africans had, of course, recognized this all along and often used mutable identities to challenge the colonial state, such as Kenyans seeking access to land outside their crowded reserves, pushing the government to formalize the arrangement.

In South Africa two opposite trends were in place at once. First, the apartheid government put every South African into a racial category, thus eliding ethnic identities for the purposes of a collective African identity. Second, at the same time, the government documented ethnicity on pass cards and in the Bantustan homelands to which every African purportedly belonged. The South African state of the twentieth century recognized that most in the country held multiple identities, and one became more important than others in a particular circumstance.

In the postcolonial era, ethnicity still matters significantly, particularly in terms of politics and access to resources. African leaders inherited gatekeeper states that were more concerned with external revenue than internal welfare. Many leaders reinforced ethnic identities inherited during colonialism as they created political parties and opportunities for single ethnic groups. But there are often other layers as well, such as religious differences. Conflict in Nigeria is not only among Igbo, Yoruba, and Hausa, the three main ethnicities, but also between a Muslim, less developed North and a more developed Christian South. One reason the South is more developed than the North is because British colonial officials built more infrastructure there, and missionaries built more schools and churches there. Thus, there are more opportunities for education, employment, and advancement in southern Nigeria than in northern Nigeria. Such colonial divisions matter in most of the postcolonial conflicts, as some ethnicities and regions received greater investments than others.

Ethnicity remains an important way Africans identify themselves and the people with whom they closely relate. Even though colonial officials, missionaries, and their African allies created and solidified some ethnic identities over others, the inherent malleability of ethnicity remains, like many other ideas and institutions covered in this book. And Africans have other identities that become important in differing contexts.

Peace Building in South Africa

The earliest inhabitants of southern Africa were ancestors of the Khoisan. More recent evidence suggests that rather than being two distinct groups, Khoi and San, with two distinct respective identities, the Khoisan were gatherer-hunters in some landscapes and during lean times, and cattle herders and sheepherders in more lush landscapes and more prosperous times. By the early centuries CE, Bantu speakers, with their economic complex of growing sorghum and millet, cattle keeping, and ironworking, had begun to settle the eastern half of South Africa where there was sufficient rainfall to support agriculture.

Europeans first came to South Africa on ships bound for the east in the late 1400s and the 1500s. Khoi were initially very interested in trade relations with the Portuguese and Dutch explorers and provided them with water and food in exchange for trade items such as beads and metal implements. In 1652, the Dutch set up a refueling station at what is now Cape Town to provide meat, vegetables, and water for ships of the Dutch East Indies Company. A few company employees lived at the station and grew vegetables and traded European goods for Khoi meat. This small-scale European influence grew quickly. Within five years, some company employees were released from their contracts and allowed to set up farms beyond the Cape station. Slaves from India, the East Indies, and East Africa transformed the small refreshment station into a significant agricultural colony. Not until 1820 did the European population outnumber the slave population. Slaves, Khoikhoi, and their mixed descendants eventually became part of the "Coloured" population of South Africa.

Some Dutch began to hunt, trade with Khoi, and, especially, raise livestock in the interior on 2,500-hectare farms registered with the Dutch East Indies Company. Quickly, Dutch settlers acquired many Khoi characteristics associated with a herding lifestyle and eventually became known as trekboers or Boers. The Boers' desire for land and cattle clashed with Khoi needs for the same things. Khoi resistance to Dutch expansion resulted in two wars, both of which they lost. Smallpox and absorption into Dutch settler society (much like gatherer-hunters absorbed in farmer societies) resulted in a severely weakened Khoi population by the first few decades of the eighteenth century. Those who survived worked as slaves for Dutch settlers, helping them with their cattle. Others essentially took up the related San identity and began to rely on hunting and gathering. San fiercely resisted intrusion on their hunting lands, but the colony waged a mostly successful war against them.

Boer expansion reached Bantu-speaking territory west of the Fish River by the 1770s, as evidenced by administrative posts near Xhosa territory. Xhosa were far more formidable opponents than Khoi or San because they lived in a more densely vegetated area and had a larger population to draw on. Xhosa had inherited the successful Bantu economic package of agriculture, livestock keeping, and ironworking. Divisions within Xhosa society, however, made it hard to unite against trekboers. One of the chief points of conflict was a particularly desirable grassland area called the *zuurveld* (sweet grass) near the Fish River.

In 1806, the British gained control of the Cape Colony as a result of political realignment after the Napoleonic War. Their conflict with the Xhosa continued in another half dozen conflicts. By the 1860s, almost 100 years after the first contact, Xhosa were unable to resist European control. In 1820, the British, concerned about being outnumbered by Dutch descendants, invited 5,000 small-scale farmers to live on the previously contested grassland area. The farming effort failed, but it did increase the English population, and soon afterward,

English became the official language. English officials replaced Dutch officials in the colonial administration. Shortly after ending the Atlantic slave trade, the British also enacted a series of laws to grant more rights to Khoi workers and abolished slavery in 1820. These acts, from the Dutch-speaking point of view, seriously upset the racial balance in South Africa.

In the mid-nineteenth century, some Dutch farmers who wanted to escape British control left the colony and settled new territories that came to be called Boer Republics. By 1840, 6,000 farmers had settled in the new territories and adopted their own governments. They were not allowed to keep slaves, but Afrikaners could buy ammunition in the British colony and Africans could not.

Meanwhile, by the early nineteenth century, Bantu-speaking societies had increasingly been pushed to marginal lands, had their traditional leaders and rights abrogated by British colonial officials, and faced a combination of bad weather, increasing population, and development of military regiments by some segments of the Bantu population. By the 1820s, Shaka Zulu had established control over a large area of northeastern South Africa. The Zulu state was a predatory state, and the violence produced waves of refugees as far as Tanzania, including significant population movements and mingling of ethnic identities within southern Africa as well.

In the 1860s and 1880s, diamonds and gold were discovered. These discoveries unleashed a cascade of events that culminated in the settlement of modern-day South Africa. The gold mines were located in the heart of one of the Afrikaner republics, and British investors came to the republic seeking fortune. This pitted British and Afrikaners against one another again, resulting in the South African War of 1899–1902. The British won the war, but in 1910, the British colony, Boer territories, and African lands were combined into the Republic of South Africa under an Afrikaner president.

Africans came to the burgeoning urban areas seeking work. Some migrated, and others chose to live in the cities. They had fought with the British in the hopes of gaining more rights and economic access to jobs and education, but that did not happen. The new Republic of South African government further carved up African territory, imposed taxes, and destroyed traditional political systems. In 1894, the Glen Gray Act forced more Africans into the labor market. Each family was given one ten-acre plot of land that could be bequeathed only to the eldest son. Thus, in future generations, all but one member of a family would be rendered landless and forced to seek other employment. In the words of the mastermind of the legislation, Cecil Rhodes, the Act would encourage "lazy" Africans to work. A ten-shilling labor tax was imposed on all those who could not prove they had been in the workforce for at least three months of the year. The 1913 Natives Land Act set out the idea of territorial segregation for whites and Africans. African land ownership was restricted to reserve areas—7.5 percent of land for 67.3 percent of the population. Later, the allocated land for Africans was increased to over 13 percent.

Afrikaners also felt marginalized in the first half of the twentieth century as the British controlled most of the capital and most Boers were farmers. In this environment, Afrikaner nationalism developed. The *Broederbond,* a secret society of Afrikaner elite seeking the preservation of the Afrikaner language and culture and working to alleviate Afrikaners from relative deprivation in their own country, began in 1919. The political arm of this movement was the Purified National Party (PNP). Both organizations held certain tenets: the nation was the basic unit of moral and cultural life (not the individual), and each nation was created by God to fulfill a unique destiny and must be allowed to develop separately along its own lines. Thus, they created Afrikaner banks, companies, and other businesses to challenge long-dominant English capital. Yet, they had one thing in common with the British: they wanted cheap African labor.

World War II was another important turning point in African history. It gave South Africa its second industrial revolution as the country transformed from a mining economy to a manufacturing one. During the war, South Africans were not able to import all the machinery needed for the mining industry, so they built engineering industries to meet the need. This led to increased urbanization again, and African populations in towns grew particularly fast. They were so numerous that the government was unable to relocate them, and housing could not be built quickly enough for them. In part due to this rapid African urbanization and employment, the National Party (an outgrowth of the PNP) won the election by a slim majority, and Daniel François Malan, the founder of the PNP, was elected prime minister. He immediately began reorganizing South African society to meet Afrikaner nationalist ideals.

Malan and the next three prime ministers were responsible for most of the legislation that came to be known as apartheid (separation) legislation between 1948 and 1966. The legal framework of apartheid was extensive and included the elimination of all voting rights for Africans and Coloureds by 1970. Every South African was given a racial designation and not allowed to marry or use designated amenities (such as toilets and transportation) across races. A series of laws were passed to restrict African urban residents, requiring either living in one town for at least 15 years or working for the same employer for at least 10 years. This was very difficult given the nature of African employment and the fact that families were often divided between rural and urban areas. When Africans did live in towns, the government secured the prime locations nearest the commercial centers for Europeans, so Africans had longer commutes and fewer economic opportunities. An education act decreed an inferior education for Africans because their role in South African society required only minimal education. Several laws were also enacted to limit Africans' ability to oppose such restrictions of their rights. They were not allowed to strike or assemble, and the government had sweeping powers to arrest citizens without trial based on what were considered Communist, illegal, sabotage, or terrorist acts. Finally, Africans could only legally live as permanent residents in one of about a dozen home territories, associated with their ethnicity, known as Bantustans. The South African government wanted these territories to receive international recognition as independent states, thus releasing South Africa from any responsibility for their citizens. However, they lacked industry and other viable economic enterprises and were mostly devoid of able-bodied male and female workers, all of whom were working in the cities.

In the face of such restriction of rights and opportunities, Africans, Indians, and Coloureds resisted. While Khoi, San, and Xhosa had also fought, often violently, the Dutch and then the British takeover of their land, the resistance that followed the unification of the South African state from the early 1900s on had a different character. Before 1960, people's resistance was less organized and more peaceful. Several national organizations were founded during this time. Abdullah Abdurahman, a doctor, founded the African Political Organization (APO) in 1902. Its members sought to convince Europeans that they were civilized enough to be included in their society. The South African Native National Congress (SANNC), which later became the well-known African National Congress (ANC), was founded in 1912 by a group of African lawyers. Like the members of the APO, they were all educated and Western-oriented. Following Gandhi, they advocated nonviolent resistance. One of their first goals was to gain voting rights for middle-class Africans and eventually for all South Africans. The Industrial and Commercial Workers Union was founded in 1919 among Coloured dockworkers, but it attracted a large following of working-class Africans who sought more aggressive tactics than the SANNC was pursuing. Mine workers struck in 1918, 1919, and 1920 over pass laws and low wages. They achieved some pay increases but not a change in the pass laws. In 1925, the ICU protested by staging walkouts and refusing to carry passes. The state responded with violence, and white farmers threw ICU members off their farms. White intellectuals established the South African Communist Party in 1921, seeking to change both the political and economic systems.

The pace of protest picked up in 1952 with a nationwide strike campaign by the ANC, called the Defiance Campaign. Thousands of people violated what they considered unjust laws: they trespassed onto forbidden areas, broke curfews, and used "Europeans only" entrances and amenities. By December, over 8,000 people had been arrested, many of them charged with promoting Communism. Three years later in a multiracial meeting, the Freedom Charter was written, calling for full rights for all South Africans. The Freedom Charter is available online at http://www.anc.org.za/show.php?id=72. After 1960, there was much more resistance to apartheid from a variety of organizations. The ANC continued to play a significant role. Two subgroups of the ANC became important as well: the ANC Youth League and *Umkhonto we Sizwe* (Spear of the Nation). The League sought more aggressive tactics than nonviolent resistance that was the hallmark of the ANC, while *Umkhonto we Sizwe,* founded by Nelson Mandela, got support from other African nations and used acts of sabotage to destabilize the South African government. They began to plan for guerrilla warfare but never implemented it. Robert Sobukwe founded the Pan-Africanist Congress (PAC). Sobukwe wanted an organization that was not Communist and would not cooperate with other racial groups. Wanting to outdo its rival, the PAC decided to hold a mass antipass campaign ten days before the ANC had planned one in March 1960. On that day several thousand men gathered at the police station in Sharpeville to protest. When a scuffle broke out and a police officer was assaulted, the police fired into the crowd. Sixty-nine people were killed, most of them shot in the back. When pictures circulated around the world, the brutality of the South African regime became clear. As a result of this action, the South African government banned both the PAC and the ANC in 1960. Nelson Mandela and many other activists were arrested in 1962 and spent decades in jail.

Stephen Biko led the Black Consciousness Movement, which was inspired by liberation theology and the Black Power movement in the United States. Like the PAC, Biko rejected cooperation with other races. In 1983, Allan Boesak, the president of the World Alliance of Reformed Churches, founded the United Democratic Front, which was aligned with the ANC. It, too, was banned by the South African government.

Despite bans, organizations continued to meet and work underground and to carry out resistance activities. Yet, it was schoolchildren in Soweto who made the international news. In 1975, the government required that both Afrikaans and English must be spoken in schools. Frustrated at the lack of English-language instruction, starting in 1976, students boycotted schools, stoned buildings, and clashed with police. In Soweto, students staged a massive demonstration, and police used force to disperse the demonstration. Two students were killed, and many others were injured; protests and rioting spread to other towns. These were the largest outbreaks of racial violence to that date. These events made it clear to the outside world that the South African state was violent and unjust.

Such a totalitarian state took tremendous resources to enforce, and it was out of step with international sentiment that had supported African independence and civil rights in the United States in the 1960s. Starting in 1978, P.W. Botha reformed apartheid in response to internal and external demands. Trade unions were allowed to register and to strike. By 1986, trade unions had a dues-paying membership of over a million. A new constitution called for three uniracial chambers—White, Coloured, and Indian—although Africans were still excluded.

The government recognized some urban Africans as legal immigrants and abolished many of the pass laws. They repealed laws banning interracial marriage and sexual relations, and some public spaces became integrated. Many things, however, were left undone. Education was still strictly segregated, and the government spent seven times as much to educate a white child as an African child. Africans were still removed from their urban homes and subject to violent raids. For most Africans the situation was still intolerable.

The recent history of South Africa is one of the most remarkable stories of the twentieth century. It begins with a small minority imposing strict racial exclusion to the extent that the majority of the population was restricted to "independent" nations with poor soil, no industry, and little infrastructure within the larger Republic of South Africa. It begins to end with a human rights' hero, Nelson Mandela, being released from jail after 27 years and becoming president of South Africa in 1994. But peace and justice were not assured through elections alone. South Africans pioneered the modern-day use of a form of justice that pays attention to victim, criminal, and community in the hopes of promoting democracy and social inclusion after bitter experiences of autocracy and exclusion.

Africans have contributed to world history by offering a recent model of restorative justice, a form of justice that has roots in Sumer several thousand years before the Common Era. Restorative justice takes a holistic approach to criminal and offensive behavior, focusing on the needs of victims, offenders, and the community alike. Retributive justice, the system practiced in the United States and many other Western nations for hundreds of years, views crime as an offense against the state rather than against individuals or communities and seeks to punish the offender. In addition, retributive justice offers little chance for victim, offender, or community to explain its actions and experiences or for the individual involved to restore his or her role in the community. Instead, lawyers are responsible for making the case for victim and offender.

The transition to multiracial rule in South Africa was relatively peaceful. Yet, the African National Congress, Mandela's party, recognized that democratic rule had been preceded by tremendous injustices by the State and by activist organizations as well. The fear was that if some of these were not dealt with, it would hinder their efforts to move forward effectively. The ANC had roughly three options before them. The first was to move forward and try to forget about the past. This was what the former ruling apartheid government wanted to do. The second option was to follow the Nuremberg Trial example after World War II and seize the military and political officers most responsible and try them for crimes. This is easier to accomplish when there are clear winners and losers, as was the case in South Africa. The third option was a Truth Commission. South Africa's Truth and Reconciliation Commission (TRC) was created in 1995 to help smooth the transition from a minority-led white apartheid government to a democratic multiracial government. Information including the number of hearings of various types, transcripts of amnesty hearings, reports of human rights violations by the National Party and African National Congress, and final reports is available at http://www.justice.gov.za/trc/.

Under Anglican Archbishop Desmond Tutu's leadership, the ANC sought to create a national court-like restorative justice system. The broadest amnesty program in history, its goal was to investigate who did what to whom in terms of gross human rights violations associated with a political objective between 1960 and 1994. If a perpetrator sought amnesty in the program, he or she had to admit fault and make a full disclosure of all the relevant facts. If granted amnesty, any pending legal proceedings or charges against the criminal were dropped. And victims were given reparations for compensation.

Twenty-three thousand victims testified over 82 weeks. Televising some of the testimony made the Commission's work part of national discourse about truth-telling and justice. The South African Broadcast Corporation aired special reports on the TRC every Sunday from April 1996 to March 1998, and the program was often the most watched. The Commission made recommendations for who should get reparations, but many were never compensated. Over 8,000 perpetrators presented their case for over 100,000 acts, and about a third of them were granted amnesty.

Most South Africans believe the TRC was a success. Even though all political parties condemned the process at one point or another because they thought it was biased, such complaints from all sides suggest that the process was fairly balanced. One of the most powerful outcomes of the process was an understanding that all parties had committed acts of violence. Some critics of the process argue that it was too evenhanded because the National Party and its adherents had been far more violent than any other party involved in the process. Political scientist James L. Gibson, who has studied the effects of South Africa's TRC, argues that it contributed to reconciliation and democracy. He also has investigated the roles that South African cultures and history played in the success of the TRC, acknowledging that the pro-democratic nature of the African National Congress contributed to the effectiveness of the Commission. Post-1994 South Africa is a modern nation with a history of strong ethnic divisions. Yet, successful work of reconciliation was founded on national identity and purpose. Its relative success can also be measured by the 20 other countries, within Africa and elsewhere, that have used a similar process to heal a country after internal conflict, including Rwanda, Liberia, Serbia, and one in Greensboro, North Carolina, in the United States.

Women in Politics

African women have played a significant role in peace building in Africa in recent years. They have been major change agents in the realms of female education and peace and security initiatives for decades. Unfortunately, though, Western media has portrayed them more often as victims of rape, dangerous circumcisions, spousal abuse, and HIV/AIDS. In 2011, two Liberian women, Ellen Johnson Sirleaf and Leymah Gbowee, won the Nobel Peace Prize after 15 years of civil war.

For almost two decades, Liberians had suffered from a civil war in which multiple warlords competed for control of sections of the population with the aim of gaining control of the capital, Monrovia. The chief protagonist, Charles Taylor, was president from 1997 to 2003. He recruited child soldiers, and his army became notorious for severing limbs of those they considered to be their enemies. The war forced 750,000 Liberians, including Gbowee's family, to neighboring countries several times.

Ellen Johnson Sirleaf, a Harvard University–educated economist, became Africa's first democratically elected female president in 2005. (For more about her life, see http://topics.nytimes.com/topics/reference/timestopics/people/j /ellen_johnson_sirleaf/index.html.) Leymah Gbowee became the head of the Women in Peacebuilding Network. You can learn more about this organization at http://www.wanep.org/wanep/. This organization grew out of a coalition of Liberian women who demanded peace. Starting in 2001, and working with women in other African countries, Gbowee rallied women across religious and racial divides and demanded that Taylor and the warlords bring peace to Liberia. In 2003, she and hundreds of other women defied a ban on street marches and gathered at city hall and along Taylor's route to Capitol Hill so they could confront him. The movement became known as the Mass Action for Peace. Even after Taylor finally spoke to them, they continued to sit in the hot sun day after day and were joined by groups of women in 15 other Liberian counties as well. These protests lasted for several months and for a period of time included a sex strike where women refused to have sex with their husbands until peace was brokered. The sex strike was not evenly carried out and had little practical effect, but it garnered much media attention.

In June 2003, peace talks began in Ghana. Some Liberian women, including Gbowee, traveled to Ghana to continue to put pressure on the warlords and Taylor to reach an agreement. She observed these warlords-turned-negotiators relaxing at luxury hotels and enjoying meals paid for by the international community. Angry that those who had caused so much suffering were wasting time and money, 200 women gathered at the negotiating hall in Accra and sat in front of the door, holding the men hostage until they reached an agreement. Security guards rushed in to arrest them, and Gbowee and others threatened to strip naked to humiliate the guards. The war did not end with that sit-in, but the women were instrumental in ending the conflict. Two months later, West African peacekeeping troops arrived in Liberia, and Taylor resigned the presidency. The women's efforts are the subject of the award-winning documentary film *Pray the Devil Back to Hell* (http://praythedevilbacktohell.com).

Nigerian women offer examples of political leadership as well. In the 1920s, they protested colonial taxes, and in the 2000s, they protested exploitative oil extraction. In both cases, Nigerian women used their role as the bearers of society to shame men into taking action. In 2002, 600 Nigerian women took 1,000 oil workers hostage by occupying an oil facility, shutting down production of a half million barrels of oil a day. Again, they threatened to strip naked if their demands were not met. After ten days, the oil executives acceded to their demands that they offer their sons employment and contribute financially to the construction of clinics, schools, and farms. This form of protest is common in Nigeria; it was successful in convincing British colonial officials not to tax Nigerian women 80 years earlier. Although threatening to disrobe may sound odd to U.S. readers, like restorative justice, it is embedded in a societal commitment to both individual and community rights. When a community is threatened with violence or economic injustice, it is up to individuals to join together to change the situation. Women's bodies, while celebrated, are also to be properly covered while in public, so displaying one's naked body shames the men with whom she is associated. In these examples in Liberia and Nigeria, women used their culturally sanctioned roles as mothers and wives to force men to behave as protectors of society rather than destroyers of it. By embracing their role as reproducers of society, Liberian women effectively brought peace to a war-torn nation.

The Liberian war in postcolonial Africa was primarily about access to resources and opportunities. Successful transitions in both South African and Liberia were multiethnic but were built on cultural values and ideals, demonstrating that ethnicity is but one possible source of identity and action still in many African states.

The Informal Economy

As economic globalization broadens, Africans demonstrate that foreign economic ideas do not necessarily overtake local ones. Africans integrate multiple forms of economic thought and operation in their daily lives. They grow food, some for external sale; engage in economic opportunities that are new and innovative; send their children to school with the hope of providing them more opportunities; and rely on and appreciate imported commodities, such as clothing, shoes, and medicine. Yet, much of Africans' daily interactions take place as a result of activities outside of the formal economy. Over the last several decades, the majority of Africans have spent some of their time in the informal economy.

Briefly, an informal economy is one that is not recognized by the government and can include both legal activities, like selling coffee, donuts, or oranges on the side of the road, and illegal activities, such as selling drugs or smuggled goods. On a two-mile walk into a university campus in Kumasi, Ghana, in 2006, for example, I would regularly do business with a variety of people on the continuum between formal and informal economic activity. These included a tailor who worked in an old shipping container. He paid taxes to the government, although he had only one employee and his "shop" was not a building meant for business. There was also a man who sold donuts on the side of the road, using just a wok filled with oil. A woman sold phone cards displayed on a small table, which she stashed behind a building at the end of the day. The last two had minimal infrastructure for their business and had no permits and likely paid no taxes on their earnings.

What we think we know about African economies comes from statistics about the formal economy; statistics proliferate about how Africans live on less than one or two dollars a day from wage labor or registered employment. How do Africans survive on two dollars a day? They don't. They have a network of obligations, relationships, debt and credit, labor, and compensation that allows them to meet most of their basic needs and provide for their families. The difference compared to the United States is that most economic transactions take place in the informal economy. Many rural Africans operate in a very different social and economic reality than that captured by official statistics, particularly tax and business records.

Scholars use the terms *informal economy* and *shadow economy* to describe these activities. Both suggest something that is not as important, efficient, or normal about such an economy. The formal economy consists of employment in an organized environment, with a formal contract and predefined work conditions, responsibilities, payments, and schedules. The institutions and organization that offer this employment pay taxes and report to the government in a variety of ways. In the informal economy, a worker has no contract, no fixed hours, and no permanent place of employment and usually earns enough each day to pay for expenses for only one or two days. The work is usually untaxed and unsupported by the government. Small-scale enterprises of the informal economy rely on local inputs in contrast to formal industry that relies on imports and foreign currency. Small farmers, street vendors, artisans, and home-based workers could all be in the informal economy. Many activities in the informal economy might be subject to regulations, such as licensing or taxation, but operate without adherence to such regulations.

Access to both imports and foreign currency became much harder with structural adjustment and the economic shocks of the 1970s and 1980s. Thus, the informal economy in many developing countries has expanded since then. It tends to decentralize capital and resources, as dozens of banana sellers compete for customers or several teenage boys seek customers for one cigarette at a time; larger enterprises tend to concentrate capital in the hands of the state or a few capitalists.

When the informal economy is the primary way the majority of a country's population makes a living, it makes sense to take it seriously. Urban geographer Garth Myers argues that it might be time to find a new language for such work and label it "(i)n(f)ormal" and "familiar." By 2000, 42 percent of the gross domestic product for sub-Saharan African countries came from informal economic activity. In Ghana at the same time, up to 90 percent of economic activity was in the informal sector, according to an action research policy organization called Women in Informal Employment: Globalizing and Organizing.

While the informal economy has been much studied as a phenomenon compared to formal economic systems, it is so predominant that it makes some sense to look at it as an economic system in and of itself, as Garth Myers argues. Its origins lie in colonial policy, particularly urban policy. Popular writer Mike Davis argues that urbanization in Africa, Asia, and Latin America over the last few decades has taken place without industrialization or development. The result has been large urban populations with limited job and economic opportunities.

Many African cities grew significantly as a result of colonial policy; without European residence and infrastructure, they would not have been much different from other settlements of the era. Dar es Salaam in Tanzania, established by the Germans, became the political and economic capital of the colony (then Tanganyika) and attracted Europeans, Asians, and Africans. In 1913, Dar es Salaam had a population of 22,500, including 19,000 Africans. It and other cities were marked by a chief colonial concern: maintaining order and peace in the city by keeping residential areas separated by race. Yet, throughout the colonial period, the chance for wage work; the opportunity to escape authority, patriarchal or otherwise, and taxation; and the educational and cultural opportunities available in cities continued to attract Africans in great numbers. These urban dwellers frequently flouted official policy and created their own homes and their own types of employment. European rules and demarcations to keep the races separate marginalized most African urban residents. In Dar es Salaam, the British (who became the colonial power after World War I) established three residential zones. Zone I was for Europeans and was marked by bungalows set in spacious surroundings. Zone II was for Asian residents, and Zone III was for Africans. Zone III was the farthest from the city center and was marked by dwellings constructed of nonpermanent materials. Keeping areas segregated was challenging and required constant vigilance. According to historian James Brennan, in 1920, native houses in Zones I and II were not allowed to be structurally improved, for example, in the hope that without improvements, the occupants would have to move.

The economic consequences of colonial urban policy were significant for Africans. Residential policy imposed severe restrictions on African entrepreneurship. Segregated areas meant limited access to the wealthier residents of the city. As a result, formal opportunities were available only through the government or industry. According to Brennan, in 1931, when the African population in the city was above 20,000, there were only two African shopkeepers in Dar es Salaam. Historian Andrew Burton has noted that in the interwar years, the African population was roughly 26,000, of whom 14,000 were skilled Africans with low-paying jobs that did not cover their monthly expenses. Unskilled workers were in an even tougher position. Thus, many urban Africans, relegated to inferior residential locations and inferior economic positions, turned to informal economic opportunities to supplement earnings or as a stopgap measure in the hopes of eventually obtaining paid employment.

Throughout the colonial era, colonial officials considered unlicensed street trading as a public health threat or a threat to licensed trade in established markets or businesses. Thus, they sought to limit its occurrence, with little effect. Moreover, activities that were not licensed provided income that was not taxed. And as urbanization increased, the colonial economy sought to control this form of development. Restrictions were placed on the production and consumption of native beer, and street hawking was deemed a public threat. These trends continued in the post–World War II era as well. Neither achieved the desired results. A 1956 survey of Dar es Salaam noted that there were petty traders of hot coffee, tea, fruit, roast meat, fish, coconuts, firewood, charcoal, flattened kerosene cans for roofing, old clothes, and peanuts, among other things. Burton reports that one petty trader told officials in the 1950s that he was forced to trade to be able to pay rent and taxes.

After independence, the Tanzanian government constructed urban policy in ways that were very similar to the colonial era both in terms of housing and acceptable economic activities. According to economist Andrew Coulson, urban settlement in Dar es Salaam grew at 10 percent per year between 1969 and 1975. Wage employment increased 5.4 percent annually, and informal sector and unemployment increased at 20 percent per year. Much like the colonial government, most independent African governments did little to create urban infrastructure to support growing urban populations. In many African cities, citizens' relationship to their government was nonexistent because the state did not provide schools, sanitation, roads, or hospitals. Political scientist Aili Tripp notes that approximately 60 percent of Dar es Salaam grew out of already existing villages surrounded by farming areas. In 1982, there were five illegally built houses for every legal one.

Wage employment did not keep up with the urban Dar es Salaam population between 1900 and 1980. Then came a series of economic shocks: oil shocks in the 1970s when the price of oil doubled and then quadrupled; declining prices led to declining terms of trade for most of the 1970s; an expensive war with Uganda in

1978 and 1979; and droughts in 1973–1974 and again in 1984. The oil shocks added to Tanzania's expenditures at the same time that the raw materials they relied on for export were earning less on the global market. Military costs and decreased agricultural harvests added to an already challenging situation.

Seeking economic growth, Tanzania made a significant change and officially abandoned socialism in 1986 and began to embrace a capitalist economy, removing subsidies and a number of economic supports that eroded an already fragile economy. Tanzania accepted structural adjustment policies from the World Bank and IMF as means to obtain loans from international financial institutions. Commonly, these steps are associated with globalization, particularly with the promotion of one set of macroeconomic ideas as a panacea for what ailed nations in Africa, Asia, and Latin America. In the case of the structural adjustment policies in the 1980s, they called for privatization of state-owned enterprises; layoff of government workers, resulting in significant urban unemployment; and an emphasis on paying for heretofore public services, such as education and health care.

In response to globalization, the informal economy expanded. Tripp's research indicates that in 1977, 77 percent of total income came from wages and 8 percent came from private sources, but by 1988, informal incomes made up 90 percent of household income in Dar es Salaam. As Davis points out, in Dar es Salaam, public service expenditure per person fell 10 percent per year in the 1980s, eroding the state's role in the city. Urban growth slowed during this period, likely reflecting recognition of the reduced opportunities available. And 60 to 80 percent of Dar's population lived in informal settlements at the turn of the century, according to Myers.

It is within this context that Tanzanians live on less than a dollar a day in Dar es Salaam. According to geographer Deborah Potts, this is sometimes called the "wage puzzle." On the ground, "poor" Africans are spending more dollars per day than that, so there is a gap between standard economic measures and the economic practices of many Tanzanians. This is not likely to change soon. Davis reports that United Nations' projections are that 90 percent of urban Africa's new workers over the next decade will have to rely on informal employment.

It was this very gap that drove Aili Tripp to conduct research in urban Dar es Salaam. Tripp wanted to know how urban dwellers in many African countries survived on reported wages when the cost of living was many times greater than those incomes. She found that Tanzanians were forced to rely on themselves as the state and formal economy shrank. She also found that households were increasingly reliant on women, children, and the elderly, reversing previous short-lived norms of the colonial and early postcolonial economies where the assumption was that men would be the breadwinners and support their families.

In most places, women are the dominant informal market participants. Tripp's study found that in 1970, 4 percent of wives were self-employed, but by late

1980, 69 percent were. By the turn of the century in Dar es Salaam, many women earned more money than their husbands did, and the majority of them are solely responsible for family income. Whereas in the 1960s and 1970s, self-employed incomes were lower than those of wage earners, with a few exceptions (such as healing and shopkeeping), in the 1980s, self-employment began to provide more than wage employment.

Moving toward the twenty-first century, African economies were generally not performing better than they had been in the previous decades. With continuing economic pressure on families to make ends meet without formal wage employment or access to land, in Ghana, men are increasingly participating in the informal economy as African families face more economic pressures. In 1997, 89 percent of total employment in Ghana was in the informal sector, according to one survey. Geographer Ragnhild Overa has argued that men in the capital of Ghana, Accra, are increasingly taking on what were considered female activities in the informal economy, such as selling vegetables, grains, and cooked food. Women have not objected to this incursion on their trade and opportunities by their male peers because they recognize that governmental failure to produce more jobs has made life difficult for all Accra residents, not just women. On the other hand, Overa found that few women are able to successfully engage in traditionally male informal economic activities, such as work associated with automobiles and furniture making.

One interpretation of a planetary situation where increasing numbers are living and working in informal sectors of urban areas, as Davis writes, is that "cities have become a dumping ground for a surplus population" who end up working in informal service industries and trade. In literal terms (in regard to economic statistics and government policy), these people do not count. But, of course, they do—to their kin and their friends, as well as the cities and nations in which they find themselves. They are a strong signal that our institutions and means of reckoning have not kept up with human reality. A widespread informal economy suggests that society rather than government is setting many of the rules of the game in an effort to cope with challenging situations. Rather than evading the state or undermining its legitimacy, the informal economy, Tripp argues, provides a "safety valve for the state," rather than inherently weakening it. That is, it directs citizens' activities toward subsistence strategies that provide a minimal existence so they are less likely to rise up against the state. The informal economy also suggests that urban residents believe deeply that they, not the state, have the right to control their means of subsistence. And, indeed, in Tanzania and elsewhere, African governments are responding to the informal economy by attempting to assist such workers by providing services and skills training, among other things.

Mike Davis and many others paint a rather bleak picture of the future of such cities and the poorer residents in them. It is worthwhile to step back from such statements and ask what African responses to challenging urban environments teach about human ingenuity and urban survival. These are not simply apocalyptic landscapes but landscapes teeming with hard-working humans who seek the best possible circumstances for both themselves and their children. In the judgments made, assumptions and metrics blind observers to the ways other people in other places have lived and do live. African urban dwellers are part of a global economy in which all have a part to play. They are no less a part of it than anyone else. And, in fact, their presence in cities and their responses to the difficult circumstances of their lives are in some ways a reflection on the choices other governments and corporations have made. To write them off is to suggest that others have no responsibility or relationship to them when this is obviously not the case.

The informal economy is everywhere. A 1983 survey reported that Sweden, Denmark, Belgium, and Italy had the highest levels of informal activity in Europe, indicating that the informal economy is an international phenomenon. The informal economy is thriving in the United States as well. Independent scholar Richard Vogel noted in 2006 that there were "no comprehensive national studies of the informal U.S. economy . . . published to date" but that the city of Los Angeles had data that provided a good picture of the informal economy there. He found that since the late 1980s, the gap between formal and informal employment in Los Angeles has been widening. An Economic Roundtable study estimated informal employment comprised 15 percent of the county's labor force in 2004. Approximately 60 percent of those in the informal economy were undocumented migrant workers. Informal employment shortchanges the public sector in Los Angeles County through loss of social security taxes, Medicare taxes, and other payments. In addition, those in informal employment tend to spend some of their wages on informal goods and services that are not taxed, further depleting public coffers. Obviously, though, informal employment is not ideal from the point of view of the employee as well. Thus, our study of the informal economy has implications for Africans and their future, as well as many other workers who find themselves at a disadvantage in the global economy.

Africans' responses to a lack of education and employment opportunities in cities invite us to learn more about global economic realities and their consequences. Instead of a black-and-white understanding of globalization that finds winners and losers, examining the totality of economic experiences in both prosperous and depressed areas results in a more nuanced appreciation of the myriad ways that globalization affects people.

Africans have responded to some of the most unimaginable challenges— total racial segregation, horrific violence, and significant exclusion from the wage economy—with both old and new ideas but, most important, with collective action through religion, nonviolent protest, and a willingness to share fragments of an undocumented economy. The better connected citizens of the North are to those for whom global politics, economics, and social ideas are not working, the better they will understand the consequences of their actions and the broader repertoire of ideas there will be to change behaviors and institutions. There is little interest in the United States or elsewhere to further promote an informal economy, for example, but its strength and ubiquity shine a light on the choices everyone in the global community makes regarding production, consumption, and employment.

Suggestions for Further Reading

Bruce J. Berman, "'A Palimpsest of Contradictions': Ethnicity, Class, and Politics in Africa," *International Journal of African Historical Studies* 37, no. 1 (2004): 13–31. A reflection on Berman's work with historian John Lonsdale, he reviews the role of ethnicity and class for Kenyans under colonial rule.

James R. Brennan, Andrew Burton, and Yusuf Lawi, eds., *Dar es Salaam: Histories from an Emerging African Metropolis* (Dar es Salaam: Mkuki wa Nyota, 2007). This is a collection on the history of Dar es Salaam, Tanzania. The first essay by Brennan and Burton is particularly helpful.

"Brief History of the Post-Autistic Economics Movement, A," peacon.net/HistoryPAE. This is from a website for what used to be called the "post-autistic economics movement" and is now called "Real World Economics." Its goal is to make economics as applicable to what people and societies are actually experiencing as possible.

Andrew Burton, *African Underclass: Urbanisation, Crime and Colonial Order in Dar es Salaam* (Athens: Ohio University Press, 2005). Burton traces postcolonial urban policies to their colonial roots. In both eras, rapid urbanization led to an interpretation of urban African residents as a less than desirable population by the political and economic elite.

Andrew Coulson, *Tanzania: A Political Economy* (Oxford: Oxford University Press, 1982). Coulson traces the history of Tanzania's economy from precolonial trade to the postcolonial state.

Mike Davis, *The Planet of the Slums* (London: Verso, 2006). This is a rather apocalyptic vision of what might be coming. But Davis does a good job of giving an overview of the urban situation globally, the causes behind it, and some of the likely outcomes.

Leymah Gbowee, *Mighty Be Our Powers: How Sisterhood, Prayer, and Sex Changed a Nation at War, A Memoir* (New York: Beast Books, 2011). Gbowee's autobiography candidly chronicles both her political activity and her personal life.

James L. Gibson, "The Contributions of Truth to Reconciliation," *Transitional Justice* 50, no. 3 (2006): 409–432. Gibson seeks to discover if the Truth and Reconciliation Commission in South Africa had an independent effect on promoting reconciliation and democracy. He feels it had a positive impact.

Garth Myers, *African Cities: Alternative Visions of Urban Theory and Practice* (London: Zed Books, 2011). Myers seeks to use the African urban experience as a means to reexamine urban theory and practice. African experiences in cities share some common elements: informal sectors and settlements and coping with colonial inheritances of poverty, underdevelopment, and socio-spatial inequality.

Ragnhild Overa, "When Men Do Women's Work: Structural Adjustment, Unemployment and Changing Gender Relations in the Informal Economy of Accra, Ghana," *Journal of Modern African Studies* 45, no. 4 (2007): 539–563. Overa finds that as more Ghanaians seek a living in the informal economy, men take up female-dominated positions. Rather than women becoming frustrated with such infringement, their frustration is with government policies that offer so few chances for formal employment.

Timothy Parsons, "Local Responses to the Ethnic Geography of Colonialism in the Gusii Highlands of British-Ruled Kenya," *Ethnohistory* 58, no. 3 (2011): 491–523. Parsons investigates what happened in colonial Kenya when European-imposed tribal boundaries no longer were large enough for more populous tribes. An arrangement that allowed Africans from one ethnicity to move to another tribal location and adopt that ethnicity did not always lead to assimilation or a change in ethnic identity.

Deborah Potts, "Urban Lives: Adopting New Strategies and Adapting Rural Links," in *The Urban Challenge in Africa: Growth and Management of Its Large Cities,* ed. Carole Rakodi (New York: United Nations University Press, 1997), 447–494. This is an examination of urban life in African cities, particularly the forces that contribute to poverty for the majority.

Aili Mari Tripp, *Changing the Rules: The Politics of Liberalization and the Urban Informal Economy in Tanzania* (Berkeley: University of California Press, 1997). This is an in-depth look at urban Dar es Salaam after the structural adjustment policies of the International Monetary Fund and the World Bank in the late 1980s.

Richard D. Vogel, "Harder Times: Undocumented Workers and the U.S. Informal Economy," *Monthly Review* (July–August 2006): 29–39. This article examines the informal economy in Los Angeles, California.

10 An African Success Story
Somaliland

To MANY both in the academy and outside of it, one of the challenges people face globally is achieving meaningful participation in the political process. African peoples can play an important role in helping to question dominant ways of thinking about political institutions and imagining different forms of organization. Such forms might be, first, better suited to African realities and, second, better able to respond to the environmental and economic challenges that many predict will profoundly shape our future. Somaliland in eastern Africa points the way to some effective means of addressing basic human needs in a rapidly changing world. What the media covers about Somalia—piracy and lack of governance, for example—bears little resemblance to the experience of half the Somali population in what is now Somaliland. Somalilanders have built effective systems based on local political and economic institutions; such institutions are one of the keys to creating more resilient and sustainable societies in Africa and elsewhere in the face of increasing global uncertainty.

As economic and cultural globalization continues to be a powerful force around the globe, part of the challenge is to retain awareness of a variety of economic, cultural, and political models and the particular geographical and historical circumstances in which they arrive and thrive. Thus, students of both African history and African politics are intrigued by Somalia over the last 30 years, and rightly so. Failure is a description that does little to help us understand the particularities of this place and its people. It is also one that after several decades might more aptly describe foreign state makers than the Somali people.

A robust, imaginative North American literature emerged in the twentieth century from those who were interested in creating more humane and ecologically sensitive societies, as sustainability scholar Ben Minteer explains. In politics, they wrote about the importance of regionalism and the public, as opposed to the nation-state. In economic development, it is recognized that local development rather than externally oriented development has been the key to economic success historically, despite contemporary calls for freer international trade as a panacea. Using these theories as a foundation for rethinking what is happening in Somaliland and in the world in relation to Somalia is one way to turn ill-informed judgment into a better-informed respect for the ways in which Somaliland helps to illuminate how peoples might have to respond to upcoming crises such as global climate change, peak oil, and economic decline. The ideals of the nation-state and unregulated free trade are likely too limited for the challenges of our present and future.

Geographical Focus

This chapter focuses on Somaliland in the Horn of Africa alongside the Red Sea. As a result of this location, it has long held strategic importance for world powers. The Red Sea is one of the main water passageways for Middle Eastern oil. During the colonial era, it was under British rule, and since the 1960s, as part of a larger Somali state, it has played a critical role in the Cold War, as both the United States and the former Soviet Union, at various times, courted and supported its leaders.

Sources and Methodologies

Many of the scholars mentioned in this chapter are political scientists. Political scientists study governments, political processes and systems, and political behavior. In many ways, political science and history are closely related disciplines. Historians are interested in politics and changes in political systems and ideas. Political scientists study the factors that make revolutions, nation-states, and civil society possible, and this inherently requires some appreciation of a people's history. There are studies that focus on political history and those that exemplify historically informed political science.

Yet, they are distinct disciplines. One of the differences between history and political science is that political scientists tend to use theories and models to explain particular events and even to think about what the future might hold. The idea of a "failed state" comes from political science and, as this chapter points out, sometimes masks significant differences within states and across states. Yet, if one needs to make some kind of assessment on a global scale of what makes some states successful and other states unsuccessful, some kind of an index, like that of the "failed state," is helpful. (Foreign Policy's Failed States Index for 2012 is available at http://www.foreignpolicy.com/failed_states_index_2012_interactive.) Historians are more inclined to focus on the particularities of a situation for its own sake rather than draw out generalities or ideas that might apply across a variety of situations. As a historian examining recent Somaliland history, for example, the colonial and postcolonial experiences of Somalilanders are crucial to understanding the contemporary state they have built.

Too much can be made of this distinction, of course, and Colin and Miriam Elman's (2001) book *Bridges and Boundaries: Historians, Political Scientists, and the Study of International Relations* seeks to encourage scholars from the two disciplines to learn from each other. It is clear from this chapter that there is a tremendous amount for a historian to gain from reading about political science and considering political systems across time, such as the kinds of political systems that pastoralists in Somalia have created and are still creating today.

Failed State or First Indigenous Modern African State?

According to political scientist Michael Walls and policy analyst Steve Kibble, Somaliland might well be "the first, indigenous, modern African form of government to achieve stability through a regime employing traditional social systems within a democratizing framework, while maintaining an emphasis on individual and collective self reliance." But it also has significance beyond Africa. Many recognize that the current era calls for greater local resilience. Rob Hopkins, leader of the Transition Town movement, argues that civilization has entered the long emergency of the triple crises of peak oil, global climate change, and economic instability. This emergency can be successfully met, he goes on, through the formation of locally focused (though not totally self-sufficient), resilient communities.

That few know about Somaliland stems in part from the fact that the global political system marginalizes some African nations by labeling them as failed states, states that do not have centralized governments able to exert control over the populace within colonially determined boundaries. The Failed States Index is a good example of such labeling. The index is based on 12 degrees of failure; on all but one indicator—external intervention—African states lead. On this indicator in 2010, Afghanistan was the leader. In all the other indices, such as human rights, factionalized (or squabbling) elites, and economic decline, an African state (or two or three) was in the lead. In regards to economic decline and illegitimate governments, an African country shared the highest ranking with one other non-African country: North Korea and Afghanistan, respectively. Somalia has been the number one failed state for three years in a row.

The failed state judgment is only the most current form of Western-judged African exceptionalism. Before that, the focus was on other signs of Africa's political and economic weaknesses—African dictators, corruption, and military takeovers. For example, Freedom House's "Map of Freedom" displays the countries of the world based on whether they have been "free," "partly free," or "not free." Since at least 2002, the preponderance of countries in the last two categories is in Africa and Asia.

Failed states follow from a view of the modern state that assumes that all states are essentially similar and should function in the same way by controlling their borders, having a monopoly on the use of force, and supervising the management and regulation of economic, social, and political processes in accordance with Western standards. The broader assumption, as political scientist Goran Hyden puts it, is "that if African states only adopt the policies used successfully in other parts of the world, they would move ahead and prosper. There is little, if any, sensitivity to contextual differences, especially in the cultural realm." Nor is there any sensitivity to the fact that a changing global political and economic environment might call for different political models.

Negative judgments and partial information reflect a power dynamic—one that often goes unacknowledged. If failed states were a truly global phenomenon, then, one might be inclined to consider that a new historical era is beginning, marked by the rise of failed states. But since the preponderance of so-called failed states are in Africa, one has to wonder if this is another example of Western interests predominating. Political scientists Martin Boas and Kathleen Jennings argue that the "failed state" label promotes Western security and interests. There are numerous states where a weakened or informal governance structure occurs, but those labeled "failed" are the ones that are perceived to be threats to Western interests, such as Somalia. These states are often regarded as a security threat and, increasingly, as possible havens for terrorism. They point out that other weak states, such as Nigeria, make it easier for business and international capital (such as multinational oil companies) and are not considered failed states. Thus, Afghanistan's, Liberia's, and Somalia's failures are to be handled militarily. Nigeria's and Sudan's (after 1998) are not. In this view, the label serves Western interests rather than satisfactorily explaining local development or offering effective strategies for change.

The Colonial Legacy

Not only did African countries inherit economic systems that were tied to dependency on very few raw materials for export, but they also inherited an authoritarian colonial state. The combination has proved challenging to overcome and partially explains the prevalence of "failed states" in Africa. Without access to diverse forms of authority such as existed in the precolonial era, and in need of significant external revenue to build a nation—roads, schools, clinics, access to clean water, and industries—many African leaders felt more beholden to outsider interests. Foreign countries and companies were the keys to the resources necessary to build a successful country. And most African countries had significant ethnic and religious divisions that needed to be bridged to achieve a meaningful sense of nationalism. But to stay in political power, African leaders often found themselves having to ally with their own ethnicity, often against the interests and needs of other ethnicities in other regions of the country. Without much experience in multiethnic societies or a government apparatus that supported expression, negotiation, and compromise (three things colonial governments did not promote at all), it is not too surprising that African leaders found themselves in a challenging situation and one in which the tendency was toward authoritarian rule inside, while ensuring that revenue flows continued from the outside.

Somali Realities

One way to read recent Somali history, as foreign policy analyst Seth Kaplan argues, is that the persistent efforts to rebuild a formal centralized state, something that Somalis only experienced in the twentieth century, demonstrate a lack of appreciation for the informal institutions that are at the heart of Somali society. Somalia has unusual ethnic homogeneity for Africa, so most Somalis share a common language, religion (Sunni Islam), and culture. All of these characteristics might suggest that Somalia was better situated to navigate the postcolonial era than many other African countries. However, Somalis share a common economy, one that mitigates against state formation. The majority of the Somali people, at least 60 percent, are nomads or have nomadic affiliations. A small percentage of Somali are cultivators, either alone or in conjunction with livestock keeping. The persistence of livestock keeping in Somalia's history is longstanding. Ioan Lewis, scholar of Somali culture, notes:

> From the president downwards, at all levels of government and administration, those living with a modern lifestyle in urban conditions have brothers and cousins living as nomads in the interior and regularly have shares in joint livestock herds. Civil servants commonly invest in livestock, including camels, that are herded by their nomadic kinsmen.

This close connection to pastoralism means that the idea of the state is alien to Somali culture and unknown before the colonial period. Political scientist Brian Hesse has quoted another Somali observer as quipping that "nomad society is essentially anarchic." The rugged individualism and suspicion of others with whom one might have to compete for pasture and water make Somalis far less likely to submit to a higher state authority.

The best-known institutions in Somali society are those of the clan and lineage. Clans can serve the same political function as ethnicity did in many African countries. Goran Hyden, drawing on work by H.-P. Mueller, argues for Africa more generally that where extensive lineage systems are still important, state institutions play a limited role. Any type of governance in the area has to reckon with the fact that Somalis do not share (and have never shared) a common large-scale political structure. Family genealogies provide basic group structure and identity. Somali are divided into six clans and some minority groups. Each clan has numerous subclans that compose, recompose, and decompose fluidly, according to business consultant Seth Kaplan. Clans might trace their common ancestry back 20 generations or more. A primary lineage has a span of six to ten generations, and marriage is forbidden among its members. These large groups are broken down into smaller *dia*-paying groups that have more day-to-day salience.

The *dia*-paying group is "the basic jural and political unit of northern Somali society," writes Lewis. It ranges from four to eight generations and could have three hundred to several thousand male members. This group's primary responsibility is to ensure justice. The groups collect and render payment of blood compensation. If a group member is wronged, the group exacts revenge or achieves reparations collectively. In the reverse situation, members would be collectively responsible for reparations. *Dia*-paying members are bound by formal oral contract. At every level, all male elder councils, *shir*, are held to make decisions. In addition, customary law governs behavior. Councils and customary law have long histories and continued to operate independently of the modern state.

During the colonial period, the land of the Somalis was divided between the British (in the north) and the Italians (in the south), the French (Djibouti) and British-run Kenya, and independent Ethiopia. British colonialism in Somaliland was marked by caution and appeasement, after a 20-year engagement with, in Lewis's assessment, the "brilliantly resourceful" Sayyid Mohamed Abdille Hassan's guerrilla movement between 1900 and 1920. For example, the British never implemented a poll tax, and there was little investment in education. Thus, many Somaliland institutions remained relatively strong. Yet, important changes did take place. During the colonial era, the British and Italians chose clan chiefs whose decisions then held more authority than the meeting of all adult males. Centers of trade introduced possibilities for relaxing clan identities and commitments as well. For example, a town dweller might choose to collect money in a bank rather than invest it in livestock. Despite these changes, *dia*-paying groups are still important, and ties with the lineages and rural kin remain significant.

At independence in 1960, the British and Italian halves merged, and many Somalis wanted to bring all the Somali people together under one leader. Today, about half of Somalis live outside of Somalia in Africa and elsewhere. This goal was at the heart of Somalia's efforts to bring Ogaden, Ethiopia, under its control almost 15 years after independence.

Clan politics dominated the first era of Somali independence. Mohamed Siad Barre came to power in 1969 in response to increasing dissatisfaction with the first prime minister and then president Abdirashid Ali Shermaake. Barre adopted a scientific socialist platform in 1970 that relied on unity and self-reliance. He viewed lineage politics and multiparty politics as obstacles to success. Barre banned collective payment of blood money and lineage genealogies and emphasized marriage as a personal rather than kinship contract. People were settled on communes where clans were deliberately mixed, and Somalis were not to refer to a person's clan affiliation but to call one another "comrade." These were unpopular steps. Yet, when threatened with loss of the presidency, he began to favor the subclans to which his family members belonged, demonstrating something his citizens already knew: clan ties remained integral to Somali society.

In 1977, in the chaos after the fall of Emperor Haile Selassie in Ethiopia, Somalia attacked the Ethiopian garrison in the Ogaden. Newly gained Soviet support of Ethiopia, however, led to Somali defeat in 1978. This defeat galvanized already existing resentment against Mohamed Siad Barre's brutal dictatorship. It also brought refugees from Ogaden into Somalia and upset existing clan structures. Guerilla groups, both clan-based and regional, formed to bring down his regime, and civil war broke out in 1988. One element of this violence was located in the North. After the failed invasion of Ogaden, more than a million Somalis left Ethiopia for Somalia, and half of them settled in the North. Barre provided aid, jobs, land, and weapons to the new citizens. But instead of using the latter for another attempt to liberate Ogaden, many formed the Somali National Movement to overthrow Barre's government. Due to these efforts and others, Barre was overthrown in 1991. The chaos that ensued in the years following has been the primary lens through which Somalia's current events have been examined. More than 2 million Somali were refugees in other African countries, the Middle East, Europe, and North America by the late 2000s.

Two important developments during this era must be noted. The first is the increasing contact that Somalis of different clans had with one another as a result of the Ogaden conflict but also as a result of famine in 1974–1975 and the resettlement of thousands of northern Somalis, mostly in the South. Since the civil war, though, most Somalis returned to their original clan areas, reinforcing local, clan-based institutions. The second is that as a result of the Cold War, the area was flush with weaponry that otherwise would not have been available. When President Ronald Reagan was in office (1981–1989), the United States gave $500 million in military aid to Somalia, $100 million more than the United States had given to Ethiopia during their 25-year relationship. Without the weapons, it is far more likely that these conflicts would have been settled in ways other than violent ones. This must be taken into account when you consider, according to journalist Charles Lemos, that Somalia's civil war has been one of the most destructive in recent African history.

Chaos or Order?

Most Western media coverage has focused on the 14 international agreements and the fifteenth change in broader Somali government since 1991 and lamented the lack of progress in building a nation-state. But there is another story to tell— one of successful, localized forms of political, economic, and judicial control in Somaliland and, to a lesser extent, in Puntland. Overall, the areas of Somaliland and Puntland are home to almost two-thirds of Somalis.

Many historically rooted institutions have accommodated the needs of Somalis over the last 20 years. Koranic schools, for example, fill some social needs, building a community of children and families with the school's teacher. *Shari'a*-based Islamic courts have become the main judicial system, providing an outlet for resolving conflicts. They are the basis of the ICU (Islamic Courts Union) that managed to gain control of the southern part of the country in 2006 in place of the Transitional Federal Government (TFG) brokered by outsiders. The ICU brought stability, particularly to Mogadishu, and even managed to reopen the international airport. No other externally introduced governments have achieved as much security and normalcy as the ICU has.

It was precisely as the ICU gained some effective control that the United States and Ethiopia militarily intervened to depose the ICU and attack terrorist targets in 2006. Local clan militias, as well as the violence perpetrated by the U.S.-backed Counterterrorism Alliance, also strengthened the ICU. The TFG, a creation of the United Nations with the support of the United States and Great Britain, is much weaker. Political scientist Brian Hesse argued in 2010 that the current TFG hung on by a thread. Further, were the central government to collapse, he argued, it would not necessarily lead to anarchy because traditional sources, such as the *shir* (elder discussions) and *sheikh* (religious jurisprudence), still exist. Other institutions, such as the *dia*-paying groups, offer security to Somali pastoralists through collective retribution, and the *xeer*, a tradition of ad hoc agreements, govern relations between clans regarding common resources such as grazing land and water.

Arising out of the ashes of the 30-year experiment in Somali nationhood is the Republic of Somaliland, in the northwestern part of what was Somalia. Somaliland has held three consecutive competitive elections since its constitutional referendum in 2001, has a parliament controlled by opposition parties, and has a vibrant economy with a prominent private sector. In contrast to the ICU government, the Somaliland government is based on clan decision making. One clan, the Isaaq, consists of 70 percent of the nation's population. Clan authority is typically emphasized as the root of Somalia's problems, but Somaliland has been able to rebuild by integrating "traditional ways of governance with a modern state apparatus," to use Kaplan's words. This bottom-up approach also strongly contrasts with the experiences of their southern neighbor, where foreign-styled and foreign-led attempts to create national governments have been forged many times, only to fail, with the exception being the locally produced and internationally feared ICU.

Somaliland has a different colonial history than southern Somalia, and its population suffered discrimination after integration into an independent Somalia. In fact, six months after union with former Italian Somalia, an unsuccessful coup sought to restore Somaliland autonomy. Also, more than half of northerners rejected a provisional constitution to unite the two territories after independence. Southern peoples and culture dominated the new government and discriminated against northerners. Northerners filled most of the technical posts, and southerners filled most of the political ones in the new national government. As civil war erupted in 1988, one target was the Somali National Movement (SNM), which was closely affiliated with the Isaaq clan and formed in the late 1970s, after the failed Ogaden invasion. Isaaq clan ties, particularly in Saudi Arabia and Britain, were integral to the success of the SNM. Barre responded to this movement by bombing Somaliland's two largest cities, killing 50,000 people and making refugees of 1 million more.

This past has brought Somaliland several advantages compared to the rest of the region and the continent: a relatively homogeneous population, limited wealth differences, a collective fear of the South that promotes a collective identity, a lack of foreign involvement, and strong traditional institutions. It is worth noting, however, that clan homogeneity is really not the most important factor for success in this instance. As Lewis notes, once the Isaaq were able to make peace with non-Isaaqis, internal divisions were likely to surface. Moreover, the Somali civil war, as well as the previous events noted above, weakened traditional institutions of interclan cooperation.

Local Political Institutions

Out of these experiences, Somalilanders have managed to forge a remarkably successful state from the bottom up, one that allows for governance and clan membership. Somaliland has yet to be recognized by the international community out of fear of escalating regionalism and factionalism and due to an international commitment to the nation-state. Lack of recognition has allowed Somalilanders unusual latitude in political construction. With that latitude, they created a system that has elements of traditional "pastoral" male democracy as well as elements of the Westphalian and Weberian state. This system has increasingly incorporated more voices and concerns through successive conferences and debate in the early and mid-1990s.

The upper house of Somaliland legislature is the House of Elders, or *Guurti*. Clan communities select this house in traditional ways. The *Guurti* can return questionable legislation to the lower house and introduce bills on religion, culture, and security. Less formalized elder influence has also been important. President Igal (1993–2002) consulted prominent paramount chiefs who were not members of the formal government body on several important issues. Thus, peripheral interests and internal pressure groups had access to state-led politics. Moreover, the traditional institution, *xeer,* manages arrangements for sharing grazing land and water resources and has been integrated into the new government. After the fall of the Somali republic in 1991, some clan elders in Somaliland sought to revive *xeer* to ensure well-being for their clans and others. Government officials in the capital, Hargeisa, have accepted the authority of these local leaders, and this is reflected in a 2001 constitution. Now *xeer* stand alongside *shari'a* and secular law as sources of jurisprudence.

The lower house, the House of Representatives, has members from no more than three political parties, and all legitimate parties must get at least 20 percent of the vote in four of Somaliland's six regions during a general election in an effort to prohibit political parties from being regionally or clan affiliated. This lower house has the power to create, amend, approve, and reject legislation from the president's council; to approve or reject ministerial appointments and the national budget; and to impeach the president. By 2003, the International Crisis Group reported that the Somaliland government administration covered 80 percent of the territory.

In addition to building a successful government that has had several successful transitions, Somaliland managed to demilitarize through a series of clan rituals with little international help. One of the government's tactics has been to remove weapons from clan control and to grant a number of recruits for the national army in exchange. They have resettled over 1 million refugees and internally displaced persons. The government has also proactively confronted piracy and international terrorism. All of these processes have created trust and confidence among the subclans, helping to promote stability. This combination of multiple traditional political and economic organizations and institutions alongside more modern ones is inherently more resilient.

Somaliland's experience outside the nation-state model fits with a variety of political and ecological thinking about appropriate political scale for a successfully engaged public. Somaliland's current experiment in building a small political unit instead of a nation reflects the early history of the United States, founded first as a collection of townships and regions rather than a nation. Somaliland's political rebuilding is also a testimony to the value of polycentric governance, or multiple overlapping arenas of political authority. Tocqueville noted that polycentric governance was one of the strengths of early American society in his book *Democracy in America*. Kirkpatrick Sale, an independent scholar, also emphasizes that diversity on all levels, including the political level, is an important part of the bioregional project. For both Kirkpatrick Sale and Lewis Mumford (another independent scholars of the twentieth century), regional governance and planning provided for a more humane existence than national government and planning. As Sale explains in *Dwellers in the Land:*

> [Bioregionalism] expressed in a deep and comprehensive form the essential ideals that I think are crucial for a viable human society on this singular planet: ecological understanding, regional and communitarian consciousness,

nature-based wisdom and spirituality, biocentric sensibility, decentralist planning, participatory politics, and mutual aid.

The last three characteristics fit most closely with the current discussion.

Perhaps most important for Africans, the majority of whom have experienced significant disconnection from colonial and postcolonial political power, polycentricity, a government structure that enables expression and negotiation among a large number of interlocking interests, allows for responsibility and engagement from its citizens. Africa has primarily become a "gatekeeper state," to use historian Frederick Cooper's term again. Local autonomy—as much economic self-sufficiency as possible—and a high level of civic engagement would mark Lewis Mumford's region. Thus, Somaliland shares several features of Mumford's and Sale's regionalism—a smaller-scale unit than the typical state and democratic institutions designed by its inhabitants. Political economist Sujai Shivakumar argues that the kind of state the international community has unsuccessfully promoted in greater Somali limits the potential of individuals to improve their communities through self-governance and locally based problem solving. Sale and Shivakumar call for planning that comes from the bottom up. Sale argues that throughout most of human history, people have lived in small, independent groups. The primary locus of decision making, according to Sale, should be the village of 1,000 or the community of 5,000 to 10,000 (about the size of a *dia*-paying group). Decisions made at this level are more likely to be correct and carried out well. Even misguided decisions are not likely to do significant damage at this scale.

Earlier in this century, philosopher John Dewey wrote about the nature of the state and reached similar conclusions about the need for states to arise out of the "facts of human activity," the vital role of public engagement, and the importance of diverse and experimental forms of government. According to this view, external attempts to rebuild are doomed to fail because they cannot adequately engage the local population in problem solving. Somaliland offers an example of some of this thinking in application.

Local Economic Institutions

Somaliland has had to rely on local and regional economic resources as well. Without international recognition, Somaliland cannot receive bilateral aid or funds from the World Bank or International Monetary Fund. Its currency is not recognized outside its borders. Foreign investors are wary of locating in an area within a failed state. It has garnered very little attention or assistance from the international community, and that, actually, might be contributing to its success. As many have argued, foreign attention and the aid that normally follows often have negative impacts, including encouraging a gatekeeper state. Rulers of aid-dependent states are often less responsive to their own people than rulers of more independent states. From a historical perspective, Somaliland's economic situation, isolated as it currently is from international recognition and aid, is possibly the best position to be in.

Somaliland's urban areas boast a thriving economy and access to basic services. In the late 2000s, the capital, Hargeisa, was one of the safest in Africa. In 2003, Edna Adan Ismail, who was the minister of foreign affairs at the time, wrote of Somaliland's industrial revolution that included aluminum factories for doors and windows, a flour mill, a mineral water drinking plant, a nail factory, stone cutting and brick making, and plastics production. Ismail concluded that economic development in Somaliland had become the envy of many African nations that enjoy international recognition. The industries Ismail highlighted are basic industries that have historically been at the foundation of building an industrial economy.

Current economic development within Somaliland is similar to the ways other areas have historically developed. Scholars like economist Antonio Serra in the seventeenth century and writer and activist Jane Jacobs in the twentieth century have recognized that "most wealth was to be found in the cities," not the states. Cities that maximized the number of different professions and activities were the ones that achieved economic development. Ensuring innovation, protecting manufacturing, and promoting import substitution and the multiplier effect of industries are the keys to success, according to economist Erik Reinert, historian Walter Rodney, and Jacobs. Somaliland, free of international pressure, is able to promote import substitution and protect manufactures, even if it means an inefficient industrial sector. In the cities of Hargeisa and Berbera, Somaliland is pursuing internally led development, increasingly from thriving city centers, rather than foreign-led development.

Much of this economic development has been driven by remittances from Somalilanders who live overseas. Estimates are that 30 to 50 percent of the republic's GDP comes from them. In the early 1990s, annual remittances were two to three times the total republic's exports. Somalia is the fourth most remittance dependent country in the world, with total revenues of between $750 million and $1 billion a year. Two-thirds of Somalia's urban population relies on remittances, and 80 percent of start-up capital comes from such funds as well. Because Somalia does not have a banking system, Somali remittance firms fill the void. These specialized *hawala* remittance agencies operate on trust. Trust is an essential element in many smaller-scale societies and often an elusive element in modern African economies. Part of the reason these agencies work is that they use *xeer* to undergird contracts and to help arbitrate disputes. Even though these remittances come from outside the country, they are Somali-to-Somali links, not foreigners giving to Somalis. Some view remittances as an ideal tool for development because they involve little overhead and minimal corruption, reach those who most need them, and are more stable than most private capital flows. They also reinforce an urban-rural divide and increase income equality; most remittances are sent to cities and middle-class Somali.

Another important feature of the Somali economy is their effective tax collection. Political scientist Peter Pham notes that taxation has historically been a means to raise revenue and build stronger relationships between state and citizens. In postcolonial Africa, by contrast, most states have virtually no taxation and little relationship to their societies. According to Pham, Somaliland has been mostly self-supporting with respect to government finances. The government collects taxes, licenses, and fees from businesses and real estate owners and collects import duties on *khat* trade, imports, and exports. There are some exceptions. In the early 2000s, Somaliland was a free-trade zone, where imports and exports were not taxed. These suggest that there is a functioning state revenue collection system but that it does not extend to the import/export trade.

Clearly, Somaliland does not exist in economic isolation, nor has it for a long time. Northern Somalis have a long history of labor migration and overseas employment in the Arabian Gulf states and on ships' crews. Somaliland livestock exports still primarily go to the United Kingdom and Saudi Arabia and other states to the east. Somaliland has economic woes as well. Through remittances, they are very dependent on employment and educational opportunities elsewhere. The open economic environment has led to the privatization of government services. There is poverty, poor infrastructure beyond the cities, and the risk of international exploitation of resources. Yet, their development is largely Somali-driven rather than driven by Western governments and aid organizations, as is the case in much of the rest of Africa.

Somaliland bolsters the argument that development is always a local phenomenon. Such a stance contrasts strongly with the dominant paradigm of development as pursued by the International Financial Institutions, such as the World Bank; major national development agencies, such as USAID; most African leaders, and many non-governmental organizations as well. For these organizations, the goal is to transform societies with large populations of poor people into societies of rich people, from developing to developed, through state policy and action. Clearly, Somaliland is not a perfect example of local development, but its combination of traditional institution-driven government and Somali-driven development represents an important step in creating a more resilient and bottom-up state.

Somaliland also boasts challenges that are common to many countries, such as weak rule of law, an undereducated citizenry, and challenges to freedom of speech. During his administration, then president Dahir Riyale Kahin extended the House of Elders' term twice by presidential decree, each time with the House voting to agree with the president's move. Members of the House of Representatives were politically weakened by this move, by redistricting under Riyale, and by the House of Elders' voting three times to extend Riyale's term in office. Yet, in 2010, the elections were finally held, and the opposition candidate, Ahmed Mohammed Silanyo, defeated Riyale. Heavy reliance on foreign remittances also shows the education and opportunity gap that still exists between Somaliland and other Western and Arabian countries. There are concerns about limited roles for women in the current government structure. Some worry that the pursuit of democracy by some in power in Somaliland might be more for the sake of international recognition than for securing the needs of Somalilanders. Its future and autonomy and success are not guaranteed, but it is an important example of what can happen when local institutions are promoted and given political and economic legitimacy.

As the United States increasingly pursues its interests through intervention, an awareness of labeling and what it obscures is important. During the same interval of rebuilding in Iraq and Afghanistan, people in a region within larger Somalia, Somaliland, have been rebuilding their own political systems despite dozens of failed external nation-building attempts. As Lewis notes, the failure of internationally led peacekeeping and nation-building efforts in Somalia over the last 20 years and the consolidation of a democratic state in Somaliland tell us more about international politics than about Somali institutions.

Rather than trying to fit all human political creation into one unitary ideal, it is time to appreciate the political and economic wisdom behind Somaliland's 30-year experience with smaller-scale, locally rooted political and economic organization. Not only is such appreciation fair, but Somaliland's embodiment of some of the most critical thinking about human institutions over the last century might be the kind of experience the world needs to learn from right now. None of this is to say that, in the future, Somaliland might not successfully merge in some fashion with a larger Somalia; one can envision a number of scenarios where this might be the appropriate response. Such a merger, however, would be far more successful if it was the result of strong local institutions first. And with a new southern Sudan, one has to wonder if its independence is similarly necessary so that such local institutions can be built. Then, perhaps someday, these will again serve them well either as an independent state or within a larger state.

Suggestions for Further Reading

Morten Boas and Kathleen M. Jennings, "'Failed States' and 'State Failure': Threats or Opportunities?" *Globalizations* 4, no. 4 (2007): 475–485. Boas and Jennings look critically at the way the "failed state" concept has been understood and operationalized by Western nations, particularly in light of concerns about Muslim terrorism.

Colin Elman and Miriam Fendius Elman, *Bridges and Boundaries: Historians, Political Scientists and the Study of International Relations* (Cambridge, Mass.: MIT Press, 2001). This book is an invitation to conversation across disciplinary lines, using three well-studied topics to illustrate how disciplinary convention has shaped the study of the topic.

Foreign Policy and Fund for Peace's Failed States Index, http://www.foreignpolicy.com /failed_states_index_2012_interactive. This is one of the more prominent measures in the United States of the failure of state regimes. An interactive map allows you learn about specific countries and the index of 12 measures that are used to create the rankings.

Brian Hesse, "Lessons in Successful Somali Governance," *Journal of Contemporary African Studies* 28, no. 1 (2010): 71–83. This is a recent survey of the ways in which Somaliland and Puntland have designed and implemented successful governance over the last two decades.

Goran Hyden, "Why Africa Finds It Hard to Develop," *Nord-Sud Aktuell* 18, no. 4 (2004): 692–704. Political scientist Hyden seeks to get to the root of Africa's recent development challenges, arguing that understanding culture and behavior is particularly important, especially the economy of affection that is prevalent in many societies, including Africa. It is important because it shapes behaviors in ways that differ from the logic of social science models.

Edna Adan Ismail, "Peace, Education and Economic Development in Somaliland," *Northeast African Studies* 10, no. 3 (2003): 275–280, www.mbali.info.doc564.htm. This is a brief report on some recent developments in Somaliland from a government official.

Seth Kaplan, "The Remarkable Story of Somaliland," *Journal of Democracy* 19, no. 3 (2008): 143–157. Kaplan focuses on the ways in which Somaliland unity and traditions have helped to build a successful state. He argues that Somaliland deserves international recognition.

Charles Lemos, "A Somali State of Mind," *By the Fault,* April 12, 2009, www.bythefault .com/2009/04/12/a-somali-state-of-mind/. Lemos examines reported chaos in Somalia, such as piracy, from the perspective of Somalis. Their fisheries are no longer under their sovereign control but exploited by many foreign entities and the dumping ground for European toxic waste. He encourages looking beyond Somalia's borders for causes of political and economic instability.

Ioan Lewis, *Understanding Somalia and Somaliland: Culture, History and Society* (New York: Columbia University Press, 2008). This is a significantly updated version of a 1978 edition of the book. Both versions are based on anthropological research done by Lewis since the 1950s. Lewis emphasizes the Somalis' pastoralist culture and its decentralized nature.

Ben Minteer, *The Landscape of Reform: Civic Pragmatism and Environmental Thought in America* (Cambridge, Mass.: MIT Press, 2006). Minteer investigates the intellectual foundations of American environmentalism through the lives and work of Liberty Hyde Bailey, Lewis Mumford, Benton MacKaye, and Aldo Leopold.

He shows that these environmentalists had a broad vision of societal reform that included conserving regional culture and identity and revitalizing democracy.

J. Peter Pham, "Peripheral Vision: A Model Solution for Somalia," *RUSI Journal* 154, no. 5 (2009): 84–90. In a response to an earlier article about Somalia, Pham lifts up "the most advanced state-building project among the Somalis"—Somaliland.

Sujai Shivakumar, *The Constitution of Development: Crafting Capabilities for Self-Governance* (New York: Palgrave Macmillan, 2005). Shivakumar is interested in locally based institutions and problem solving. This is in contrast to the position of most development economists that the only way to achieve development is through nation-states.

Michael Walls and Steve Kibble, "Beyond Polarity: Negotiating a Hybrid State in Somaliland," *Africa Spectrum* 45, no. 1 (2010): 31–56. Walls and Kibble examine the ways in which Somaliland has created a state structure out of both long-standing local traditions and the colonial legacy. Their focus is on the challenges that Somaliland still faces in terms of democratic representation and the regional context.

Conclusion

INCREASINGLY, AMERICANS and others assume that with advancements in technology, societies will be able to outwit the environment, political leaders, or bad economic decisions and continue to live as they always have regardless of damage to the landscape, its resources, or the needs of other people or species. Yet, as many have begun to realize, this approach to life is not sustainable. The experiences of Africans discussed in this book offer other models for coping with challenging circumstances. In the media, however, Africans and their societies are not often portrayed as reservoirs of wisdom and important practices.

African history offers those outside the continent a unique balance of long-term and nonhegemonic recent experience that broadens the possibilities for crafting societies. Every human society is shaped by the imagination, but whatever possibilities are perceived must fit within a longer historical, ecological, and economic trajectory. They cannot exist only for the short term or for a single period of unprecedented growth or change, such as the Great Acceleration.

This kind of understanding of African history is both liberating and grounded. Understanding Africans' history can offer readers a chance to explore their own history with a sense of how it is different from or similar to those of many African societies. Thus, it can provide a sense of grounding in one's own cultural experience and knowledge. It also helps readers to relate to the world around them in ways that are more fulfilling. It enables an opportunity to discuss and imagine very different ways of thinking about the economy, politics, and society. There is much to be learned economically, socially, politically, and ecologically from the long-term and contextualized history presented here.

Even though this is a unique historical moment, the concerns and problems facing us are not new. In the past, however, humans were fewer in number and had less powerful technology. It is not always easy to envision how to adapt smaller-scale ways of operating to a twenty-first-century framework. The first step, however, is to consider how and to what extent these ways might be relevant in contemporary societies. The histories and experiences of Africans are important because they provide a sense of what is possible beyond our own particular circumstances and experiences. They promote greater and broader visions than would be possible without them.

Learning from Africans' experiences with global economics over the last 100 years or so illuminates the ways in which some ideas, such as development, have come to play an important role in the welfare of millions. A strong belief in free trade and trickle-down economics has created wider economic disparities than ever before. Such disparities impact all of us. Free trade within the framework of comparative advantage promises entire countries a better existence, at least in terms of the quantity of goods available to its citizens, based on specialized production. As many African countries have found over the last century or so, specialized production of raw materials locks them into an economically dependent relationship from which it is very hard to escape.

Yet, they have in their past different ideas about what an economy is and whom it is meant to serve. In Buganda, people came together to create communities based on diverse skill sets, recognizing that specialization on an individual level was necessary, but within a community different skills were useful. In Somaliland, Somalis hold strongly to their pastoral tradition, suited as it is to the climate, while weaving these traditions into more recent political and economic institutions. In matrilineal societies when there is no strong identification with the father's family—and thus the nuclear family—it is expected that resources will be evenly distributed among members of the extended family. This might look like socialism (and thus have a negative taint), but it is more accurate to consider it a mechanism for ensuring that everyone has access to the resources he or she needs for a reasonable existence. In a smaller-scale society, it is harder to enjoy excessive wealth and comfort when those close by are suffering. And, as recent studies show, societies where people feel there is greater economic parity are better for all.

Africans' experiences also highlight how a focus on Western ideas and economic institutions masks others ideas and institutions that are making a difference in the global economy, such as entrustment, African self-help, and African contributions to our own health care system. A more careful and balanced look at the characteristics and activities that shape Africans' relationships with the rest of the world is in order.

It is not likely that Americans or others will return to creating small-scale communities from the ground up, as Bugandans were doing 800 years ago, or that they will form matrilineal groupings, let alone societies. It is possible, however, to promote and enact laws and policies that conform to the ideals of these historical institutions elsewhere. We could choose to develop communities and regions as places where a diversity of skills, talents, and professions is embraced and where extended family members are part of our economic community. And we could make sure that all kinds of economic activities that contribute to human welfare, whether informal or not, are acknowledged within the global economy.

Similarly, in terms of family relations, there are valuable and socially beneficial lessons to be learned from our long history of evolution. For example, grandparents played a vital role in human welfare in our evolutionary past. While the circumstances have changed, it is shortsighted to assume that we have outgrown all the usefulness that grandparents might offer. In Africa, at least, grandparents are still very important. Millions of African children who have been orphaned due to AIDS continue to rely on grandparents as caregivers. On the other hand, as the younger generation leaves rural areas for the cities or even foreign countries, the extended family ties that have been part of African cultures for millennia are unraveling.

Rather than making old age a stage of life during which people are often separated from younger family members and meaningful work, we should build on trends that are already in place where older citizens continue to make important contributions to society. Parents and grandparents should be incorporated into families as they age, rather than sent to a separate residence where someone else will care for them. Grandparents are part of our evolutionary and biological inheritance; recognizing that is an important part of our successful future.

Our deep historical past also reminds us of the tremendous challenges involved in developing the vegetables, grains, and animal products upon which society depends. Humans are still an agricultural people. Distancing ourselves from the skills involved and from a sense of gratitude for the foods we have inherited is risky. As much as humans have made certain plants and animals dependent on us, we, too, are dependent on the same plants and animals for survival. In the early twenty-first century, we are inheritors of an incredibly rich and difficult past, and this realization should make us humble. It is quite likely that we face a difficult future. A warming planet, with the change in growing seasons that it brings, threatens some of the foods that early humans domesticated, such as wheat.

We must recognize the value of spreading political and other types of authority across society, as seen in the practice of heterarchy, rather than concentrating authority in the hands of few, as has become the case with the United States and many other oil-rich nations. The U.S. government and its politicians have alliances with corporate giants that weaken the practice of democracy. Of course, heterarchy has existed in the United States and elsewhere for hundreds of years. We should consider the benefits of smaller-scale societies, or bioregionalism, where every citizen would contribute to the prosperity of the region. Many governments have checks and balances at the federal level. Yet, the independence and integrity of many branches of government are in peril. What if we looked at local politics from the perspective of a particular region in terms of its resources and geography and how we could create active democratic societies on a local level? The people of Somaliland are striving to achieve just this balance between local institutions and those of a modern nation-state.

Ecologically, long-term climate change in Africa is at least partly responsible for human evolution. This suggests that significant climate change has some profound benefits. Yet, the human suffering caused by these changes is lost in the historical record. In addition to the more typical climate changes of the past, human-induced climate change is occurring. It is important to understand how the climate has altered Africans' lives in the past for both good and ill. Contemporary human suffering is already visible in environmental refugees from a shrinking Lake Chad and increasingly arid pastoral lands in Kenya. Africans' experiences with climate change suggest a need to be adaptive rather than assume that humans can overcome whatever challenges might arise. A variety of livelihoods suited to a particular climate is more secure.

The ingenuity, adaptability, and resilience that Africans have shown with respect to both their environment and more recent political and economic challenges can serve as essential lessons for us no matter where we live. Learning about our own histories and the histories of those in other countries can provide an important and vital foundation for a more resilient and humble future.

Index

adaptability: in face of climate change, 8, 69–72, 79–83, 223 (*see also* Lake Chad); and pastoralism, 72–76

Afrasan speakers: agriculture, 54–55, 56, 71; ancient Egypt, 71; in East Africa, 86, 87, 89, 90, 128

African agriculture: African language groups, 54–58; bananas, 57; colonial effects, 58–61; early experiments, 53–54; gender roles, 58–59, 63; maize, 60–61; modern economy, 61–63; southern Africa, 57–58; sugar, 61; sustainable agriculture, 64; Ufipa, 58–59

African contributions: development in Africa, 175–178; development in the United States, 173–175; economic thought, 195–201 (*see also* informal economy; Tanzania); peacekeeping, 176–177; peacemaking, 192–195; restorative justice, 192–193; U.S. medical profession, 173–174; women in politics, 193–195

African history: long-standing traditions and ideas, 3, 5; *longue durée*, 4, 5, 13, 15–17, 26, 27; new approaches to education, 6–7; new ideas about economics, politics, and society, 9–12; new perspectives, 1, 4, 20, 220–223; sources, 4–5, 6, 9, 20–26, 48–49, 68–69, 86–88, 106–107, 111, 114, 122–123, 138–139, 158–159, 183, 205–206

Afrocentrism, 22

age grades, 90, 91; and heterarchy, 108

agriculture: and animals, 47, 48–49; challenges of, 50–51; disruption of ecosystems, 52–53, 64; domestication of *H. sapiens*, 63; population growth, 63–64; process of domestication, 48–49; role in history, 46–47; why people began, 51–52. *See also* African agriculture

Anthropocene, and agriculture, 52–53

anthropology, 48, 122–123; source for gatherer-hunters, 48

archaeology: and heterarchy, 105, 108; source for domestication of plants and animals, 48–49; source for human evolution, 23–26. *See also* paleoanthropology/paleontology

Ardipithecus ramidus, 23, 28, 30, 37

Ariaal, 73–75; government, 77

Australopithecus afarensis, 24, 30

Australopithecus sediba, 24, 30

Bantu speakers: in eastern Africa, 86–87, 89; interaction with gatherer-hunters, 90–92; loan words, 89; now dominant, 90–93; in southern Africa, 58, 94–95; tradition, 85. *See also* matriliny

Buganda: banana farming, 57, 111, 114; heterarchy, 114–116; history, 111–113, 114; *kabaka,* 111, 115–116; queen mother, 126–127; sources, 105–106

climate change. *See* global climate change

colonialism, 155–156; and African authority, 105, 116–119; concerns with desertification, 76; and development, 8–9, 159; economic change, 161–163; failed schemes, 164–165; goals of, 161–163

development (economic), 7, 156, 159–161; African contributions, 175–178, 192–201; African leaders, 97, 165–166, 167; African understanding of debt and credit, 151–153 (*see also* wealth in people); definition, 160; development era, 163–169; era of poverty reduction, 168–169; failed schemes, 170–171; measures, 157–158, 160–161; Somaliland, 214–216; structural adjustment policies, 167; Tanzania, 158, 164–169, 176; weakening the African state, 169

early human ancestors, 21, 28, 29; perspective on history, 1

East Africa, four major language families, 86

economic measurement: alternative measures and Africa, 160–161; Gini coefficient, 160; gross domestic product, 157–158; Western influence, 157–158

environmental history, 6

ethnicity: and climate change, 72; and ecological niche, 73, 108; in history, 184–186; Native Authorities, 185–186; South Africa, 186, 190

gathering-hunting: adopting other languages, 90–91; changing views of, 50, 54, 58; in comparison to agriculture, 50–52; duration of lifestyle, 46; not hunter-gatherers, 49–50; interaction with pastoralists, 73; and moral

Kathleen R. Smythe teaches African history, global economic development, and sustainability at Xavier University in Cincinnati, Ohio. She is the author of *Fipa Families: Reproduction and Catholic Evangelization in Nkansi, Ufipa, 1880–1960* (2006) and several related articles about mission Christianity in Tanzania, including "African Women and White Sisters at Karema, Mission, 1894–1920" in the *Journal of Women's History* (2007). This book and more recent works use historical investigation and a transdisciplinary perspective to shed light on the choices humans must make to ensure the continued welfare of all planetary life. Recent articles include "An Historian's Critique of Sustainability" in *Culture Unbound* (2014); "Rethinking Humanity in the Anthropocene: The Long View of Humans and Nature" in *Sustainability: The Journal of Record* (2014); and "Transformative Community Service Learning: Beyond the 'Poor,' the 'Rich,' and the Helping Dynamic" in the *Journal of Higher Education Theory and Practice* (2012). She is currently at work on a book manuscript tentatively titled *Rethinking Humanity in the Anthropocene: The Long View of History*.

Smythe is an avid hiker, biker, and gardener. She aspires to slow living and thrives in community.